ROUTLEDGE LIBRARY EDITIONS:
JAPAN

THE JAPANESE POPULATION PROBLEM

THE JAPANESE POPULATION PROBLEM

The Coming Crisis

W. R. CROCKER

Volume 73

Routledge
Taylor & Francis Group
LONDON AND NEW YORK

First published in 1931

This edition first published in 2011
by Routledge
2 Park Square, Milton Park, Abingdon, Oxon, OX14 4RN
52 Vanderbilt Avenue, New York, NY 10017

Routledge is an imprint of the Taylor & Francis Group, an informa business

First issued in paperback 2013

British Library Cataloguing in Publication Data
A catalogue record for this book is available from the British Library

ISBN 13: 978-0-415-85236-4 (pbk)
ISBN 13: 978-0-415-59336-6 (hbk)

Publisher's Note
The publisher has gone to great lengths to ensure the quality of this reprint but points out that some imperfections in the original copies may be apparent.

Disclaimer
The publisher has made every effort to trace copyright holders and would welcome correspondence from those they have been unable to trace.

THE JAPANESE POPULATION PROBLEM

THE COMING CRISIS

by

W. R. CROCKER
Balliol College, Oxford

LONDON
GEORGE ALLEN & UNWIN LTD
MUSEUM STREET

FIRST PUBLISHED IN 1931

PRINTED IN GREAT BRITAIN BY
UNWIN BROTHERS LTD., WOKING

TO

THE MEMORY OF

MY BROTHER

FRED LINDO CROCKER

1905–1929

ἱερὸν ὕπνον
κοιμᾶται. Θνήσκειν μὴ λέγε τοὺς ἀγαθούς.

CALLIMACHUS

PREFACE

Much has been heard in recent years about the Pacific being the new storm-centre of international rivalries and about the threat of these to world peace. There has been a good deal of exaggeration in many of the estimates of the threat, but in so far as they do contain any measure of truth it is due to the pressure of population in Japan.

In the following pages an attempt is made to ascertain precisely in what this pressure consists and to indicate from the knowledge thus gained the form it will probably take in the future. Such an attempt involves showing not only the present relation between the number of inhabitants and the economic resources of the country but also an analysis of the structure and movement of the Japanese population, of the agricultural potentialities of Japan, of the prospects of importing food in return for exporting manufactures, and of the possibilities of finding relief through acquiring outside lands or outlets for emigrants. Further, the relation of all this to international affairs is stressed throughout because there is little doubt that the foreign policy of Japan, already being shaped by such considerations, will in the future be still more decisively shaped by considerations arising from the size and growth of her numbers.

The Japanese population problem is interesting, not only because it is a living case of "over-population" (a term to be understood with the qualifications implied within) and because of the bearing it has on international relations over the Pacific region, but it is scarcely less interesting for the light it throws on the condition of several other countries to-day. Great Britain is one of these. Italy is another.

Italy's condition is remarkably similar to that of Japan. It is significant that some of the European powers are beginning to feel uneasy about the future foreign policy of Italy. The misgivings of France are now notorious. Such uneasiness is not without some justification. The steadily changing relation between Italian numbers and Italian economic resources is not a reassuring phenomenon, and probably is one that cannot avoid having an unpleasant manifestation in international politics during the next generation.

It has given the author considerable confidence to find that so many of the conclusions concerning the position of Japan drawn in the recent book[1] of an authority of Professor Warren S. Thompson's standing are in substantial agreement with the conclusions arrived at within. Professor Thompson's book unfortunately arrived after the present MS. was written, and as a consequence it was not possible to include some of his brilliant suggestions in it. The author would like, however, to take this opportunity of acknowledging his many debts to Professor Thompson, whose studies in demography, from his first work on Malthusianism and onwards, have been a constant help to him, in method no less than in matter.

Though pains, either of theoretical investigation or of travel, have not been spared in the collection of the facts and in applying the technique of demography to interpreting them, and though the method pursued is as far as possible strictly quantitative, the book is written for the general reader and has therefore imposed upon itself the limits of a general treatment.

Footnotes, however, have been retained. They serve to acknowledge sources and the author's obligations to other students; also they give references so that if a reader desires further to pursue a matter authorities are indicated. (A bibliography is added for the same reason.) But as glancing down

[1] *Danger Spots in World Population*, Warren S. Thompson (Director of the Scripps Foundation for Research in Population), New York, 1930.

at a footnote may be an interruption to a line of thought, nothing essential to the main discussion has been put into them, and it is not necessary for the general reader to take notice of them. Graphs and diagrams have been omitted because their inclusion would have necessitated a higher price for the book; and maps, for the same reason.

The research that has gone into the making of this monograph was made possible by the author's election to a Fellowship of the Commonwealth Fund, the generosity of which and the considerateness of whose Director, Dr. Edward B. Reed, and Assistant-Director, Mr. Whitemore Littell, were unceasing throughout an instructive two years' sojourn in the United States. Help of various kinds but always essential has been received from many students and friends, and although it would not be possible to mention all the names here, he cannot forbear mentioning Dr. Yamato Ichihashi (whose high standard of scholarship he is only too conscious of not having met), Professor of Japanese History in Stanford University, California; Carl Lucas Alsberg, M.D., Director of the Food Research Institute; and Professor and Mrs. Harold Hotelling, of the Mathematics Department, in the same University; his old teacher, Professor H. Darnley Naylor, Emeritus Professor of Classics in the University of Adelaide, who has added yet again to a long list of obligations; and Miss Edith Ellis, of the Society of Friends. Dr. F. G. Tryon, of the Brookings Institution, very generously consented to the publication of some of the data presented by him at the *Round Table on Mineral and Energy Resources for Future Populations* of the Sixth Institute of the Harris Foundation, Chicago University, 1929. In Japan Mr. Mori, of the Central Statistical Bureau, Mr. Nagai, of the Statistical Section of the Ministry of Agriculture, Mr. Higashiura, of the Imperial Agricultural Society, Professor Sasaki, of Tokyo Imperial University, Mr. Kanaya, Director of, and Mr. Kano, Industrial Statistician to, the Tokyo City Bureau of Statistics, and Mr. Azari, of the Japan Office of the I.L.O., have all rendered help with a charming courtesy. Essential help was also received from the statistical sections of the League of Nations, both of the Secretariat, and of the International Labour Office, and from the Government Departments in Tokyo and Washington. But above all are his thanks due to Mr. B. H. Sumner, Fellow of All Souls College and Fellow of Balliol College, Oxford, and to Mr. K. N. Bell, Fellow of Balliol College and sometime Fellow of All Souls College, Oxford.

The author alone, however, must accept responsibility for what is within.

His friend Mr. R. O. Sinclair helped him through the drudgery of proof-reading.

September 1930

CONTENTS

JAPANESE POPULATION PROBLEM

CHAPTER I

INTERNATIONAL RELATIONS IN THE PACIFIC

I. Is the Pacific the New Storm-Centre?

". . . it may be said that after the close of the War of 1914–18 the storm-centre of international affairs, which for the past half-century had hovered over the Near and Middle East and for the previous four centuries over Central Europe, had apparently shifted to the Pacific area."

Taken from a standard and authoritative work on international affairs this sentence is not an unfair representation of an opinion that is, and for the last decade has been, widely current.[1] Explicit reasons for the opinion are seldom given, but behind it may generally be detected the feeling that some predestined force of historical *entwicklung* is unwinding itself and in the unwinding brings forth the primacy of the Pacific. As one writer puts it, "the world left behind it the Mediterranean era centuries ago, and it is now leaving behind it the Atlantic era. The curtain of the new world drama is about to rise on the Pacific."[2] That is to say, the Pacific region is not only the new storm-centre of international politics, but is becoming the new pivot of world affairs as well.

Rare as it may be to find explicit reasons, recent bookmaking and recent journalism are rich in allusions and innuendos to the importance not yet recognized of this or that movement in the region. A glance at any half-dozen books published on that part of the world in latter years will quickly reveal what forces are forming the current opinion.[3]

[1] *Survey of International Affairs*, 1926, p. 392. It need hardly be added that the use of this quotation—wrenched as it is from its context—implies no criticism of the brilliant and penetrating work from which it comes.

[2] Y. Tsurumi, *Contemporary Japan*, p. 156.

[3] Cf. N. Roosevelt, *The Restless Pacific*; Etherton and Tiltman, *The Pacific: A Forecast*; Sir F. Fox, *Mastery of the Pacific*; W. B. Pitkin, *Must We Fight*

There is, for example, the common feeling of astonishment as men recognize on the one side the very large and very disproportionate share of wealth and power on this earth that is in the hands of the "White" or European races, and on the other side the very large proportion of the world's population that the non-European—and poorer—races amount to. Placing the two facts in juxtaposition—which in truth are not under a bushel but there before the eyes of all men to see—they at once proceed to argue that the non-European races will not much longer tolerate this maldistribution of opportunities and the position of inferiority to which it relegates them. They can point to the ominously bitter resentment engendered in one Oriental country by the *Exclusion Law* of the United States, and to the persistent resentment manifested towards the formerly discriminatory nature of the *White Australia Policy* and the immigration restrictions of other British Dominions.[1] The cup is running over: the non-Europeans look back and see little but a long record of arrogance and concessions snatched by force, and their anger appears menacing. And as the non-European races of any account in such a reckoning are the Asiatic, and among the Asiatic the Mongolian, books are written on the Pan-Orient movement and the Revolt of Asia, sometimes a finger pointing to the rumblings of Islam and sometimes to signs that betoken a conscious working for Mongolian consolidation.

Japan?; C. B. Fletcher, *The Pacific Problem*; E. G. Marks, *Watch the Pacific!*; Y. Tsurumi, op. cit.; A. J. Brown, *Japan in the World of To-day*; C. H. Sherrill, *Have We a Far Eastern Policy?*; M. Harrison, *Asia Reborn*; S. Rice, *The Challenge of Asia*; Upton Close, *The Revolt of Asia*.

[1] Cf. Consul Eitaki's letter, quoted in *Commonwealth of Australia Parliamentary Debates*, 1908, p. 11486. Also correspondence between Japanese and Australian authorities printed in Senator Pulsford's pamphlet of 1905, *British Empire and Relations of Australasia and Asia*, and in Appendix B, Fletcher, *Problem of the Pacific*. Also discussions à propos the Geneva Protocol in League of Nations' *Official Journal*, 1924, *Special Supplement, No.* 24, pp. 40–57, 80–83, 88–91; Temperley, *History of Peace Conference*, Vol. VI. From the 'Nineties up to the present day Japan's attitude has been constant: immigration may be restricted, but not in such a way as to discriminate against Japanese as such. Up to the present it has been discrimination, and its implications of racial inferiority, not restriction itself, that they have resented.

Were such fears less prevalent they might be dismissed at once as the merest fancy of the excitable. But since they are so prevalent it will be worth underlining the two obvious facts that do make them the merest fancy. In the first place, not only do the European races outnumber the Asiatics, their populations increasing at a markedly faster rate than the populations of Asia, and their peoples dominating most of the surface of the earth, but (and this is even more to the point) the capacity for organizing their common opinion and desires into political action, and the material force for making their political action effective, are beyond comparison greater. Were a conflict ever to arise the victor could not be in doubt. But a conflict can scarcely arise; for, in the second place, far from having any unity of sentiment Asia is riven into a diversity of elements that have no capacity at all for cohering. It is possible to speak of *a European* because the common heritage of Graeco-Roman and Christian culture has given Europeans a small corpus of ideas and feelings that they hold in common. But it is not possible, even in this limited sense of community, to speak of *an Indian*, let alone *an Asiatic*. Islam, Buddhism, Confucianism, Brahminism—to name these is enough to suggest the heterogeneity of Asia;[1] and within each of them is such a multiplicity of sects and schisms that common action on behalf of the common name is not conceivable.[2] Chinese and Japanese—and only through the closest co-operation of these two peoples would a pan-Asia revolt or even a Mongolian *bloc* be possible—seem parted by differences in temperament that cannot be bridged. Personal association with either peoples reveals differences between them not less than the differences between, for example, Norwegians and Italians. This clash in mind and temper may in future years have effects for Asia like the effects in Europe of the clash between Teuton and Gaul. It is

[1] Sir Frederick Whyte, *Asia in the Twentieth Century*, Chap. I.

[2] Islam is perhaps the only religion in Asia with any power for common action; though Islam in Asia is held by some students to be waning rather than waxing. In any case, the common action, if it could ever be organized, though but in part, would be directed against other Asiatics.

not for nothing that a sober Japanese statistical compilation in referring to the backwardness of the textile industry of China can explain it as being in part "probably due to the thievish and corruptible propensity of the Chinese".[1] Equally significant are the records of the two Pan-Asia Congresses, records that must be as discouraging to the protagonists of that movement as any reverse ever met with by men who launched a desperate cause. At the Second Congress, which met at Shanghai in 1927, there were 15 Chinese, 13 Japanese, 6 Hindus, 1 Arab, 1 Turk, and 1 Afghan, all self-elected deputies. They had scarcely announced their several manifestos when they broke up in confusion, the delegates of Japan and China at a deadlock of discord over a very local Asiatic matter.[2]

Whatever part the countries in the Pacific may play in the world to-morrow, the facts above would seem to indicate clearly enough that it will not be due to a Revolt of Asia or to any coalition of the peoples on the Oriental shores of the Ocean.

Other writers not concerned with the fanciful are pointing out the livelier economic life on and around the Pacific region to-day, and are foretelling a future which spells primacy. Dr. Joseph Bonnet, for instance, a French economist, believes that the axis of commerce is tending to move to there; and behind his opinion he has, at least in large part, the opinion of the Economic Section of the League Secretariat.[3] If commerce is being displaced or is to be displaced from the Atlantic to the Pacific there are the inferences of History to be applied at once to the process, inferences that leave little doubt as to the connection between economic pre-eminence and cultural leadership as the story of Nuremberg or the Italian or Flemish cities reminds us. But is the axis tending to the Pacific? or can it tend there? For the moment the Pacific is still one of the economically less important oceans of the world. The commerce carried over its waters is far smaller than the commerce carried

[1] *Japan Year Book*, 1927, p. 513.

[2] Reports of this meeting appeared in the *Trans-Pacific*, 29.10.27; 12.11.27.

[3] Bonnet, in *Journal des Economistes*, 1929, p. 268; and League of Nations' *Memo. on Production and Trade*, 1926, p. 39.

over the waters of the Atlantic—the commerce between the United States and the Orient, to take an instance, is considerably less than the commerce between the United States and Europe. And although Pacific commerce will in the future surely increase, there is ample reason for thinking that it will never become greater than that of the Atlantic. The paucity of the basic metal and power reserves over the Far East as a whole—of iron and coal and oil and hydro-electricity—mark it out for an industrialization on a lower scale and most likely mark it out for a different economic order from that of Europe or North America.[1] At all events the paucity of reserves promises that the region will not reach a higher economic level than that of the more favoured regions of the world. Nor have the Pacific islands anything in their power to add to this economic secondariness, notwithstanding any future that they may enjoy as the playground of Hollywood or as external National Parks for the vacationing American. Rather than the Pacific supplanting the economic status of the Atlantic, the facts suggest that it will be permanently subordinate to it. And in any case what of Africa? what of the Indian Ocean? what of South America and the accident of its geography that heavily overweights the Atlantic and underweights the Pacific side? Whatever in the future may raise the Pacific to the pivot of world politics, it will not be economic primacy.

A region, however, it can be readily admitted, requires no claims to economic primacy in order to become the centre of diplomatic tension. The accidents of strategy have before to-day turned deserts and mountain wastes into objects of ambition and sources of scorching hatreds, and set into activity all the smooth, slinking, tigerish motion of the Foreign Offices. There are men who think nothing of race ferment in the Far East, and nothing of the economic future of the region, but who yet regard it as a storm-centre, some believing that the tumult of war is possible, others that it is even probable. Yet what do we find when we pass in review each of the Powers

[1] Vide infra, Chap. V.

in that area? We observe that China, by reason of her poverty and her disorganization, could not undertake a war for at least a generation or so to come; that Russia, with much less military power than had the Government which lost the Russo-Japanese War, must live through many days before it could contemplate campaigning on a considerable scale in the Far East; and that France and the Netherlands need not be reckoned with as major factors in the situation. Great Britain, the United States, and Japan remain. As a consequence of the arrangements made at the Washington Conference Great Britain agreed not to improve her fortifications at Hong Kong—her only strategic foothold in the area[1]—and thereby in effect withdrew from those waters to Singapore, about 2,000 miles from south China, which is too far away to serve as a base of operations in Chinese or Japanese seas. And as a consequence of the same Conference the United States agreed not to improve her fortifications in the Philippines and Guam, and thereby in effect withdrew to the Hawaiian Islands, more than 5,000 miles from the Orient, a distance likewise too great for offensive operations in Oriental seas.[2] Naval strategists are agreed that over 500 miles from a base is beyond effective striking distance.[3]

This is an interesting situation. It means, for example, that a war between Japan and the United States is impracticable, if not impossible, because both Powers are strategically beyond the striking range of each other.[4] They are like two men each armed with a weapon that is effective within a hundred yards, but because they are fated never to get closer to one another

[1] Wei-hai-Wei could not be regarded as a strategic foothold. Lord Balfour in fact offered at Washington to return it to China. Cf. Arnold Toynbee, in *Manchester Guardian Weekly*, Feb. 21, 1930.

[2] Cf. Ichihashi, *The Washington Conference and After*, pp. 83 et seq., 109 et seq., for the arrangements made at Washington about fortifications and bases in the Pacific.

[3] Cf. Admiral Bubnov, Chaps. VIII and IX in N. N. Golovin, *The Problem of the Pacific in the Twentieth Century* (transl. C Nabokoff).

[4] For the same reason fears about Japan's suddenly seizing the Panama Canal or attacking Australia are absurd. The inherent difficulties of Japan's conducting a war against Australia are overlooked in such a book as C. B. Luffmann, *The Harvest of Japan*, Chap. XI.

than two hundred yards, their weapons are useless. Both would be wiser to save the expense of buying them.[1] Aviation or some as yet unknown factor might intervene to end the stalemate; or the United States might become willing to exert all the immense force of her wealth and numbers in a prolonged and terrific struggle; but it is not likely that she ever would become willing. China and Russia impotent, and Great Britain and the United States withdrawn from the arena, leaves Japan supreme. Only Japan could be an aggressor. Ignoring for the moment whether Japan could have any conceivable motive in becoming an aggressor, it is doubtful, from a series of military considerations, whether Japan could attempt an aggression on China or Siberia with success. In any case the opposition of the chancelleries of the world and the opposition of the League of Nations, an opposition which in both cases could be made operative by an interference with the supplies, possibly the petroleum, that Japan is obliged to import from abroad, would act as the strongest deterrents. Nor is any Japanese Government, after the empire's recent experiences of Chinese boycotting, likely to undertake a struggle with China except for unusually urgent reasons. In any case it is patent that the new facts of strategy, which the Washington Conference has imposed upon the geographical and political facts, have created a situation in which international war, purely from the military point of view and irrespective of motives or incentives to fight, is so difficult as to be impracticable.[2]

The common opinion as to the political importance of the Pacific thus appears to need considerable modification. That it should have arisen, however, is intelligible. It is probable that an undue concentration on European or other non-Pacific issues, in days when the world has been steadily growing less and less

[1] Vide article by Hon. F. W. Eggleston in *Edinburgh Review*, Vol. CCXLVII, p. 330; also cf. H. C. Bywater, *Sea Power in the Pacific*, for the pre-Washington Conference strategical facts.

[2] No discussion is offered here of an attempted Japanese aggression on the East Indian archipelago. From the military point of view it would probably be successful. But because of the relative defencelessness of the archipelago it would be *seizure* rather than *war*.

divisible into independent unconnected political entities, has led some writers to convert the neglect into attentiveness by a method of over-emphasis. But this explanation cannot be carried far. The opinion is not of recent origin. Seward, Abraham Lincoln's Secretary of State, used words not unlike those quoted from recent writers. There are stronger inducements to it than an undue preoccupation with European issues. The example of historical analogy was there to invite the opinion. The rather meaningless generalization about civilization beginning with a Mediterranean era and then passing through an Atlantic era has led men to complete the syllogism by saying that the Pacific is the next and culminating stage; an argument by analogy of that dangerous order which destroys actual thinking through the very appearance of its unanswerable reasonableness. And what seems unanswerable in the light of the Law of History is fortified by the sheer size of the area under consideration and the plenitude of the population around its shores. Thus an American admiral, writing on the politics of the area, is led to say that "we sometimes forget that its mighty expanse covers one-quarter of the whole globe and that it contains half of the globe's entire water surface". Both arguments, that of historical analogy and that of size, are combined in another book published in America where the author, after using the well-worn phrases about the rising of the curtain on the new world drama, clinches his point by adding that the Pacific is "seventy times as large as the Mediterranean and twice as large as the Atlantic". Its political significance apparently is to be seventy times as large as that of the Mediterranean and twice as large as that of the Atlantic. Valuable as is the quantitative approach to political problems, cause and effect are not so ruthlessly connected as this.

It might be claimed indeed that no region of the world could in these days of economic and still more of political interdependence be parcelled out into such separable divisions as *the Pacific Area*, and it might also be claimed that what in appearance has been a Pacific problem has on analysis turned out to be the repercussion of some diplomatic clash in other parts of the world, as was undeniably the case sometimes during the first decade of the twentieth century.

It is sufficient here, however, to emphasize the fact that the Pacific region is to-day and for the immediate future from every point of view unusually pacific. It discloses no issues that can be compared with the issues which ruffled the chancelleries of the Powers in the quarter-century beginning with the break-up of China in the 'Nineties—a period that witnessed forced concessions, leaseholds, spheres of interest, non-alienation agreements, the Boxer uprising, international rivalries in Manchuria, following hard upon one another in disturbing procession. For not only did the Washington Conference innoculate the region militarily, it innoculated it politically as well.[1] The issues outstanding were, if not settled, at least filed down to a smoothness in which they ceased to irritate the international body politic, particularly by the Nine Power Treaty relating to Chinese sovereignty and to the re-defined principle of the *Open Door*. Since the Conference at Washington the political situation in the Far East—and therefore in the Pacific[2]—has become stabilized so that it is now less of an international storm-centre than at any time during the last forty or fifty years. There are no first-class explosive issues in the region to-day, none, for example, that can be compared with the issue of Reparations and International Debts, and none greater than the rising issue of Italy's population problem.[3]

[1] Ichihashi, op cit.

[2] As will have been observed, the "Pacific" in a political sense turns out to mean the Far East, or matters rising out of the relations of other countries with the Far East. This assumption seems universal in the books.

[3] The single issue that did arise after the Washington Conference as a dangerous international question was the U.S. Exclusion of the Japanese from its immigration quota in 1924. Although Japanese official announcements have not ceased to speak of it as an issue still not closed as far as Japan is concerned, the tension between the two countries has become less and less, so that feeling is now anything but inimical. It is a "sore spot" still, but not a dangerous issue.

II. China—Manchuria—Japan

To say that the political importance of the Pacific area has been exaggerated, or to say that the issues there are less considerable than some international problems elsewhere, or are less considerable than were the issues in the same area for many years prior to the Washington Conference, is not of course to argue that there are no issues at all, either for the time being or for the future.

It is notorious—to take a case in point—that few countries in recent years have been receiving so much attention in the Press as China. Extraterritoriality, Tariff Autonomy, the Settlements, are words before the eyes of all. There must be urgent grounds, surely, for so much interest. There are grounds enough in all truth for an interest in the politics of China; yet the fact remains that notwithstanding the wise statesmanship which the relationships of the Powers with her will require, there is nothing in these relationships and nothing in the condition of China that can be regarded as a first-class issue in international affairs.[1] For the basic truth about China is her lack of governance—a domestic affair; and from this lack of governance all the other facts proceed.[2] Hers is the condition that Sir John Fortescue described for fifteenth-century England. The comparison indeed does not sufficiently indicate the devolution, almost the dissolution, of authority that prevails in that country. China, as one writer well says, must be regarded as a cultural not as a political society.[3] In a younger world this did not matter, especially as Chinese never required much government;[4] but in the world of to-day some centralization

[1] Manchuria is excluded from China in this section, for reasons that will be made clear later.

[2] Cf. W. H. Mallory, *China, Land of Famine*, pp. 64–83; Eric Teichman, *Travels in North-West China*. This book, written by a British Consular officer, gives an admirable insight into Chinese conditions, and is illustrated with excellent photographs. Cf. also Teichman, *Travels in Eastern Tibet*, p. 134.

[3] H. M. Vinacke, in *A History of the Far East in Modern Times*.

[4] Sir Frederick Whyte, in *Asia in the Twentieth Century*. It is relevant to note here a sentence written by M. André Siegfried: "As everybody knows, Europe before the war had hardly more of a sense of unity than China," *Foreign Affairs*, October 1929.

of governmental functions is not to be avoided. All the agitation of the nationalists and all the brawling of the Tuchuns take life from this need: on the one side is the attempt to turn a cultural into a political society, on the other the resistance to that attempt. The country is passing through the throes that sixteenth- and seventeenth-century Europe passed through when building up the omni-competent State. Perhaps the pangs are sharper, just as the task is harder. The magnitude and the difficulty of the project are not to be denied: the slow and painful and empirical efforts exacted in the evolving of new forms of government, above all the forms of a sovereign State, are now well known from the researches of historians into Mediæval and Renaissance administrative history. Yet for all this, the centralizing programme and the events that arise from that programme remain a Chinese domestic rather than an international issue, even though foreign States are bound to be interested. Indeed, the privileged status of foreigners, that has seasoned with such pepper the oratory of the nationalists, is not a cause of the Government's weakness, but a manifestation of it. So long as security of foreign lives or property could not be counted upon because of there being no adequate Government in China, so long were extraterritorial privileges unable to be avoided. While admitting with all frankness the inferiority of the type of European that was and still is common in China as in other Eastern countries—men who were there for the single purpose of making money and making it as quickly as may be, Philistine business men unhampered by any touch of *noblesse oblige*—the student cannot but admit that "the unequal treaties" were imposed because no competent State existed. At all events the somewhat vociferous attention that has been directed to them, in particular to the anomalies in them, must not withdraw our attention from the significant fact. The same fact—lack of governance—is still behind the turmoil of the country to-day.

Nor is there anything in the existing privileges—which have been modified and with the passage of time will be modified further and further—that threaten to create an international storm-centre. The integrity of Chinese sovereignty and Chinese territory is secure: the Powers have imposed a sort of self-denying ordinance upon themselves, so that the danger of its infringement and the still greater danger of international crises arising from efforts of the Powers to grasp an option here or a territory there, no longer haunt the scene. Further, the steady conciliatoriness that has characterized their behaviour during the last eight years may be expected to continue. The civilized world cannot but be interested in the spectacle of so large a community—perhaps amounting to one-fifth of the population of the world—and one with such gifts of vitality and moral culture, working out the political habits and administrative forms that Englishmen began learning from the days of King Henry of Anjou. They look on not without sympathy; only in the very improbable case of China, after years of unsuccessful effort, dissolving into anarchy would a first-class international issue arise and would the Powers be obliged to intervene.[1]

If China has been a name to conjure fears, Manchuria has sounded more ominous still. It has indeed a significance for international relations that China has not. Lying, as it does, at the point where the territories of Russia, China, and Japan converge, it has an obvious strategical importance.[2] Lying, too, between Japan and China, an unfilled land of rich resources, as large in area as three Japans, between the crowded populations of the two first Oriental Powers, its economic importance is no less obvious.[3] The strategic and economic incitements to possess it, or to prevent a rival from possessing it, have been dangerously exacerbated by the ambiguities of its juridical status. Legally a part of the Chinese Republic, it is in fact autonomous, first

[1] For authoritative accounts of recent happenings in China, vide *Survey of International Affairs*, 1925, Vol. II; 1926; and 1927.

[2] The Russo-Japanese War was largely the outcome of this.

[3] For economic facts about Manchuria, vide *Manchuria: Land of Opportunities*, 1922, and *Report on Progress in Manchuria*, 1907–28, 1929, both published by the Southern Manchurian Railway. The latter is particularly good, though of course not claiming to give a severely objective treatment.

under the ex-brigand, Chang Tsao Lin, and now under his son.[1] And before Chang's day, in the time of the Chinese Empire, the single tie between the two countries was their common fealty, since the seventeenth century, to the same dynasty, itself of Manchu origin. The emperors barred the boundaries of the country to the Chinese, and left it to the sparse population of Manchu pastoralists who drove their flocks over the plains and through the breaks in the forest. In the north the Russians have held a special position from the middle of the nineteenth century, which from the 'Nineties onwards was concreted with a railway system joining Manchouli on the Siberian border with Vladivostok on the ocean (a short cut between Russia and her Pacific port) and which was left undisturbed by the shock of the Russo-Japanese War.[2] Even yet it has not slipped out of the grasp of the Soviets. In the south, Japan, from the time of her victory over Russia in 1904, has been largely *de jure* and wholly *de facto* ruler. The base to this stage, occupied by these players, is a population neither Japanese nor Russian, not accurately numbered but ranging between 25 and 30 million, and almost entirely Chinese. During the last twenty years, but especially during the last six, there has been a migration of men into Manchuria perhaps as spectacular as any such movement in history. For several years not less than a half to one million men have entered the country annually, and they have entered it from China.[3] Whatever the play and whatever the players that may hold the scene for the present in Manchuria, the sheer numbers of this swamping mass leave no doubt as to who will hold it in the ultimate future.

[1] Chang Tsao Lin actually declared Manchuria autonomous; but later he co-operated with the Chinese Republic. The *de facto* autonomy was well revealed in the Chinese-Eastern Railway affair of 1929. Mukden appears to have decided to restore the *status quo* as demanded by Russia without consideration of the wishes of the Nanking Government. Nanking officially styles Chang's son Governor-General.

[2] Vide Clyde, *International Rivalries in Manchuria*.

[3] For the migration, vide *Report on Progress in Manchuria*, 1907–28, S.M.R., Dairen, 1929, pp. 12–14. Also *Foreign Affairs*, October 1928; *Far Eastern Review*, June and July 1928; *Trans-Pacific*, 24.9.29; and *Kinney*, *Modern Manchuria and the S.M.R.*, pp. 1–3.

For the moment the Japanese are pre-eminent. The local Manchurian Government under Chang's son and successor is in harmony with them. Moreover, the Washington Conference not only left them in possession of their Kwantung Lease and the Zone along the Southern Manchurian Railway, but left their claim to a sphere of influence in Southern Manchuria and Eastern Inner Mongolia undisturbed.[1]

Far more important than their political status and its security is their economic entrenchment. The coal deposits at Fushun, Penhsihu, and Yentai, and the iron fields at Penhsihu and Anshan are in their hands; and their railways are as the very arteries and sinews of Manchurian prosperity. Nearly half of Manchuria's foreign trade goes to Japan. Japanese investments amount from £150 to £200 million.[2]

In fact it is difficult to see how the extension of Japanese interests has not amounted to an encroachment upon the old Russian sphere. By building a line from Toananfu to Tsitsihar (which, though built for and is now operated by the Chinese, has the same gauge as the S.M.R. lines and has S.M.R. officials associated with it) they are bound to drain traffic which is already served by the Chinese-Eastern Railway, the backbone of the Russian sphere; and more threatening still, in building this line they cut the Chinese-Eastern Railway into two at Anganki and so hold a gate between Siberia and the short route to Vladivostok.[3] Moreover, a hundred miles or so south

[1] Perhaps it is more accurate to say that the Open Door Declaration of 1922 left the status of the old spheres unsettled. Though it expressly forbade the creation of new spheres, there is nothing to indicate that this prohibition was to be retrospective. Japan's claims to her sphere were virtually conceded by the Consortium. Vide Ichihashi, op. cit., pp. 196, 201, 305; also Clyde, op. cit., p. 209.

[2] Vide *Progress in Manchuria*, op. cit., p. 2. For further information as to Japan's stake in Manchuria, vide infra, footnote 2, p. 168.

[3] Vide railway map of Manchuria. There is a map in *Progress in Manchuria*, op. cit.; also in *Survey of International Affairs*, 1925, Vol. II. A map is given in *Asiatic Review XXV*, p. 734. Perhaps the text as it stands does not make it sufficiently clear that the Toananfu-Tsitsihar line is Chinese and not Japanese. It is operated by the Chinese and is under charge of the Chinese Dept. of Communications. On the other hand, the line was built by Japanese capital and under the direction of Japanese engineers and its gauge is that

of the Chinese-Eastern they are projecting and in part have already built a line running parallel to it from Changchun through Kirin to the Korean coast, which not only encroaches on the Russian sphere but would hit Vladivostok another hard blow economically.[1] It has also been reported[2] that they are now projecting a system of lines that will push through the heart of the Russian sphere up to the borders of Siberia, thus linking all Manchuria with a 4-ft. 8-in. Japanese gauge. It is well known that the S.M.R. (i.e. the Southern Manchurian Railway Company) was negotiating for a heavy loan from the J. P. Morgan Company of New York during 1928, but for some reason the negotiations were cancelled at the end of the year or early in 1929.

Of course the significance of Japanese railway policy in Manchuria can easily be exaggerated. Railway competition after all is ordinary economic competition, and as such is not unknown in peaceful Western States. And there seems much soundness in the plea that the country needs not less but more railways. Nor can there be any question as to the services that have been rendered and are being rendered by the Japanese railways, the record of which is as uniformly high as that of Japanese administration there.[3] In fact it is on record from an official of the S.M.R. that the company does not regard railway competition as a vital or even as a first-class issue.[4] The connec-

of the S.M.R. lines, 4 ft. 8 in., not that of the Chinese-Eastern lines, 5 ft.; also there are some Japanese officials on the management. Moreover, the *latent* opposition of interests is not so much Japanese *v.* Russian as Japanese *v.* Chinese.

[1] Cf. *Progress in Manchuria*, op. cit., pp. 45–6. For an instance of rivalry between the two railway systems and their terminal ports—Dairen and Vladivostok—vide *Trans-Pacific*, 20.6.29; 18.8.29; 21.2.29; and 28.2.29.

[2] In *Survey of International Affairs*, 1925, Vol. II, op. cit., p. 350. The map issued by the S.M.R. in 1929 does not show some of the lines nor the projections mentioned in the *Survey*, and rather curiously no references have been made in the 1926 and 1927 volumes of the *Survey* to this highly controversial question. Also *Asiatic Rev. XXV*, p. 713, and *Round Table*, August 1928.

[3] In addition to running the railway as the most efficient in the Far East, the company runs schools, hospitals, research institutes, and does other social work, some details on which will be found in *Progress in Manchuria*, op. cit. Also vide U.S. *Commerce Reports*, 25.3.29.

[4] Kinney, *Modern Manchuria*, p. 8.

tion, too, between the railways and the Japanese Government, that now sometimes breeds suspicion as to politics masquerading in the cloak of business, can in due time be severed and what is a legitimate economic corporation be dissociated from political affairs. This indeed is what Mr. Matsuoka, until lately the Vice-President of the S.M.R., himself a Government official and in no small measure responsible for the railway's fine record, looks forward to, and even appears to regard it as shortly practicable.[1] Until that time it would seem to be placing no undue expectations upon the reasonableness of human behaviour to believe that in the event of a conflict of interests arising between the railways of Japan and Russia, or (what is less unlikely) China (China too has her lines in the country, owning wholly or in part and operating one-half of the total mileage),[2] adjustment can be reached through discussion.[3]

In any case it can be taken for granted that the Japanese will insist on reasonableness at the least. The juridical status of Manchuria may be indefinite and the human material—with Chinese in the first heat of nationalism and the Russians eager at home to pursue an active policy abroad—may be inflammable, but the Japanese, under the pressure of their necessitousness, will pursue a policy of no uncertainty. They have, in fact, been direct and precise in announcing their intention to suffer no interference with their essential interests in Manchuria. As Mr. Matsuoka has said, while nothing contrary to the real interest of China is contemplated, on the contrary the Chinese will continue to benefit from the advance of civil order and prosperity, Japan has now "reached a point where she can no longer afford to deal with these matters except in the spirit of candour".[4] The late Prime Minister, Baron Tanaka, and the present Foreign Minister, Baron Shidehara, who

[1] Vide Mr. Y. Matsuoka, in *Far Eastern Review*, August 1929.

[2] *Progress in Manchuria*, op. cit., p. 48; Kinney, op. cit.

[3] The Japanese official attitude is reasonable and conciliatory, as shown in their *Report on Progress in Manchuria*. They urge, too, the desirability of co-operation (e.g. pp. 7–8).

[4] In *Far Eastern Review*, August 1929, p. 345 et seq.

represented opposite schools of foreign policy, have spoken in similar terms.[1]

It is not probable that Japanese interests will be seriously challenged. Treaty rights endow them with a legal sanction until nearly the end of the century.[2] And if any violation of the treaties be attempted Japan has at her command all the force necessary to implement them. Neither the Chinese nor any other Power in the Far East can challenge her to combat of arms. And though a combat is probably not likely to arise and though it is evident that Chinese feelings will be studiously considered, we must be clear as to Japan's intention, and as to her ability to carry out that intention, of preserving her treaty rights in Manchuria. Before the time when the treaties expire it is probable that all political interference or interest will have been withdrawn, the entrenchment of her economic interests being deep enough for them to subsist in the hands of private enterprise. The Japanese rulers may be relied upon not to hamper themselves with the embarrassment of political associations so soon as these have become unneeded. But until then no Japanese Government, be the party what it may from which it is formed, will have any alternative regarding the fundamentals of Manchurian policy. For here is a national interest more vital, in the nearly unanimous opinion of Japan, even than the interests of the British Empire in the approaches to India or of the United States in the Caribbean.

For what reason is it that Japan's stake in Manchuria means, or is thought by Japanese to mean, so much to her well-being?

[1] For Baron Shidehara, vide *Survey*, op cit., 1926, p. 395 and appendix. Numerous statements by Japanese officials or authorities as to Japan's interest and policy in Manchuria can be found in the files of the *Trans-Pacific*, e.g. Baron Sakatani in 11.8.28; also 18.8.28, 25.8.28, 3.10.29 ("Should Japan Buy Manchuria?"). Also vide *Die Neue Rundschau*, Sept. 1929, art. "Welt Politik in Mandshurie, by Georg Cleinow.

[2] As a result of the arrangements following the Twenty-One Demands. Vide Ichihashi, op. cit., pp. 293–5. Of course some of the Chinese Nationalists refuse to admit the validity of these treaties, and it is possible that some future Government of China may challenge or attempt to repudiate them.

III. The Major Issue

This question brings us face to face with the basic factor in the foreign politics of the Pacific region—the pressure of population.

Pressure of population is general in the Asiatic corner of the Pacific. In that corner are nearly one-third of the human race, and if India, just beyond, be added, more than one-half. So near to the margin of subsistence are these huddled millions living that a drought or a flood or any other derangement in the food supply destroys them in their hundreds of thousands. This of course is no new lot for them; but the knowledge that in other countries around the Ocean—in Australasia, in the Southern Islands, and in the Americas—population is less dense and the struggle to live less fierce is new knowledge; and the opportunity and the will to benefit from the opportunity are very different from what they were a century ago. This seems a perilous state of affairs—a few million transplanted Europeans confronting a thousand million Orientals; the very apparition indeed that has haunted the fancy of many an Australian and has invigorated the immigration Code of his Government.[1]

There is no lack of evidence as to the persistent outward thrust of the most numerous of the Oriental peoples—the Chinese. On all sides of the Ocean, the immigrant from China is found beating against the closed doors and matching the intransigeance of Exclusion Codes with a quiet subtle unrelenting watchfulness.[2] Throughout the islands and in the lands on the borders of the Pacific he shows his extraordinary power

[1] Cf. *Commonw. of Australia Parl. Debates*, e.g. Senator Cameron or Senator O'Keefe, Aug. 31, 1910 (2260); ibid., Nov. 1910, 6138; ibid., Sept. 1920, 4551, 4722; *Queensland Parl. Papers*, 1907, Vol. I, No. 11; Piesse, in *Foreign Affairs*, January 1926, pp. 481–3.

[2] Cf. account in Harada, *Labour Conditions in Japan*, p. 105, as to Chinese attempting to enter Japan notwithstanding the immigration law exclusion; or in *Economic Record* (Australia), Nov. 1927, as to their attempting to enter New Zealand; also *Survey of International Affairs*, 1928, p. 456 et seq.; and Dept. of Overseas Trade Report on *British Malaya*, 1929; Teichman, *Travels in North Western China*, p. 192; Harrison, *Asia Reborn*, p. 235; Also cf. W. H. Mallory, *China, Land of Famine*, pp. 5, 19.

to survive and to flourish—in Siberia, the Philippines, Hawaii, California, Chile, Peru, Tahiti, Australasia, the Netherlands East Indies, British Malaya, and beyond. He now outnumbers the Malayans in British Malaya;[1] in the Netherlands East Indies he is supreme over large sections of the economic field; in far-away Tahiti he dominates it absolutely;[2] in Siberia the Russians have been forced to protect themselves from his invincible economic power;[3] in all places he prospers and is feared, and in most the barriers are now held up high against his further entrance. Were they not held up one wonders what would happen—surely a steady outpouring from China into the sparser lands until all disparity in pressure of numbers was at length ended.[4]

The millions of Brown men to the south of China show none of the Chinese's formidable traits. Not that their plight is happier; on the contrary the density of numbers and the results of the density are probably not greater in China than for instance in Java (though the Javanese mitigates these somewhat by a superior hygiene). But the lassitude that is born of their climate seems to condemn them to a passive acceptance of their lot.[5]

A pressure of population in Japan would be a very different matter. The Brown men suffer it complacently. The Chinese may beat against the doors, and though sometimes they may even elude the scrutiny of the sentinels, in general they fall back upon or remain within their own boundaries and there allow any excess of numbers to work its own drastic course. Japan, on the other hand, has long reached a stage where the usual Oriental cure to over-population—starvation or a recession in the standard of life—would not be possible. Not only would a reduction in the standard of life bring about (for reasons to

[1] Department of Overseas Trade report on *British Malaya*, op. cit. Chinese immigration has been prohibited since July 1930.

[2] As far as a visitor could judge without access to official statistics, trade on the island is almost entirely in Chinese hands; especially were they playing with admirable adaptability the rôle of mine host in the local estaminets.

[3] See H. K. Norton, *Far Eastern Republic of Siberia*, p. 194, etc.; F. Nansen, *Through Siberia* (1914), pp. 340–1.

[4] For an excellent sidelight on Chinese Immigration, vide Coolidge, *Chinese Immigration*; also R. L. Stevenson, *Across the Plains*.

[5] Cf. Count Keyserling, *Travel Diary of a Philosopher*, Vol. I, Parts 2 and 3.

be indicated within) far-reaching social disturbances that are not to be thought of in China or the East Indies; but Japan is unique in the Oriental Pacific as a country with an organized and organizable public opinion which can be brought to bear upon a strongly unified government. China and the Philippines and the East Indies all have their population problems; but their problems have only a domestic and no international significance; they have not the conception of a standard of life, the force of a mobilizable public opinion, and the omni-competent State, that Japan has.

So although pressure of population is general along the Asiatic shores of the Pacific, only in Japan has the pressure any implications for international politics. One implication is now being shown in the question of Manchuria. To speak of Manchuria as an international danger zone may be exaggeration, but it is not foolish exaggeration—the elements of inflammability are plentiful enough; but we can be sure that any combustion that may burst forth will be quelled by Japan, and her own interests maintained. All parties and all opinions in Japan with any claim to attention are unanimous on that point. They are unanimous because they believe that Japan already cannot subsist without the food and industrial materials that she draws from there, and that in the future she will of necessity be drawing upon them in larger and larger amounts. It is conceivable (though not probable) that other Powers may form a *bloc* against Japan's policy. To oust her from Manchuria, however, will be a war to the death. Such an attempt is not easily imagined. In any case the truth remains that Japan's policy, not only in Manchuria, though dramatically there, but elsewhere too, in short her whole foreign policy, is determined and will be shaped by this belief as to her numbers being greater than can be sustained at home. In order then to understand, not only the determining forces of Japanese policy, but also what is the major issue, incomparably greater than any other issue, in the Pacific region to-day, we must analyse her problem of population.

CHAPTER II

THE JAPANESE BACKGROUND

Before proceeding to analyse the population problem of Japan it will be worth while delaying for a little to remind ourselves of the geographical environment and of the historical background of the Japanese people as well as of some of the more outstanding of the national traits.

I. Geographical

Japan proper consists of one long narrow island with two smaller islands at the south-west end and another at the north-east end, and with innumerable tiny islands beyond these and along the main shore-line. It stretches from the latitude of Morocco to that of England.

As the ship nears the land the traveller descries jagged mountain masses and a predominant colouring of green; a view that strongly recalls the north island of New Zealand or the typical volcanic islands of the southern Pacific. Nor is this first impression misleading, for when he disembarks and pushes into the country, he finds that Japan is a typical Pacific island, or rather a series of Pacific islands. That is to say, the landscape is made up of blocks, sharp-edged and crumpled blocks, of mountains, useless for agriculture because though generally not very high, they are nearly always too steep for cultivation. And the flats and valley bottoms and blunter hills where cultivation is possible are relatively few and always crushed in between mountain and mountain or mountain and sea. On these bottoms and less steep hillsides rice and other plants are grown, and for century after century have been grown, by a toilsome exacting culture. The abiding impression is green: green hillsides covered with bamboo or pine or maple, and green chequer-board fields covered with rice; and rather an atmosphere of mountain wastes and the loneliness of unpeopled forests. For in Japan there is this strange combination of miles of untouched natural land with yet an overcrowding of human beings: the humanity is pent up in thick density on the flats and valley bottoms, and the rest of the country is left over to the wilderness of the forest-clad ranges.

It is of course an attractive landscape, and in parts one of great picturesqueness. But, to an Englishman at least, it lacks that beauty which comes from the hand of man. There is nothing here of the gentle loveliness of the Cherwell valley or the hills of Somerset, nothing here to compel that intimate solicitude for the countryside which sent W. H. Hudson, Richard Jeffries, and so many other Englishmen of literature prying into the hedgerows, turning over the mossy stones, seeking out the veriest minutiæ of all its life and associations. The proportion of wild land in Japan is too great: it overwhelms one. And where the hand of man has been applied—on these hard-worked fields—one scarcely escapes the feeling that it has been applied too laboriously, at a cost that is cruel. Occasionally one chances upon a road lined with the gnarled and twisted pines that were painted so often by the masters and recaptures for a moment something of the quaint prettiness which still belongs to much of Japanese life; but more often one is on overcrowded, overworked valley floors, or in the loneliness of the mountain wastes. Hemmed in by too many men or by too many trees, one rarely looks out on a wide view and the far horizon: not only is there a lack of the intimate beauty of the English countryside, but a lack of the spaciousness which has led American Hotel Proprietors' Associations to speak (with a religious thankfulness) of God's Great Prairies and God's Great Out-of-Doors.

Nor is one generally conscious of the immense antiquity of the order of life around him. There are no grey stone walls to awe him, none of the mellow memorials that the younger civilization of Europe has erected to itself. The Buddhist temples, many of them built before our cathedrals, impress only after a conscious effort. For the temples, the palaces, the villages, are all built of wood and of a low structure, and the more they age the more they fade into the trees around them, and, forgetful of its great past, one is once again left with an impression of the typical Pacific volcanic island; still, a picturesque Pacific island. R. L. Stevenson would have delighted in Japan.

That stone was very rarely used until recent years, but wood instead, was probably due to the prevalence of earthquakes in Japan. It is estimated that on an average there are four tremors a day and several severe earthquakes every year. How disastrous the worst of these can be was shown to the world in 1923. This part of the Japanese environment has had an effect on more than the architecture.

Not only earthquakes have emphasized the incalculability of natural forces. Typhoons sweep some part of the land in the latter part of every summer, laying low in a few minutes the crops, which the farmer has tended so patiently for months. One sees from whence has come the national trait of not repining at reverses. In other ways, however, the climate is as congenial as the landscape is attractive, though by reason of the winds somewhat warmer in summer and somewhat colder in winter than the corresponding latitudes in Europe.

II. Historical

It was on this background that a history older than our own yet both strangely similar to and strangely dissimilar from it has unwound itself. Until the rise of the Tokugawa Shogunate, in 1603, the Japanese story might be called typically feudal, and it covers much ground of a kind familiar to English historians: knights and chivalry, barons' wars and usurping prelates of a powerful church, serfs, guilds, self-subsisting manors, even tithings and frithborhs, are all there. In administrative history the parallels are sometimes so close as to be astonishing, the mysterious dual rule from "household government" being included as well as a nearly identical process of working out the Unified State.

During the Tokugawa Shogunate, life, though often hard and penurious, was perhaps as agreeable for the minority and as tolerable for the majority as it has ever been in any place or time. Peace and good order were maintained throughout the country; a fair balance was held between population and economic resources, the number of people remaining stationary for nearly two hundred years; and in the *Sih No Ko Sho* division of society there was a rough but workable method of apportioning social status according to economic and social contribution. The aristocracy was of course marked off from the rest of the people, containing within itself the three orders of Imperial nobility (depending on the secluded Emperor at Kyoto, where they lived elegantly but impotently), the Daimio (vassals of the Shogun, and at whose seat in Tokyo they were obliged to spend half their time), and the Samurai (a class comparable to, but more numerous—there must have been two millions of them in a population of thirty millions—and very much poorer than our squires). The Samurai were the backbone of what is most characteristic in Japanese culture—courtesy, self-discipline, honour, and Zen Buddhism. They are of special interest because though living in extreme simplicity (to us it would be great poverty) they evolved a way of life and for many centuries lived it on perhaps a higher æsthetic and spiritual level than has ever been done by any large number of men. They had their faults of course, and they had some rather self-destroying eccentricities like holding it bad taste to be thrifty and good taste to be ignorant of the value of the different coins; but the best in Japanese civilization is due to these poor and austere aristocrats, with at once so much of the Cavalier and so much of the Calvinist in them. After the aristocrats came the peasants as the next class; after the peasants the artisans; and at the lowest were the traders and merchants. (The Eta, the outcast class, still existing to-day and at present not less than a million in number, cannot be noticed here.) Throughout this period Japan was shut off from the rest of the world: foreigners were forbidden to enter, and Japanese were forbidden to leave the country. Seclusion was actually practised: it was not merely a policy.

The Tokugawa Shogunate lasted from 1603 until 1868, when for various reasons, partly "intellectual", partly feudally political, but probably mostly economic, its structure and strength caved in, and the Emperor was restored to power. The restoration was only less curious than that the Imperial House (whose lineage is the oldest in history) was still surviving to be restored. Seven centuries had run since it had lost power and the actual government been usurped by the Shoguns. These shogunates were regent dynasties, sometimes lasting for generations, in the case of the Tokugawa family lasting for nearly three centuries. Sometimes the shoguns became feeble and another family seized power—but nominally only as regents (*Shikken*), and the feeble shoguns remained in the shogunate, so that dynasties arose which actually ruled the land but theoretically only as regents for another family whose own status was also only that of regents. At one period this triple arrangement—Emperor, Shogun (regent for the Imperial House), and Shikken (regent for the Shogun House)—lasted as long as two centuries! It is surely one of the strangest compromises in history, and well exemplifies the non-extremist compromising spirit of the Japanese character. Throughout the seven hundred years, however, the Imperial family had lost nothing but its power: it lived on at Kyoto, provided with sufficient revenues, surrounded by its own nobility, and secure in a certain prestige. But actual power, save during the Shikkenate, lay with the Shoguns. As one member of a Shogunate family, with a literary turn and an engaging candour, once wrote: "The moon changes every month, but I am always the full moon."

The long reign of the first restored Emperor, Meiji, stretched from 1868 to 1912, and is contemporaneous with that brisk westernizing of certain parts of Japanese life that made the European world realize for the first time that such a people as the Japanese were actually in existence. A constitution, railways, Western legal forms, compulsory popular education, top-hats, swallow-tail coats, two modern wars, and many other aids to the Good Life as then conceived were quickly, yet methodically, introduced.

The process made Europe aware of the existence of the Japanese, but scarcely more. It did not make them realize for how very long these people had existed nor that they possessed a civilization of unusual quality. At the spectacle, however, of so small and so recently discovered a country defeating the great Russian Power in 1902–4 Europe was sincerely astonished, almost incredulous. But still uninformed of the country's past. The impression remained—nor is it wholly dissipated to-day—that a people latterly in a condition analogous to that of primitive tribesmen had somehow yet very suddenly taken to adopting the forms of European life. It was perplexing; and rather disturbing; in fact it soon became the "Yellow Peril".

Europeans did not, and most of them still do not, realize that the chief superiority of their civilization over Japanese civilization was due (to borrow some lines of Mr. Belloc) to:

> Whatever happens, we have got
> The Gatling gun; and they have not.

For some cause, which as yet is not at all clear, the Europeans had got the Gatling gun, and the mental technique that produced the Gatling gun. They had got hold of Natural Science and (from it) Technology—a method for investigating Nature and, as a consequence, for partly controlling it. They had got hold of steam engines and medicine and industrial chemistry. These things are spectacular as well as being useful: they gave and still give an appearance to European civilization that is unduly impressive when compared with that of Japan.

This, then, is the explanation of "the marvellous rise of Japan". It not only explains the "rise" but it explains too why the Western world knew so little of the Japanese until so late a time and why it began to know so much about them in so short a time. (It apparently does not take very long to acquire the Gatling gun technique.) But it is not only the secret, it is also the misfortune, it may even be the tragedy, of Japan; for the captivating appearance of the Gatling gun civilization has impressed her scarcely less, sometimes more, than it has impressed Europeans themselves. In this mental plight many Japanese are not content with merely taking over the Gatling gun; they hanker after all the ways of the Gatling gunners as well. It is of course a foolish confusion of mind on the part of such Japanese, and none the less foolish because easily understandable; but it is even more dangerous than foolish because they may lose their gold in pursuing what will turn out to be only the glamour of gold paint.

For though we have been taking the Gatling gun as a symbol we should to-day more fittingly have taken the mechanical dish-washing machine. It cannot be too frequently repeated that Japan's impression of the West comes via the United States. More of the Japanese students going abroad to study go to the United States than to Europe; and Americans visiting Japan far outnumber the Europeans. But these factors, though they doubtless count for something, are as nothing beside the powerfully capitalized and highly mechanized disseminators of American culture. American gramophones and gramophone records are reckoned by some observers as one such; and although these are to be heard cheekily grinding out their cacophonies in every corner of the Pacific, from Samoan grass huts to Malayan *pesars* and from there to Chinese slums, they appear to be a solecism rather than a menace. The true disintegrating factor is the American cinema, a sinister phenomenon which is not pleasant to contemplate by anyone who has seen something of its popularity and influence among the non-Caucasian peoples. American students repudiate it and deplore it no less than Europeans. We are not here concerned with the apparent irresistibility of its march over the entire world to-day; nor with the effect it will produce in the coming decades on the prestige of any European people governing and developing a primitive colony (for the great leveller to-day is not Communist propaganda but the cinema film, and in the silent world revolution that it is gradually working the levelling is mostly downwards); nor with its disruption of the standards and disciplines of older life-systems. The question for us is whether Japan as a whole can resist the almost universal fascination of the way of living portrayed and held up for imitation in the film. Alongside the flashy colour of film-life the quieter and economically poorer life of the Japanese appears dull and inferior: the inward anarchy and the ugliness of the former is unobserved or forgotten, and stronger and stronger grows the temptation to leave their gold and to pursue the gold paint. Every day in every week hundreds of thousands will gain their cheap and perhaps chief amusement by looking at pictures of and from the mechanical dish-washing civilization; and gradually they come not only to admire and want the mechanical dish-washing machines (which are worthy of all admiration) but all the ways and standards and habits of the people that invented them.

The Japanese, then, perhaps even more than the Caucasians, need reminding to-day that the quality of a civilization is not quite so flawlessly identical with having electric potato-peelers as seems sometimes to be thought, and that Progress comprehends somewhat more than erecting separate baths to all hotel bedrooms. Plato had not a single electric button in the house, while Shakespeare worked without the summer-time aid of a Frigidaire. There is still something to be said for the Athens of Pericles when compared with the Detroit of Mr. Henry Ford, and there may even be something for Kyoto when compared with Chicago.

III. Cultural

It is difficult for a European who does not know this people and their country to realize the quality of the culture that has been developed on those small unfruitful islands off the coast of Asia. On first going to Japan one encounters what he has never encountered before—universal politeness. Courtesy is all-pervading and it is exquisite. And if he be fortunate enough to go into Japanese homes he will not easily lose the impression of the first experience—at the threshold a member of the family helping to remove his shoes and to don the slippers that are worn indoors, the smiling welcome and the low and repeated bowing of the host and hostess, and (in hot weather) the hostess's artless fanning of him, and throughout an attentiveness and considerateness that cannot be wearied. The training in and the instinct for *politesse* is so diffused among all the people that members of one class are as carefully courteous to members of another class as they are to members within their own class. That semi-unconsciousness of the existence of servants which is so often to be seen in Europe would never be tolerated in Japan: for although the servant bows profoundly to the master on his entering or leaving a room the master in return bows as lowly and smiles as pleasantly as the servant. The same graciousness is observed by the poorest artisans and peasants to one another. An excursion to the popular beach near Tokyo is only less surprising than what follows when two heavily laden porters collide with one another. The ugly vice of wrangling seems hardly to exist. It is the same instinct for *politesse* which forbids any sign of annoyance or impatience, and which requires all criticism to be conveyed by hints and indirect suggestions. What we regard as candour they would regard as grossness. It is such obliqueness no doubt that led to their former reputation for dishonesty, one of the silliest untruths ever uttered by one people of another.

It has been not infrequently complained that such elaborate courtesy is merely external. Precisely at what such a criticism is driving is never clear; for if delicacy in social relationships makes them smoother and pleasanter, that, it might be assumed, would be sufficient justification for it. If the complaint means that the politeness is not the outcome of an inward considerateness it is not true, for this is even greater than the considerateness and courteous helpfulness that one finds among so many American men. It is to be seen not only in the politer social relationships but especially in such relations as those between master and man, employer and servant. It is not easy to treat a working-man as a "hand" in Japan, or to dismiss him unprovided for when a turn in the market makes it profitable to reduce the personnel. If a man is dismissed he is given an allowance that appears generally to be equivalent to about three months' wages and sometimes an extra sum in addition. Nor can a landlord evict a tenant when and how might be most convenient to his interests: the tenant must be informed weeks ahead and even then he expects to enjoy many weeks of grace besides: the landlord seems to be fortunate if his house is free within three months. Most curious of all is the obligation that employers feel (and generally carry out) not only to pay wages throughout a strike but to give a lump sum to the strikers to see them through the expenses incurred during the strike.[1] It is for this reason that the doctrine of the class-war and much of the other philosophy of the European Labour Movement is so peculiarly unsuited to Japan, and it may be no bad thing that the Labour movement there continue weak or ineffective until the Japanese Labour leaders develop more originality, and instead of borrowing alien formulas *en masse* they evolve a programme of their own and one that has some relevance to the conditions of Japanese life.

Inward virtue or disinterestedness or idealism is a large part of the average Japanese character. True patriotism (in addition to a merely intense nationalism) and the self-denial on which it is nourished are a conspicuous example, ranging from the Young Men's Societies (dating from the Middle Ages and to-day comprising several million members, which have much of the spirit which one might find in an adult Boy Scout Movement, but the good deeds they do are such things as clearing waste land and improving the standard of agriculture as well as improving their own minds and bodies) to groups like the Patriotic Savings Association (for contributing a daily mite

[1] Cf. series of articles in *Japan Weekly Chronicle*, July 1930, on Japanese Labour, by E. H. Anstice, B.A.; also Harada, *Labour Conditions in Japan*.

towards paying off the National Debt). But a still better illustration of Japanese idealism is afforded by their religion, particularly in its higher reaches. Zen Buddhism is a good instance. Its central teaching is that one should attain to one's "Buddha Nature"; that is, to realize what Bernard Bosanquet has called "the real self", or, as the Quakers have it, to follow "the inner light". All, men and women alike, can by their own individual efforts and without any aid or interference from priests attain to the Buddha Nature. Priests are as redundant (and they may even be hampering) as temple ritual. Silence is the chief means to this mastery over self. Zen Buddhism, it is clear, has a great deal in common with Quakerism. Its main contribution to Japanese life has been a serenity and a stoicism that cannot be easily disturbed by the accidents and pitfalls of life.

While Zen Buddhism is the religion of only a minority sect its emphasis on inward serenity and stoicism is an emphasis on qualities that form part in greater or lesser degree of every Japanese. To show any lack of mastery over emotion is to show the least pardonable of the weaknesses. The heaviest sorrows must be borne with a placid, even a smiling, face. Thus, too, physical courage is the *sine qua non*: to fail in this is to deny one's very manhood or womanhood. The many stories of the heroes' "friendliness with death" do not exaggerate the place of this trait in the national character. No people possesses the essentials (as contrasted with merely a love of bright uniforms and martial music) of the military tradition more pronouncedly than the Japanese. It is probable that another equally noticeable trait has its roots in this part of the national character—non-nervousness. An American biologist, Professor E. S. Morse, who went to Japan in the early days, not long after the restoration of the Emperor, has recorded his surprise at the relative absence of nervous diseases in Japan. A visitor to-day is equally struck with the absence of anything approaching neuroticism. A Japanese never seems to fidget or to become self-conscious, but to remain calm and untouched by even the suggestion of excitability.

The religion of Japan has another interest to the Western student for the light it throws upon the Japanese character. The national religion is Buddhism, but how different is the Buddhism from that of the tropical peoples. The distance between them is vividly suggested by visiting Kandy, the Buddhist centre in Ceylon, with its untidy temples and littered courtyards and beggar-infested approaches, and then visiting Kyoto or Nara in Japan. One moves in different worlds whose only possession in common is the common name of Buddha. The robustness of the Japanese character could never find satisfaction in this Southern Buddhism and has accordingly transformed the religion it originally borrowed almost beyond recognition. In this, as in every other respect, the common notion of what is "Eastern" will not fit the Japanese.

For notwithstanding all their sensitiveness, robustness of both spirit and body is another national trait. The æsthetic gifts of the race are too familiar to need recounting here—their heritage of paintings (probably not even Italy has a greater), their music (of which much more notice deserves to be taken in the West), their delicate crafts of cloisonné, lacquer, ceramics, damascene, and brocading, above all the dress they have evolved (Europe has nothing to compare with the Kimono) and the houses they live in, combining as they do a rare simplicity with a rare elegance, are all witnesses to these. Æsthetic gifts are often dangerous gifts; but the national robustness deprives them of any danger among the Japanese. Where else is there a national habit of climbing mountains to see the Autumn moon, or of scaling summits to catch the view at sunrise? It is good to love the Autumn moon from mountain peaks, but many times better if you have to labour up some height to satisfy the love. Their love of beauty (a very real thing) is generally somehow related to Nature and is almost a love of the beauty of Nature. Love of Nature, in fact, is the basis of Shintoism (a religion existing side by side with Buddhism—one can be and generally is both Buddhist and Shintoist—and is most briefly though crudely explained as being a compound of venerating Nature and venerating Ancestors) and its cult strikes the foreigner as often being little more than an excuse for taking a walking tour along an avenue of Cryptomeria, or up to some mountain point, usual places for the Shinto shrines.

As would be imagined from this, physical cleanliness is another characteristic trait. Just as there are no politer people than the Japanese, so too there are none cleaner. The peasant looks upon his daily bath as being as indispensable as his food. The poorest poor are never squalid, and their quarters never become the leprous excrescence upon the district that European slums are. To pass through what the Japanese consider to be the worst areas in Yokohama astonishes one after seeing the slum areas of industrial England, or of Pittsburg or Chicago in the United States. As we know them there are no slums in Japan; and, what is better, there seems to be no aptitude for forming them.

A people who have evolved such a happy scheme of social relationships as the Japanese can be expected to have been successful with the best but most difficult of all relationships—the family. They have been successful, perhaps to a degree reached by no other people. The home-life is charming, and particularly charming is the treatment of children. No children could be better used than the average Japanese children, and none too could be better behaved.

Why family life has been so successful is not easy to say. Perhaps it is partly an outcome of the Japanese conception of sex as a whole, a point in which their civilization appears to have been rather more successful than the European. Perhaps too it is partly due to the rather different conception of the sphere of women prevailing there from what now prevails in Europe and America. The phrase customarily used in this connection is the *Japanese status of women*; but such a phrase has connotations which are misleading. The distinction between Western and Japanese women appears to be, not one of *status*, but one of *spheres*. Her status is certainly higher than the status Milton, and probably Carlyle, would have given to women. (It is fitting to recall here that the Married Women's Property Act dates from the second half of the nineteenth century, and that Mary Wollstonecraft was conducting her crusade at the opening of the century.) The Japanese woman's sphere is clearly demarcated: she is "the honourable lady of the house". It is assumed that she will be a wife and mother, not a professor or an engineer or a political agitator. And although she enters the carriage after, not before, her husband, or may wait upon him and his guests at table, we must not be misled. She is no chattel (to use the feminists' favourite phrase): the arrangement in the home is not one-sided, but carries reciprocal burdens and advantages. It is true that the vast majority of women did not choose their husbands, but it is equally true that the vast majority of husbands did not freely choose their wives. Marriages are arranged—or until recently were arranged and among the majority still are arranged—by the respective families. It would seem that where the family is held to be of the importance that it is in Japan (the family covers many more units than our family, its cohesion is incomparably greater, and its protection over the individual member just as the obligations it exacts from him, are also incomparably greater) a matter like marriage cannot be trusted to merely individual fancy. The results of this attitude seem to be a sufficient justification for it.

It is evident that in this respect the present customs of Europe divide it fairly sharply from Japan. In nothing is Western individualism more fiercely animated than in love. In these latter decades, when the individualism is being carried to its logical conclusion, many Europeans are beginning to feel great doubts about it. The chaos of spirit that is laid bare in contemporary Western literature seems to be the chaos of an individualism run to seed. In the pursuing of individualistic love, affection is becoming lost. At all events, in Japan family life is reared on the quieter but more stable foundation of affection. And when it is said that Japanese culture is threatened in its very centre by the American film, it is meant that the objective of affection is in danger of being rejected for the objective of individualistic love; and the danger is not the less because the

American film offers (unintentionally) the crowning indictment of the latter.

The system of social relationships in Japan has been a very great achievement, and perhaps no part of it has been greater than the family system. But the same genius extends to other relationships—to political and to economic—and in them all is the emphasis on group welfare as against individual advantage. The dormitory system and the welfare work in the cotton factories is a small example in a difficult field. It is something so good as this that the Japanese are in danger of losing.

A strong group instinct is of course not without dangers of its own. The eccentric, the pioneer, the originator, has small scope for rendering his valuable (if sometimes disturbing) contributions to society. Perhaps too the power and status of the policeman in Japan is another manifestation of the less attractive side of the group instinct politically. It is a very unpleasant manifestation. One is not complaining of the policemen as individuals, but of the power and status of the police body. A primary care in any State that seeks to preserve a reasonable degree of personal freedom is to hedge in the power of the police to the utmost that the legitimate performance of their functions will allow. No tyranny is worse than that of a privileged police. They generally manifest only the lower strata of a country's culture and are probably below the average ethical standard, for otherwise they could not be doing such work. Such a tyranny is at its worst when it is linked with a habit of prying and spying and the despicable arts of the political detective. It is a regime the less defensible in Japan because in no country (except perhaps in China under happier auspices) do the people require less policing.

That police could be stationed in so great numbers in cities like Tokyo—in numbers almost sufficient to restore law and order to Chicago itself—without touching the sense of humour of the rulers suggests another trait: the Japanese, notwithstanding their persistent cheerfulness, are not strong in the subtler kind of humour. Irony is not in use. But it is a defect quite deprived of its usual seriousness by the national light-heartedness. Even the most prying policeman often shows a wide and teethy grin: for the Japanese have a great deal in common with Dr. Johnson's friend, "old Mr. Edwards", who tried to be a philosopher but had to give it up because cheerfulness would always come breaking through.

The lack of a sense of the subtler humour—and the rapid imaginative insight that goes with it—may also be at the root of their acquiescence in the present educational system, or rather educational methods. These encourage memorizing at a serious expense of thinking, and produce mere sand-heaps of knowledge instead of minds with an edge to them. To a sympathetic foreigner they, particularly in the higher grades (colleges and universities), seem as unworthy of the people as the power and status of the policeman and of the Defence officials.

Not only does the Japanese temperament lack the subtler humour and an animated imagination, but it feels little of the pathos of the human record. In all their wealth of paintings there are no Mona Lisas smiling a "smile that is not of this world". There are no Beethovens in the Japanese story, giants weeping grandly at the tragedy of human struggle; no Dantes; no St. Johns. Their very success in making the compromise between human ideals and human nature forbids that there can be. The Japanese does not aim at the sun or walk on air. His civilization (and the compromise on which it is based) does not reach the altitudes; it rests on the safer middle heights. The magnificent soaring idealisms and the magnificent crashing failures in the Western story are alike unknown. Though always pretty, it is, perhaps, seldom great. Let us not for this reason be disdainful of the Japanese compromise. Wisdom is justified of her children, and the Japanese have shown how much can be done on the middle heights. Moreover, while the Western story is largely a story of objectives unattained, the Japanese is a story of actual achievement. If the West could lessen the wastage from its failures it might be ready to spare its

Beethovens. At all events, for good or for evil—though surely to the loss of the old superiority of the poesy of the West—this seems to be the resolve now taking shape among a large proportion of the people to-day. Out of the chaos of values so evident in modern Western literature and life there seems gradually to be forming a resolve to make the compromise on a lower level, down to the easier or the safer middle heights. Our natural misgivings at this abandonment of the two-thousand-year-old effort of the Western world will be the less if such people show any signs of making the success there that the Japanese have made.

To do more than hint at a few of the outstanding characteristics of this unusual people is not possible here. Nothing can be said of their remarkable gracefulness—every act and every movement of the average woman and child is instinct with grace; nothing of their art, or their ethnic origins, or their present constitutional arrangements. And perhaps not enough has been said of the weaker aspects of their civilization. But from the little the reader may have learned of them, both the good and the bad, he will follow with the greater interest the condition, one might almost say the accident, in which they are finding themselves, because of the changing relation between the numbers of their population and the economic resources of their country.

CHAPTER III

PRESSURE OF NUMBERS IN JAPAN

I. Is there a Population Problem in Japan?

Whatever the realities may turn out to be, there are at least the appearances of a population problem in Japan. The population of Japan Proper numbered over 62 millions in 1928; in 1878, fifty years before, it numbered only half this figure—it had doubled itself in less than two generations. And in 1928 the Birth Rate was 34·4 per thousand. For the period 1921–5 it has averaged 34·3 per thousand, while the Birth Rate in England for the same period was 19·9, and in Germany 21·8.[1] Since 1922 more than six millions have been added to the country's inhabitants—that is, more than the entire population of Australia.

In the opinion of some observers there are factors, even more powerful than those they find in Roman Catholic countries, working against a fall in this very high birth rate. Social customs and the importance which religious tradition gives to leaving male heirs to carry on the veneration of the family ancestors allow of slight hope, in their opinion, for a thinning, rather the promise of a thickening of the present density.[2] Mr. M. Inouye, who is a Japanese business leader and officially connected with the Government, publishes a calculation, according to which the 60 odd millions of to-day will have grown to 108 millions by 1965.[3]

The density is already greater than that of any European country. The area of Japan (excluding the colonies) is 147,651

[1] Figures computed from those in League of Nations, *C.E.I.* 4 (1). They can also be found for Japan in *Finc. and Econ. Annual*, or *Résumé statistique de l'Empire du Japon*, or *Japan Year Book*; for Germany, in *Statistisches Jahrbuch für das Deutsche Reich*, 1926, p. 24.

[2] A standard book for the moral education of women in Japan before the modern education system was adopted says that "a woman who does not bear a child within three years after she is married should leave her husband's home". Vide Harada, p. 96. But the attitude in Western Europe was not so very dissimilar a century ago.

[3] In *Jap. Year Book*, 1928, Suppl. 20.

square miles or 382,315 square kilometres; that is, somewhat larger than the United Kingdom but smaller than California and less than half the size of New South Wales. And only one-sixth of its area is cultivable. There are nearly 1,000 persons to every square kilometre of arable land; in Holland, where the numbers are highest for Europe, there are 800,[1] while agriculture is of distinctly less importance to it than to Japan. Travellers are unanimous as to the minuteness and economy with which the land is utilized: "Not a foot . . . is wasted. Even the hillsides are terraced to the very summits with almost incredible labour."[2] This is the dominant note in every account, for indeed it is an obvious fact and could not escape the most casual tourist. One writer tells how he saw the outer crater of a volcano in Kyushiu being tilled while sulphurous smoke was rising from the centre of the new crater.[3]

Such being the case, the reader would naturally believe that

[1] The following table is condensed from Tableau I in *Population and Natural Resources*, *C.E.I.* 39, League of Nations, 1927:

DENSITY OF POPULATION IN JAPAN AND ELSEWHERE (1925)

Country	Population	Arable Land (Kilometres)	Density
		Millions	
Japan	59,737,000	60·2	993
Holland	47,416,000	9·2	802
United Kingdom	44,150,000	59·2	800
Belgium	7,812,000	12·2	640
Italy	40,548,000	132·3	307
Germany	62,569,000	204·8	305

Also vide U.S. *Trade Information Bulletin*, 642; Prof. Shimizu, in *Japan Year Book*, 1929, p. 41; and Professor Nasu, in *Proceedings Second Conference Institute Pacific Relations* (ed. Condliffe), p. 341.

According to Sir D. Hall in the presidential address to Section M of the British Association in 1926, it requires from 2 to 2½ acres of cultivated land to support a unit of population among the European peoples (*Scottish Geog. Mag.*, 1927, p. 47). In Japan the present figure is about ¼ to ⅓ of an acre.

[2] A. G. Brown, *Modern Japan*, p. 42; cf. King, *Farmers of Forty Centuries*; Copeland, *Rice*; Amer. Bankers' Assoc., *Japan before and after the Earthquake*; U.S. *T.I.B.*, 642, p. 2.

[3] J. E. Orchard, *Geographical Rev.*, 1928, July.

there must be little chance of extending the arable area. Some students think that an extension can be effected, but that at the utmost it will not suffice to feed the new additions to population made during the next decade or two;[1] others go so far as to say that there is virtually no chance of extending the acreage at all.[2]

And no relief can be expected from emigration. Apart from the overwhelming physical difficulties in the way of either seizing or arranging a field for several million emigrants, most specialists are agreed that emigration cannot remedy over-population. The room left by drawing off the surplus is immediately filled: the pressure of numbers is like the pressure of the tide against a barrier: remove the barrier and the tide immediately pours in to fill the newly emptied space.[3]

The present seems gloomy for Japan, and the future prospect gloomier still. We are prepared for stories of peasant riots and industrial disputes; for statistics suggesting that nine-tenths of all the families, in a land where families are much larger than in Europe, are living on less than £10 a month; and for an unusually large proportion of the population being required to engage in gainful employment—as much as 50 per cent., while in the United States the proportion is only 39 per cent.

The Japanese Government appears to have reason enough for its preoccupation with the matter. The interest indeed is not confined to the rulers: if a traveller were asked to single out the first subject engaging public opinion in Japan to-day his answer would be the population problem. It has gripped the imagination and the thinking of the whole nation. Journalists, politicians, students, all have the same story—our increasing numbers. The Tanaka Government was calculating on a 30-million addition by 1957.[4] It appointed a commission of

[1] J. E. Orchard, *Geographical Review*, 1928, July; Yamamoto, *Kyoto Univ. Ec. Review*, July 1927.

[2] E.g. Prof. E. M. East, *Mankind at the Crossroads*, pp. 72–3.

[3] Cf. Prof. Gregory, *Contemporary Review*, Nov. 1929; a convenient statement of the American point of view can be found in H. P. Fairchild, *Immigration*. Emigration is discussed at some length in Chap. VII, infra.

[4] *Trans-Pacific*, 24.9.27.

distinguished members to study the subject of providing the extra food that would be needed and in 1928 set up a permanent body (the *Jinko Shokuryo Mondai Chosakai*) for the same purpose. Schemes for land development in the colonies were elaborated, and also for hastening on industrialization. "The fundamental solution of the Food versus Population Problem is the one grand aim of the present Government's economic policy," declared the Minister of Finance.[1] Perhaps most significant of all is the fact that the Government of a country which a few years earlier had debarred Mrs. Margaret Sanger from disseminating contraceptive information now began discussing the subject itself, one minister pleading strongly for a favourable consideration.[2]

Yet none of the evidence that has been adduced above is proof that Japan has entered or is entering upon a condition of over-population. The conflict between numbers and economic resources is no new thing; above all is it no new thing in Japan. There are observers, not without claims to an opinion, who do not hesitate to declare that if there be any pressure of population to-day, it is not more but less stringent than in former times. The English-language newspaper, *The Trans-Pacific*, for example, says that there can be no question about the average Japanese being better off in 1927 than ten years earlier. The reports on Japan by the British Department of Overseas Trade speak confidently of a rise in the standard of living. And another observer has published indices which, if accurate, would demonstrate that production in Japan has definitely outstripped population, not population outstripped production.[3] A rise in the standard of living that such a calculation argues would be the more striking because it has been accomplished in the face of persistent economic abnormality over the last ten years, when slumps have been followed by natural disaster and natural disaster by foreign political disturbances and political dis-

[1] *Trans-Pacific*, 24.9.27.

[2] Ibid., 24.9.27; cf. 14.2.29; Harada, *Labour Conditions in Japan*, p. 96.

[3] Ibid., 14.1.28; Dept. Overseas Trade, reports on Japan, 1921–2, espec. 1922–3, p. 20; D. K. Overell, in *Trans-Pacific*, 7.7.28.

turbances by financial collapses, one set-back after another in disastrous sequence.

The case then is not clear. On the one side are the appearances of an acute problem—appearances sufficiently convincing to captivate the Government, its experts, and the publicists, as well as the people—while on the other side is the assertion of responsible observers as to the country being better off. Even if their assertion be denied, there are the effects of this chain of economic disasters and the depressions following on them to be accounted for. In order to clear the confusion only one course can be pursued, and that is to pass beyond the generalities and to wrestle with the facts in an arithmetical manner; in brief, to balance up the statistics.

As is shown elsewhere (in Appendix I) there are some special difficulties in the way of making a statistical examination of Japanese demography and economic life, and, as a consequence, some special limitations will be imposed.

Another difficulty is that of language. Though the Japanese Government publishes a number of statistical annuals in English and French, and though the international compilations and the Year Books of the French, German, Italian, and other European Governments publish some Japanese figures, there is a wealth of information both in the form of statistics and competent estimates and in the form of specialist monographs which is published in Japanese only, and as Japanese is a language beyond the time or the capacities of the average student, it remains inaccessible.

A quantitative analysis then can be undertaken only with great difficulty and with the assurance that the results will be less complete and must be more cautiously qualified than usual. It would be particularly unfitting to assume that they *prove* anything; but unless otherwise indicated they will suggest trends and point the general direction that Japanese life is taking with sufficient unambiguity.

II. The Quantitative Tests

It must be understood that we are not concerned in this analysis with discovering what number of inhabitants in Japan would result in the highest possible income to each inhabitant, or with ascertaining whether Japan is over-populated in the sense of having exceeded that number. The Optimum Density, as this theoretically perfect volume of population is called, is, in our present state of knowledge, a concept entirely beyond any means of statistical demonstration or even of approximate ascertainment. And in a study of this nature, which is interested primarily in the political implications of Japan's population growth, it would be irrelevant to digress in search of illustrations to a concept which is so remote from our purpose as to allow a community, all of whose members enjoy the standard of comfort of millionaires, to be over-populated so long as the income of each member could be enhanced by a reduction in the number of members. Yet it is well to recall the concept, if only to emphasize the poverty of information that we still labour under as to the connection between numbers of population and the average economic return to each. Since our present knowledge, or rather ignorance, is what it is, the only condition which we can assume to manifest over-population or, to use a term that is less objected to among the experts, undue pressure of numbers, is where a pronounced increase in numbers is accompanied by a continuous decline in the standard of living, and where there are no other forces that can be clearly singled out as explaining the decline. Our concern, therefore, will be to determine whether there has actually been an appreciable fall in the wealth and welfare of the average Japanese, and to judge from the several tests applied whether the fall—in the event of there being a fall—is due to a plethora of numbers. The comparison to be made is not between the present conditions and the ideal of the Optimum Density, but between the present conditions and the realities of the recent past. Such a procedure as is thus dictated to us will have no satisfying mathematical neatness or precision about it, and a deal of conjecturing from inadequate or ambiguous data will still be unavoidable; but it is the least unquantitative that is open to an investigator. At the worst our position will be that of the candidate in Geometry who remarked after an examination that though he had not exactly proved the proposition set before him he had at least made it appear highly probable; and generally our position will be less embarrassing.[1]

The tests to be applied for ascertaining whether there has been a decline or not in the wealth and welfare of the average Japanese are: (1) a comparison between the increase in National Wealth and the increase in Population; (2) a comparison between the increase in National Income and the increase in Population; (3) Movement in the per capita consumption of rice; (4) Movement in real wages; (5) the operation or not of Diminishing Returns in agriculture.

As for the movement in the per capita wealth of the nation the Government Bureau of Census has made the following estimates:

NATIONAL WEALTH[2]

Year	National Wealth	Per Capita	Per Capita when Price Changes are Eliminated
	Million Yen	Yen	Yen
1913	32,043	606	606
1919	86,077	1,530	608
1924	102,343	1,731	720

That is to say, between 1913 and 1924 the national wealth per capita has increased by as much as 20 per cent. That the

[1] On the Optimum Density, vide Cannan, *Wealth*, 1914; L. Robbins, in *London Essays* (to Prof. Cannan), and in *Economica*, April 1929; H. Dalton, in *Economica*, March 1928; A. M. Carr-Saunders, *Population*; H. Wright, *Population*; and A. B. Wolfe, in *Population Problems* (ed. Dublin).

[2] Figures for National Wealth supplied by Statistical Bureau of Dept. of Commerce and Ind., but the price changes have been eliminated by calculations of author, the U.S. Fed. Reserve Wholesale Price Index for Japan being used.

estimate for 1924 is near the truth is suggested in an independent estimate made by Mr. Hideome Takahashi, whose results are very similar to those of the Government Bureau of Census.[1]

As for the National Income the Bureau of Statistics in the Imperial Cabinet gives the following figures:

THE NATIONAL INCOME[2]

Year	National Income	Per Capita	Per Capita when Price Changes are Eliminated
	Million Yen	Yen	Yen
1913	2,334	44	44
1919	5,911	103	44
1924	12,882	209	104
1925	13,382	201	103

Though official these are clearly inaccurate estimates. There is in fact only one satisfactory method of estimating the national income, and that is by adding up all the incomes within the State.[3] There is evidence, however, for the approximate truth of the 1924 and 1925 estimates, and there is independent evidence too for a rise in the National Income, as will be indicated later, though we can be sure that it would not have risen as steeply as the figures here would represent.

Both the tests so far taken suggest an increase in capital and an increase in income markedly greater than the increase in population. If we could correlate them with figures comparing the increase in the volume of physical production with the increase in population, and in result obtained a similar trend, we should feel less uncertain as to the significance of the tests. But figures for physical production are not in existence; and in their absence and in the unsatisfactory nature of the first two estimates we can hardly venture to make any inferences from them without strong independent corroboration.

[1] Results of Mr. Takahashi's calculation communicated by the U.S. Dept. of Commerce.

[2] Vide, p. 56, footnote 2.

[3] Cf. Professor Bowley, in *Journal Roy. Statist. Soc.*, 1929, Vol. II, p. 165.

Probably in no other country in the world, certainly in no other country with a modern civilization, does the staple food amount to so large a proportion of all the food consumed as does rice in Japan.[1] It amounts to more than half the total diet. The first change or improvement that the poorer classes make in their way of life when coming upon an increased income is to lessen the proportion of rye or barley—"muji" as they call it—that is mixed with their rice. No better single indicator as to the movement of the standard of living could therefore be given than by the per capita rate of rice consumption:[2]

RICE CONSUMPTION PER CAPITA

(In Quintals)[3]

Year	Production	Imports (Minus Exports)	Available	Consumption per Capita
	Millions	Millions	Millions	
1909–13 average	90·87	4·23	95·1	1·81
1922	109·49	7·98	—	1·97
1923	100·26	9·71	—	1·82
1924	103·38	13·30	—	1·91
1925	107·96	14·98	—	1·98
1926	100·53	14·40	—	1·82
1922–26 average	104·22	12·07	116·29	1·90
1927	112·30	16·96	129·26	2·10

Absolute accuracy is not claimed for either the figures or the calculations based upon them, but they are sufficiently accurate to point the trend, and the trend, as the final column shows,

[1] Cf. E. C. Grey, *The Food of Japan*, League of Nations, 1928; and Professor Nasu, *Proceedings Inst. Pacif. Relations*, 1927 (ed. Condliffe), p. 355.

[2] "Its price [i.e. of rice] regulates the prices of all the other necessaries of life," says Professor Saito in the *Economic Journal*, 1918.

[3] Figures for Production and Imports are taken from *Internt. Yearbook Agric.* for years 1922 to 1927–8; figures for population were taken from the *Financ. and Econ. Ann.*, and the per capita calculated from the two sets of figures thus gained.

For other estimates or for the figures before 1909–13, cf. U.S. *T.I.B. Rice Trade in the Far East*; the Sec. to Ministry of Agric. in Supplement to *Japan Year Book*, 1927; Professor Nasu, op. cit.; Harada, p. 77; Dr. I. Takano; also Ohara Research Inst., both quoted in S. K. Inoui, *Trans-Pacific*, 12.9.29.

is clearly an ascending rate of consumption per capita. The average Japanese is eating more rice now than twenty years ago—he has increased his amount by 5 per cent. More than one investigation has been made on this subject and though varying in details they all agree in showing an increasing rate of consumption, and they show it from the 'Eighties and 'Nineties of the last century. Further confirmation is given in the decline of the area under barley and rye and the decline in the consumption of these cheaper cereals. Since the consumption of rice is the chief element in the standard of living, it is apparent then that notwithstanding fluctuations and, latterly, some halting in the upward movement, the standard of living in Japan as a whole has been steadily rising for the last forty years or more.[1]

It will be interesting to discover whether the movement in real wages confirms this suggestion of an ascending standard of living.

Of course a decline in real wages is not necessarily an indication of undue pressure of numbers. There are many factors that might depress them. The slightly downward movement in England during the decade prior to the War is now generally agreed among economists to have had its impulse in other forces than that of population.[2] At the most this is a negative test: if over a sufficiently long period of time and for a sufficiently representative section of the community the movement is definitely upwards, we can conclude that the size of the population, notwithstanding any other effects it may be exerting, is not depressing the standard of living. From our point of view there is, then, no undue pressure of numbers.

[1] The per capita consumption of some other foods has also risen steeply —e.g. fish and (to a much lesser extent) wheat. Fish is consumed in twice the quantity per capita as ten years ago, according to Professor Nasu, op. cit., p. 359.

[2] Vide discussion in *Economic Journal*, Dec. 1923, etc., between Mr. J. M. Keynes and Sir William Beveridge. Also Warren S. Thompson, *Population: A Study in Malthusianism*, New York, 1915; and Prof. F. W. Taussig, in *Economic Journal*, March 1925.

MOVEMENT OF REAL WAGES[1]

Year	Wage Index	Wholesale Price Index	Retail Price Index (1914—100)
1921–3	100	100	—
1921	96	102	—
1922	102	98	236
1923	102	99	221
1924	104	103	221
1925	103	103	218
1926	103	93	199
1927	101	87	189
1928	102	—	184

With all their inaccuracies and with all the qualifications that must be made to them the above statistics can be regarded as pointing the direction in which the wage-earners' standard of life has been moving. Indeed it is the opinion of Dr. Ayusawa, of the International Labour Office, perhaps the best-informed student of the subject, that real wages have been rising continuously from the 'Nineties onwards, the only reverse being in the War years, when the depreciation of money worked its

[1] Wage Index supplied by the Statistical Bureau of the U.S. Dept. of Com. and Industry, Wholesale Price Index by same, and Retail Price Index by Bank of Japan. The same result can be got from figures in the *Report of Tokyo Chamber of Com. and Industry*.

Qualifications must be made to these figures too. The wage index is based upon wages in thirteen cities and may be regarded as satisfactory. There is no cost of living index, however, whereby the movement of real wages could be determined precisely. In its absence we have to fall back upon price indices, and as there is no retail price index based on the same years as the wage index we have included a wholesale price index. As both indices refer to Tokyo alone they are not strictly comparable with the wage index; but as prices in Tokyo would not be markedly different from prices in the other cities they can probably be used without notable violence to the truth. No other measure is available in any case.

A more serious objection to this estimate of real wages is that money payments are a very inadequate indication of what the worker is actually receiving in Japan. Under the semi-paternalistic system of that country payments and allowances are made which are unknown in the West—workers' dormitories where free lodging and often board at half or less than half the cost price are given; bonuses as a general rule and not as an exception; allowances on discharge; and there are even cases of workers on strike

well-known effects on workers' incomes.[1] The ascent has shown no slackening in recent years, real wages being higher in 1928–9 than in 1926–7. The diminution in the number of strikes in the years since 1919–21 is probably one outcome of the rise in wage-earners' conditions.

Wages and workers' conditions indeed are much higher than is usually thought in the West. The common belief that the Japanese working man can be satisfied with a bowl of rice and a few coppers a day is an illusion that the British Department of Overseas Trade reports have very rightly been at pains to dispel.[2] A detailed investigation carried out by the Statistical Bureau in 1926–7, covering the income and expenditure of 3,406 working-class families, numbering over 14,000 members, found that the average family income amounted to 94·31 yen a month, that is, about £9 9s. 0d.[3] This seems to be higher than the average working-class family income in France,[4] considerably higher than that in Italy, and not very far behind the average English working-class income. Not only have wages risen

receiving strike expenses (Harada, pp. 12, 138, 144, 225; also U.S. *T.I.B.*, 642; and Ayusawa, cited infra). The question then is whether these payments and allowances are declining while money wages are on the ascent; for if they are declining the upward movement in money wages may be cancelled out or may even turn out to be a downward movement. After examining the money wage movement for the various trades, however, one finds that workers in the building or metal trades, where allowances are on a much smaller scale than in the textile trades, have been experiencing a movement in money wages not appreciably different from that of the textile workers. More reassuring still is the fact that these indefinite and extra receipts form, after all, but a small fraction of the whole, so that even if they were eliminated they would scarcely cancel out the advances in money wages; and in point of practice we know that they have not been eliminated and there is little or no reason for believing that they have materially altered.

[1] Ayusawa, in *International Labour Review*, Feb. to April 1929, and in *Industrial Conditions and Labour Legislation in Japan*. M. Albert Thomas, however, did not reveal in his report entire satisfaction with labour conditions, notably with the non-ratification of the Washington Convention. *Report of Albert Thomas to Governing Body of the I.L.O.*, March 1929, pp. 8–10.

[2] Dept. Overseas Trade, reports on Japan for 1921–2; 1922–3, pp. 5, 20–1.

[3] Vide *Jap. Year Book*, 1929, p. 258, or *U.S. Labour Review*, March 1928, p. 200; and April 1928, p. 127.

[4] But cost of living is lower in France, and probably in Italy.

to this degree, but working hours have been reduced.[1] In brief, conditions among the wage-earning class in general have been improving, and are hardly behind the Western European level.

There is little doubt that in so far as the tests taken are valid the standard of living in Japan shows a continuing ascent and especially during the last decade. The stable food is being consumed in larger amounts and the wage-earner has been becoming better off. But how far are these tests valid? The wage-earners after all constitute but a minor proportion of all the bread-winners in a country where half of them are farmers and considerable numbers are still engaged in village or domestic industries. Also it is possible that the increased wages of this minority class may be due to an unequal distribution of burdens and advantages within the State: the taxation system and the tariff schedule, for example, may be operating in such a way as to subsidize urban industry at the expense of the farmers. This to some degree is certainly happening in Japan just as it has been happening in U.S.A. Precisely to what degree cannot be said because complete data do not exist; but to a sufficient degree, we can be sure, as to deprive real wages of any claim to be necessarily representative or indicative of conditions in Japan as a whole.[2] Rice consumption per capita therefore remains as the indicator of a rise in the standard of life. Is it an adequate test? Not wholly. For this cereal is not only the staple food but a mark of social status as well; a Japanese family's standing is connoted by the absence or presence of cheaper grains mixed in its diet, somewhat as a family's standing may be connoted by the practice of dressing or not dressing for dinner. Human vanity, and its pathetic manifestations in doing the utmost to appear well with one's neighbours, will suffer most things before withdrawing from

[1] Act of 1923 came into force in 1926, regulating women's and youths' hours; and in 1929 night work for women was abolished and hours of labour further regulated. Vide Ayusawa, op. cit., and Harada, p. 164 et seq.

[2] Cf. *Financ. and Econ. Ann.*, 1928, p. 14 et seq. That the interest on agricultural capital is only half or less than half on other capital is illustrative of the same maldistribution of burdens.

that struggle. An increased consumption of rice may therefore represent not so much the fuller satisfaction of physiological needs as an attempted satisfaction of more insistent "social" demands or ambitions. This observation may not be worth much, but it must be reckoned with in any effort to estimate the significance of the increased rate of consumption. For a double reason—because it is the staple food and because it is a mark of social status—a reduction in its consumption will be long and strenuously resisted. Among the denials and economies that distress will impose this will be among the very last. Food consumption in fact, except among populations of the very poorest kind, is not an adequate indication of the standard of life: men do not live on bread alone, and their standard is indeed low if only that need is to be reckoned with. Food consumption, though one indication, is not by itself an adequate indication of the standard of the Japanese population. The standard of living may be on a downward grade for a considerable time before it will manifest itself in the rice consumption: in order to keep up the rice consumption there may be in operation—as there was in England during the War when tennis courts were turned into vegetable plots—what is known as a "transference of resources", in the case of Japan longer hours and harder efforts at work, for example, by the farmers, the majority class, a concentration on raising the nation's food that holds them more and more relentlessly to this single task. Is this phenomenon at work in Japan? To ascertain whether there is a decline in the wealth and welfare of the country as a whole we need a test that is more general than the last two, and above all one that will not be disguised by a scarcely visible "transference of resources".[1]

In other words, we need to know whether the rice is costing more to grow—whether the basic class in the community is working longer and harder to raise the staple food; in brief, whether Diminishing Returns are in operation.

[1] For a discussion of "transference of resources", vide Harold Wright, *Population.*

The whole argument indeed for the possibility of over-population anywhere ultimately rests on this conception of Diminishing or Non-Proportionate Returns. The agriculture, for example, of any given country provides food for so many men. Let it be assumed that at 1900 it provides food for 30 men to every square mile cultivated, at 1910 35 men, 1920 40 men, 1930 43 men. It is possible that a square mile will yield to the efforts of the 43 men not only as much per man as it yielded to the efforts of the 30, but even more. At some time, however, the point must be reached when a further increase of men will result in a lesser yield per man, if for no other reason than that the productivity of any constant unit of soil is not infinite. Otherwise the population of the whole world might be sustained on a square foot of earth, or indeed on the smallest microscopic speck that still remained soil. The cultivable land of Japan will support an increasing population at a standard of life that does not diminish only up to a certain point; beyond that point it demands more work and yields less in return to each of the workers. Has the agriculture of Japan reached the point where a given yield from the soil is demanding more effort to extract it?

III. Diminishing Returns

The common denominator that has been spoken of here as *effort* consists of hours of human labour, animal or other non-human work, quantity of seed sown, outlay on implements, outlay on water and water-works, and amount of fertilizer applied. Of these elements fertilizer and labour are to an overwhelming extent the most considerable in Japan: not only are the other elements relatively unimportant, but they are also nearly constant in amount each year. The presence or absence of Diminishing Returns in Japanese agriculture will be determined by the application of fertilizers and labour.

The author had hoped to have shown here the amount of fertilizers expended on each acre of rice-land (rice-land being taken because the bulk of Japanese agricultural effort is centred on it) and the yield of rice from each acre over the last twenty years; in other words, the amount of fertilizer expended on raising each bushel of rice. This would have demonstrated conclusively whether Diminishing Returns were or were not at work. But the statistics necessary for such a calculation do not exist. After making, however, rather long and tedious calculations from such data as do exist, and from personal inquiries in Japan, an estimate of fertilizer consumption has been made and the author feels justified in assuming from this estimate that a bushel of rice has in the last decade been taking more fertilizer to produce,[1] not markedly more, yet quite definitely more.

[1] Statistics for the consumption of nine of the principal "market" fertilizers (i.e. those fertilizers which the farmer actually buys) have, with rare generosity, been supplied both for quantity and for value for each year after 1912 by Professor Sasaki, of the Institute of Crop Science in the Faculty of Agriculture at Tokyo Imperial University (who, however, must not be held responsible for the use to which the author has put them). By summating the items for each year and dividing the result by the total cultivated area for the same year has been ascertained the average amount of market fertilizer expended on each acre. This figure has then been compared with the acre-yield of rice in each of those years.

Several objections to this procedure of course at once suggest themselves: (1) These nine "market" fertilizers do not cover all the market fertilizers. The reply is that those omitted are inconsiderable. (2) "Market" fertilizers altogether, however, amount to rather less than half the total fertilizers consumed. Green manure and excretum preponderate. The reply is that Green manures rather than declining have increased and also it is probable (despite several opinions to the contrary) that the amount of excretum has not declined; that is to say there is no decrease in the amount of non-market fertilizers used. (3) The calculations deal with the amount of fertilizer put on *all* the arable land, not the amount put on the rice-land. This, too, is not a final objection because the acreage yields of the other crops have moved nearly parallel with that of rice; that is to say, we can assume a fairly continuous distribution of the total volume of fertilizers consumed among the several crops.

This statistical estimate as to a bushel of rice costing somewhat more to grow seems to be corroborated by the following facts: (1) The per acre yield of rice, though fluctuating widely from year to year, has trended slightly downward since 1920, and now on the average is only a little higher than the yield of 1913. This suggests that despite the growing population and therefore growing demand for rice the yield has already reached its economic maximum. (2) The price of rice for eight years now has been higher than the General Price Level; yet despite this the rice grown over a large part of Japan, probably one-third or more of the rice crop, is costing more to grow than it sells for, and it is only grown by virtue of "sweated"

Labour is a still bigger item in the costs of growing rice than fertilizer. According to a recent regional study made by the Imperial Agricultural Association (of Japan), fertilizer amounts to rather more than a quarter of the total costs, labour to more than a third. Another and perhaps more satisfactory method of costings would show a higher percentage for both. At all events labour is a bigger element than fertilizer. Has the outlay of labour been rising in recent years to produce a bushel of rice? In the absence of actual figures the only means we have of estimating whether the hours of human labour have become longer is to ascertain whether there are more men compared to an acre who are in agriculture now than at some prior date. But here again there are no statistics. Nevertheless it appears certain that there are more men. There are undoubtedly more men on an acre now than there were fifty years ago, because the farming population has since then increased more rapidly than the area under cultivation; but whether it has increased more rapidly during the last two decades is a more difficult matter.

farm labour. The distress among the Japanese peasantry is very serious. Cf. p. 93 et seq., and pp. 101–2. (3) Rice from Indo-China and from Formosa can be imported at slightly more than half the price of Japanese rice. The superior quality of the Japanese article and the higher standard of living of the Japanese farmer would partly explain the greater cost, but they cannot account for the whole of so wide a discrepancy. Its cause seems to lie in the uneconomic cost of Japanese rice-culture. (4) The poor profitability of agricultural capital seems a further corroboration. The interest earned by agricultural capital is around 4 per cent., a very low figure for Japanese interest rates. It seems to be low primarily because land values are far too high in relation to what they can yield, and land values are high because of the pressure of agricultural population. This pressure is such that men are content to work a piece of land merely for subsistence, earning in return nothing for their skill, nothing for their management, often nothing for their capital, only "sweated" labour rewards.

It is understood that Dr. H. Ando, Director of the Government Agricultural Experimental Station, has made a study of the consumption of market fertilizers. This unfortunately is not available in English; but according to a reference made to it in Nasu, *Land Utilization in Japan*, Dr. Ando concludes that "the cost of increasing the amount of fertilizer per unit of area is *generally* less than the gain resulting from the consequent increase in production" (p. 243). This is contrary to the conclusion one would draw from a recent study made by the Imperial Agricultural Assn. for a number of farms, 1922–7 (kindly translated by N. Hayashi, M.D.), and from the present author's investigations.

Over some areas it has so increased; and there is good reason for believing that it has for the whole of Japan Proper (excluding the north island, Hokkaido).[1] And there is definite evidence in certain areas as to there having ceased to be a parallel connection between the per acre expenditure of labour and the per acre productivity;[2] that is to say, there is a Diminishing Return to the labour output.

So in reply to the great question, Are Diminishing Returns being shown in Japanese agriculture? we cannot give an answer of positive facts. We can give only an estimate. But it is a carefully considered estimate and, it would seem, the only one deducible from such facts as are known. According to that estimate it is taking more labour and more fertilizer to produce a bushel of rice in Japan now than it took twenty years earlier: in order to extract a bushel from the soil more has now to be put into it. It is true that at the moment it is not much more. Moreover, not all the land nor all the farmers are working under Diminishing Returns. Some farmers are still prosperous, some land is still profitable. But the evidence indicates fairly clearly that a majority of the farmers are working under Diminishing Returns.

Such farmers obviously could not live on farming alone. The question that arises at this point is how then do they manage to carry on, and where do they find additional income to meet the losses on their rice-culture, in particular to pay for the fertilizer (which is officially estimated to eat up two-thirds of all the cash that passes through the farmer's hands) they have put into it? They get it from subsidiary or outside work. Thus it is computed that about one-third of the farmers (significantly the same proportion, it may be remarked in passing, as those farmers who are officially estimated to end the year in debt) do some kind of work not connected with their farms; and a still greater proportion engage in sericulture; a work connected with farms.

[1] It is of course useless to compare the number of farm households (for which there are statistics) with the arable area since we do not know how many persons there have been in each household.

[2] Vide Nasu, *Land Utilization in Japan*, pp. 162, 191.

The farmer's deficit is being met by his subsidiary occupations, and of these sericulture is far the most important. Silk in fact has saved the situation. The raising of silk-cocoons is not new in Japan, but as a widespread subsidiary occupation of farmers and as a work that can be done in three and not, as previously, in only one of the four seasons of the year, it is new. It is a development that has been in process during the last twenty or thirty years. Between a third and a half of the farmers are now officially estimated to be sericulturists as well as farmers; and if all branches of sericulture were included the proportion would probably be greater. The recruits increase annually. It is the men faced with a deficit who naturally, where at all practicable, have gone into silk culture.

In general then the increasing cost of growing the extra bushels of rice—the extra bushels that have gone to swell the amount now consumed by nearly everyone and that have also helped to augment the wage-earner's income—is being met from the profits of silk, the profits themselves coming in turn from the prosperity of America, whose citizens can afford to buy such a commodity. But because the increasing cost of rice production is, as a matter of practical business, being paid for and therefore can still be carried on, primarily by reason of this silk development, we must not forget that there is still the increasing human effort to be reckoned with. The tedious work of rearing silk-worms is ultimately paying for it. How tedious that is would be too long to recount here, but a hint may be seen from an economist's account: the silk-worms "when small require the most painstaking care, and when large they eat enormous quantities and at the most unconventional hours. Having gorged at 11 p.m. they demand another feast at 3 in the morning. . . . Such work is akin to being on both day and night shifts" while it lasts.[1] For the present everything works, the only difference being that the farmer's hard lot is made somewhat, yet not spectacularly, harder. The significance of the phenomenon is for the future. It is when we

[1] D. H. Buchanan, in *Quarterly Journal of Economics*, August 1923, p. 559.

project the unmistakable trend twenty years or so ahead of now that we see its ominousness. Every extra bushel extracted from the soil will cost more and more.

How many more bushels will Japan probably be needing twenty years or so from now? Will the farmers be willing to expend the additional effort, even assuming that they can expend it, in raising these? Or can Japan find some way not now used of producing them, or if not producing them, of finding them? These queries summarize the population problem of Japan. For the time being it is a manageable problem and not out of hand. The real problem lies in the future: will it remain manageable? Before attempting any answer to that question we must first know what size the population is likely to be, above all to know whether the enormous rate of increase in recent years is likely to continue.

CHAPTER IV

THE FUTURE POPULATION

I. On the Movement of Population in General

The races of European stock doubled their numbers between 1700 and 1800, and between 1800 and 1900 more than trebled them, rising from about 175 millions to 580 millions.[1] Among the European races the population of England numbered about 8 millions in 1800, and four times that figure in 1900;[2] and besides this enormous addition to the population at home millions of men and women were sent out to America and the colonies. Reflecting over such multiplications men have become fearful for the future. By means of a little arithmetic they have calculated that at such a speed of expansion the human race will amount to so and so by 1950, so and so by 2000, and obtain figures that are beyond any means now known, or beyond any means feasibly predictable, of raising food and clothing for them. In order to show the dangerous potentialities of human reproductive power, one expert has computed that two persons could multiply to 1,700 millions persons in two thousand years, which is about the present population on the earth. Competent sociologists and competent statisticians are alike of the opinion that the recent rate of population growth could not safely continue.[3] This can be granted. The rate of the nineteenth century could not continue for many centuries, and it is doubtful whether it could continue for another century.

[1] Cf. Prof. Warren S. Thompson (Director of the Scripps Foundation for Population Research) in Pitkin, *Must We Fight Japan?*, p. 317. Such figures do not claim to be exact, of course; but they are sufficiently approximate to show the broad truth.

[2] That is, England and Wales. The actual numbers were 8,892,500 in 1801, and 32,092,000 in 1901. Vide *Summary Tables of* 1901 *Census*, Cd. 1523, p. 1.

[3] Cf. e.g. Sir G. H. Knibbs, *Shadows of the World's Future.* It is worth noticing here, however, that since the end of the War, since 1900, and of course before then, Production has quite definitely and quite considerably grown faster than Population throughout the world as a whole. Cf. M. Theunis at World Ec. Conference, 1927, president's closing address; also cf. League of Nations *Memo. on Production and Trade*, 1913–27.

There is, however, no reason for believing that it will continue. The fall in the birth rate has gone too far for that. This indeed is the first fact to be grasped in connection with the subject of population to-day. From the commencement of this century all but a few European countries have shown a steady decline and some a decline long before the commencement of the century. Because the death rate has also been declining a considerable excess of births over deaths still remained, thereby obscuring the true trend; but since the War a rapid shrinking of the natural increase has been in evidence. The birth rate in England, for example, was 35·5 per 1,000 in 1871–6; in 1928 it had fallen to 16·7; the natural increase was 11·6 per 1,000 in 1906–10, in 1928 only 5·0 per 1,000.[1] England's case is but an epitome, though in a heightened form, of the cases of the European races as a whole.

These figures would indicate a drop that was sharp enough; yet the true birth rate has fallen even more steeply than these crude rates show. Being crude rates they take no account of age-composition (i.e. distribution of persons according to ages in the total population); that is to say they ignore the fact that an unusually large proportion of the European population is now, and for some time has been, in the middle or reproductive years of life. The aggregate number of children born annually may not appear so very few when expressed as a percentage of the total population; it is when we express them as a percentage of all the families which are now at the reproductive period that their true significance becomes clear. Nor do the crude rates tell us anything of the fact that this age-composition, favouring a high aggregate of annual births at the present, is about to change to one favouring a low aggregate and one that will depress the natural increase even though families become notably larger.

It is obvious then that in mentioning age-composition we have mentioned a factor of basic importance in the movement

[1] From *Registrar-General's Statistical Review of England and Wales*, 1928, Tables I, II.

of population.[1] Crude rates of births and deaths, the ordinary way of comparing the number of births and deaths in any given year with the total number of the population, can tell only how fast that population has grown that year. Of the actual springs to the growth they tell nothing. Whether families are becoming smaller or larger, or whether the rate of natural increase is likely to change or to continue is not indicated in such rates. To compare, for example, the crude birth rate of 30 per 1,000 in one community with the crude birth rate of 25 per 1,000 in another is not necessarily to compare the fecundity of the two communities, although it be the usual "popular" method of doing so. It is possible that the average parent is having fewer children in the community where the crude birth rate is higher than in the community where the crude birth rate is lower, because the proportion of men and women in the reproductive ages in the former community is larger. Such an age-composition (with its higher proportion of persons in the child-bearing years of life) would normally result in the total number of births being higher and therefore the percentage to the whole population also higher even though families had less children. The crude rate is swollen to its bigness because there are more families. Thus to compare the crude birth rates of France with Australia or of England in 1910 with England in 1930 is spuriously to minimize the one and to magnify the other.

By reason of the changing age-composition of the European races the decline in the crude rate—i.e. the decline in the number of children added to every 1,000 of the population each year—is bound to proceed much further even though families become larger; and as families are not likely, for some time at least, to become much larger, the decline is about to slope down very steeply. There is going to be a smaller and smaller pro-

[1] The sex-composition is sometimes an important fact, as e.g. in immigrant countries like Canada or recently belligerent countries like France or Germany. In Japan the official figures show a slight excess of males, a very unusual condition. It may be due to statistical inaccuracies; and in any case it is not great enough to have much effect on the movement of population.

portion of families in the reproductive period; and there is going to be a larger and larger proportion of elderly people. The economic or the social or indeed the political effects of this silent deep transforming of the *personnel* of nations cannot be noticed here; it remains for us to take cognizance of the fact that not only is the birth rate about to drop more sharply but, for the same reason, the death rate—the number of those dying each year out of every thousand of the total—is bound to rise. Death reaps his richest harvest at the extreme ends of the field—among the young and the old. It is these who are still few in proportion to the whole. The young are not likely to increase their proportion, but the old will increase markedly in the coming years; and with their increase the death rate, whatever improvements may be made in medicine, will increase too.[1] The higher death rate in France is largely (though not wholly) due to the higher proportion of old people there, just as the very low death rate of Australia is largely (though not wholly) due to its low proportion of old people. Population experts in the United States are counting upon the death rate of that country increasing to perhaps 16 or 17 per 1,000 within the next few years. In 1925 it was 12·2.[2]

A falling birth rate and a rising death rate will work an obvious effect—a sharp diminution in the natural increase. And unless some rather improbable counterfactors arrest or retard their movements, both rates will ultimately reach the same point, one falling to it, the other rising to it, so that there will cease to be any natural increase at all and the population will become stabilized. A stationary or nearly stationary population is in sight for most of Europe at least. So closely within sight

[1] On the age-composition and its implications, vide A. L. Bowley, *Econ. Journal*, June 1924; League of Nations, *Natural Movement Population First Quarter Twentieth Century, C.E.I.* 4 (1); S. de Jastrzebsky, in *Journal Roy. Statistic. Soc. XCI*, Vol. II, 1928; Dublin and Lotka, *Journ. Americ. Statistical Assocn.*, 1925; Dublin in *Population Problems* (ed. Dublin); *Journal Roy. Statistic. Soc.*, 88, pp. 25 et seq. (especially discussion by Bowley and Stevenson).

[2] For the remarkable changes in the English age-composition between 1901 and 1928, vide *Annual Report of the Chief Medical Officer of Ministry of Health for Year* 1928, p. 12, etc.

is this for England that the population will have ceased to grow before the end of another decade,[1] and unless the number of children in the average family increases the population will decline markedly at the end of the century.

Unless more children are born to the average family in Northern and Western Europe than have been usual since the War—and in the United States since 1927—and unless the life-prolonging effects of modern Medicine are extended further than they can ever be expected to extend, these populations will not only cease to grow, but will gradually dwindle out of existence. Recently Herr Kuczynsky, developing methods that Professor Bowley had used with such excellent results in England, and later Messrs Dublin and Lotka in the United States, has made a series of interesting calculations showing that in spite of an apparently safe margin of natural increase, the true reproductivity, when reckoned, as it should be reckoned, with reference to the abnormal age-distribution, is not great enough to renew the present numbers of Northern and Western Europe, and that England, for example, is replacing less than nine-tenths of her population.[2]

Most students of the subject have in recent years been so preoccupied with the possibilities of man's overcrowding the surface of the earth that the opposite case, the vanishing of the human race, has only lately been recognized; and as might be imagined it is now being recognized with not a little perturbation of heart. From the panic of "Standing Room Only" we

[1] Professor Bowley in 1923 estimated, on a conservative basis, that the maximum would be 48 million odd, which would be reached in the 'Fifties. It is now agreed that the peak will be reached before then. Significantly, there were more deaths than births in the early months of 1929.

[2] R. R. Kuczynski, *The Balance of Births and Deaths*. The essential idea of this work was apprehended by Dr. T. H. C. Stevenson in 1925, and applied several years earlier by Dr. Bowley. Vide *Journ. Roy. Statistic. Soc.*, 88, p. 25. For Messrs. Dublin and Lotka's contribution, vide *Journ. Am. Statistic. Asso.*, 1925. Vide also Dr. Lotka's review of Kuczynski in *Journ. Am. Statistic. Asso.*, 1929. Also L. C. Connor, in *Journ. Roy. Statistic. Soc.*, 1926, pp. 53–66. For a recent application of such an analysis to the U.S. population, vide P. K. Whelpton, "Differentials in True Natural Increase," *Journal American Statistical Association*, Sept. 1929.

pass to the panic of the "Empty House": scarcely have we regained our composure from the disturbing computations of the over-populationists than we are assailed with the equally disturbing computations of Italian and German statisticians and the forebodings of the French *League of the Fathers of Large Families*, and are left to sustain ourselves on what hardihood we may draw from the sight of Signor Mussolini's fiery strivings to salvage some part at least of the Latin heritage by compensating every Italian parent of a sixth child with a portrait of himself.

To speak, as responsible students have spoken, of certain populations being "doomed to die out" is not a wise, though it may be a natural, way of drawing attention to a new or neglected aspect of the subject. Indeed to decry this decrease of numbers in such terms when Europe is urgently needing a decrease could be done only by a more than customarily engulfed expert. Whatever diminution may take place will in any case be gradual and will not betake us unawares. Nor does such a view allow for the normalness of a stationary or nearly stationary population. In the past—so far as the scanty data available can be used for any deductions—a stationary or very slowly expanding condition has been the rule. A great burst like that of the later eighteenth and the nineteenth centuries has been the exception. Consider what we know of the population of England or France from the early Middle Ages up to the end of the seventeenth century. In Japan itself numbers were stabilized for nearly two hundred years. Consider too what we know of the animal world and the rough balance that is held in it between numbers and food supplies. Not only is an accelerating movement exceptional, it is economically less advantageous. The economic condition of France, for several generations a very sound one and now probably the soundest in Europe, is not unconnected with the very slow growth of the French population over the last hundred years.[1]

[1] It is worth noticing that this vast increase of the eighteenth and nineteenth centuries was almost certainly not due to an increase in the birth rate. It

As to why the birth rate, not merely the crude rate but the true rate, the size of the average family, should be falling, here is one of the most perplexing problems confronting students of the subject of population; and not until a great deal of painstaking research has been made into the biology of population will any satisfactory suggestions be forthcoming. For the time being the experts, with very few exceptions of note, tend to ascribe it to the practice of contraception.[1] Eighty-five to ninety per cent. of the decline, in the opinion of Professor East, of Harvard University, is due to that practice.[2] It is not to be denied that contraception is being practised; and it is probable that the practice will be extended. Also in support of such an opinion as that of Professor East is the strong presumptive evidence which comes from the fact that the size of families tends—only *tends*, be it observed—to diminish as their economic and social status rises, a condition that would seem to argue against any self-regulating biological factor. But to explain the fall as being due, or even primarily due, to contraception is merely

is probable, very highly probable, from general historical evidence—the available statistics of course are of little use if only because they take no account of the age-composition—that the birth rate did not change appreciably. The increase was due to a change in the death rate. More children were not born to a family, but more of those born continued to live and to become themselves the parents of children. The lowering of the death rate is often ascribed to advances in Medicine and Hygiene. Such an explanation, however, overlooks the fact that had our forefathers in the seventeenth century enjoyed the medicine of the nineteenth and twentieth centuries their numbers could never have mounted to 40 million because the economic technique of the day could have provided sustenance only for 4 or 5 million. The lowering of the death rate was due to a general rise in the standard of living which in turn was due to the ever-increasing volume of production being brought about by the economic revolutions; the reduction of the terrible infantile mortality and the prolongation of life were but one element in this rise in wealth and the standard of living. The great expansion of the Russian population in the second half of the nineteenth century was clearly not due to advances in Medicine; the unhygienic peasant saved more of his progeny because the economic changes put more food, etc., at his disposal.

[1] Cf. H. Wright, *Population*; A. M. Carr-Saunders, *Population*; *Population and Parenthood, 2nd Report National Birth Rate Commsn.*, 1918–20; also A. B. Wolfe, in *Journal Pol. Econ.*, Oct. 1928–Feb. 1929, on Pop. Problem Since War.

[2] Edward M. East, *Mankind at the Crossroads*, p. 192.

an assertion which the asserters themselves would admit to have slight basis of quantitative knowledge; and it is certainly too simple an assertion to explain the whole phenomenon. Too many relevant facts cannot be accommodated within it.

The decline first appeared in Normandy in the early nineteenth century and from the Catholic peasants of that province (whether such people at such a period could in general be practising birth control must be judged as the reader thinks fit) spread to other parts of France. Nor was it long before a similar movement appeared in Ireland, another land of peasants and of Catholics. The effects of the decline on the population of France are known to all men. Not all parts of France, however, have a low birth rate: it is fairly high in Flanders and Auvergne, to take examples from the opposite ends of the country;[1] and what is more arresting, it is higher in the towns than in the rural districts,[2] a very singular fact and one that hardly harmonizes with the contraceptive explanation. Again the average birth rate of France is much lower than that of Italy as a whole, yet it is higher than the birth rate of Piedmont.[1] In England the rate among textile workers is notably lower than among coal miners: can we assume, as we must assume if the contraceptive explanation holds good, that birth is being controlled or restricted in the one region or among the one working-class group but not in or among the others?[3] Nor is it likely that the decline which is taking place in Spain and Italy, Roman Catholic countries with innate inhibitions of the strongest potency against contraception, could be due to this practice. As will be seen later there is no unmistakable shrinking

[1] Vide *League of Nations*, *C.E.I.* 4 (1), op. cit.

[2] Cf. *Revue d'Econ. Politique*, Mars–Avril 1929, p. 343. The division of land, in requirement with the French law of inheritance, is the usual explanation of the low general birth rate in France and therefore presumably of the lower rate in the country; but this is pure assertion. An acquaintance with the households of French peasants where the family is small makes it very difficult to believe that they are consciously limiting their families.

[3] A suggestion as to these differentials is made by C. T. Brunner in *Economic Journal*, 1925, p. 81.

—and a shrinking that has been taking place for the last two decades—in the size of families in a certain Oriental country which we can be certain was not due to contraception. It is pertinent to ask, moreover, before leaving the subject why, if contraception be so widespread, are such a surprisingly large proportion of first-born children conceived *ante nuptiales*—more than one-fifth of all the first-born children of New Zealand, for example, about the same for Australia, and undoubtedly more for most countries.[1] Such parents, if any, it would be imagined, might willingly avail themselves of such a device as contraception. The predominant impression, indeed, left on the author's mind after attending a conference of population experts in America last year, at which several obstetricians interested in birth control clinics spoke, was the very great difficulty in the way of getting contraceptive information or material and then when got the insecurity as to its effectiveness. This, in fact, leads us to the supreme difficulty in the way of the contraceptive explanation of the fall in the birth rate: the records of the failures of contraceptive efforts among patients at Birth Control Clinics themselves.[2] These are well known to specialists but, it is imagined, will come as a considerable surprise to the average person. If the clinics, with every advantage of equipment and expert knowledge, experience so many failures, how can we assume that the generality of people are practising methods so much more efficacious as to turn the birth-rate movement in the way that it has been turned in recent years? In fine, whatever part birth control may be playing in depressing the birth rate, it is not the only factor, and such

[1] Vide *New Zealand Official Year Book*, 1928, p. 123; Comm. of Australia *Year Book*, 1928, p. 949; also *Population and Vital Statistics, Bulletin* 39, p. 94, Austr. Bur. of Statistics.

[2] Vide detailed investigation carried out by L. S. Florence, *Birth Control on Trial* (foreword by Sir Humphry Rolleston). It is understood that Mrs. Margaret Sanger has recently prepared a record of the cases going through her clinic. Convenient bibliographies on the whole field of contraception can be found in the *Eugenics Review*. It must be understood that most of the birth-control literature is propaganda, and therefore of very slight scientific value. It seems, too, to be impregnated with an unnecessarily philistine attitude to marriage.

little evidence as can be marshalled on either side suggests that it is not the primary factor.[1]

Of the work that has been done on the biology of population perhaps the most relevant in this connection is that of Professor Raymond Pearl showing the effects of density on the rate of reproduction in fruit flies, domestic fowls, and wheat.[2] In all cases a marked and more or less precise decline is correlated with the density of the flies or fowls or wheat stalks.[3] Another American biologist has shown that any curtailment or interference in the food supply of an animal colony has a marked effect on the number of births in it. What food is to animals the standard of living, in which food of course constitutes but a part, is to human beings. If a conception of or a desire for a higher standard dominates the thinking, or if the present standard is pressed upon by economic exigencies, the result may be the same as limitation of food among animals; that is, a smaller number of births. That some automatic self-regulating factor may be at work maintaining a balance between numbers and the standard of living is suggested by the possibilities of its operating biologically. More needs to be known, for example, about death *in utero*, and more about the implications of the claim that *couche fausse* may happen in the earliest stages without the subject knowing it. The statistician too has a wide field in investigating changes in the average age of marriage[4]

[1] Also vide an important study by W. T. Russell, "A Study of Irish Fertility, 1870–1911", *Metron*, 31.3.28.

[2] Raymond Pearl, *Biology of Population Growth*, 1925, Chaps. I, II, VI, IX. Also cf. pp. 1–90 in *Journ. Roy. Stat. Soc.*, Vol. 88. Other relevant and significant evidence is claimed to be given in studies of fecundity in aristocracies, e.g. of Sweden or Belgium, records for which, of course, are much more extended than for ordinary population statistics; but the author has not been able to examine these studies.

[3] The association of these facts with a somewhat discredited theory of population has, perhaps, deflected attention from the truth that they are experimentally ascertained knowledge which can lose nothing in validity or significance on account of the accident of such association.

[4] The marriage rate is declining over Europe as a whole, in Mediterranean Italy as well as in Scandinavia. Statistics can be found in publications of the Institut. Internat. de Statistique or in *Annuaire Statistique de la France*, e.g. Vol. for 1926, p. 202 et seq. Though this decline must be partly responsible for the decline in natality, it cannot explain the whole phenomenon.

and in the ages of child-bearing.[1] Meanwhile we can only know as a fact that natality is declining, and that the usual explanation of contraceptive restrictions will not account for all of the decline. By overlooking the inadequacy of such an explanation we may lose sight of what is much more interesting and much more significant, namely the possibility of Nature, through the infinitely complicated and little understood mechanism of mind and body, bringing about an equilibrium between numbers and environment.[2]

II. The Rate of Growth in Japan

During the five years 1922–6 the number of births in Japan averaged 34·3 per 1,000 per annum. In 1928 the birth rate was 34·4 per 1,000—England's birth rate for the same year was 16·7, or less than half the Japanese figure. As has been pointed out earlier, it has been estimated by the Government that at such a rate of expansion the population will have added 30 million to its present 60 million by 1957, and according to the figures published by Mr. M. Inouye, it will have become 108 millions by 1965.[3] But will this rate continue? That is the crucial question.

From the glance which we have just taken at the movement of the European and extra-European populations we saw that among them a rise in the death rate is imminent and that the

[1] The decline in child-bearing is greatest for ages beyond 30 to 35, cf. League of Nations, *C.E.I.* 4 (1), op. cit.

[2] The present condition in the Irish Free State perhaps ought to be mentioned here. The marriage rate (true as well as crude) is extraordinarily low, and the age of marriage extraordinarily late. Yet despite this abnormal proportion of bachelors and spinsters the number of children is not abnormally low because of the high birth rate—the highest in Europe. Vide *Irish Free State Census*, 1926, Vol V.

[3] *Japan Year Book*, 1928, Suppl. 20. It is worth noting that Mr. Inagki calculates on purely statistical and therefore unacceptable premises 91–2 million by A.D. 2000 (Nasu, p. 352); while Professor Raymond Pearl, by means of the logistic curve, calculates 86 million by A.D. 2000 (Pearl, *Studies in Human Biology*, pp. 621–6). Neither of these estimates has more than a technical statistical interest. For the limitations of such extrapolated curves, vide Knibbs, *Eugenics Rev.*, Jan. 9, 1928.

birth rate is falling even more steeply than appears on the surface. This double movement, bringing a stationary, perhaps even a slightly diminishing, population within sight, was detected only after examining the deaths and births in the light of the age-composition.[1] How does the natural increase and the accelerating birth rate of Japan, which lead some Japanese students to expect a 50-million addition within the next three decades, stand in the light of the age-composition of the present population?

Our first interest is naturally with the size of the group that can become the parents of children. This is given in the following table:

SIZE OF REPRODUCTIVE GROUP IN JAPAN[2]

Country	Total Females	Females aged 15 to 49	Percentage of Females 15 to 49
Japan	29,723,000	14,108,000	47
France	20,352,000	10,684,000	52
England and Wales	19,811,000	10,713,000	54
Germany	31,632,000	17,446,000	55

The size of the reproductive group in France and also of two other countries is added for purposes of comparison. It has already been remarked that the population of France is now nearly stationary. As such it offers an acceptably approximate indication of what would be the age-composition of a theoretically normal (or stabilized) population, and also of what no doubt is rapidly becoming the age-composition of most of the European and extra-European countries. We thus see that notwithstanding the very high number of children born each year in Japan the group that can give birth to them is considerably

[1] A recent interesting case is the study of U.S. Population by Dr. P. K. Whelpton, op. cit. The crude rate of natural increase of the native white population in New York State, Connecticut, and Massachussets was 4 per 1,000 in 1920, yet the true rate was actually a decrease of 6 per 1,000.

[2] Figures are for 1925 or census-years nearest to 1925. *Aperçu de la Démographie des divers Pays du Monde.*

below normal in size—5 per cent. lower than the French (and the theoretically normal) group and 7 per cent. to 8 per cent. lower than the English and German groups. Yet it is with this much lower proportion of child-bearing persons that Japan has a crude birth rate in the census-year, 1925, of 33·8 per 1,000 inhabitants as compared with 18·9 in France and 18·3 in England for the same year—a crude rate that is nearly twice as high as their rates.

Not only then is the crude birth rate in Japan very high, but an analysis of the age-composition reveals that the true birth rate is even higher than this very high crude rate. A comparison between the fecundity (as contrasted with the merely crude birth rates) in Japan and in several other countries is given below:

COMPARISON OF FECUNDITY[1]

Country	Births	Women aged 15 to 49	Average Children Born to Each
Japan	2,210,000	14,708,000	·15
France	813,000	10,684,000	·07
Italy	1,181,000	9,820,000	·12
England and Wales	848,000	10,713,000	·07

These tables would seem to argue little hope for a halting in the rate of increase in the Japanese population: for if an unusually small reproductive group is giving birth to an unusually large number of children each year, what will be the number of children born when the reproductive group has grown to a normal size? To state the question only in this way, however, is to ignore aspects that should not be ignored. It is not enough to know that fecundity is very high at the moment. We must also know its movements during the last two or three decades,

[1] The figures are for the last census-year of each country, all between 1921 and 1925, and are taken from the collections of Inst. Internationale de Statistique at The Hague: *Aperçu annuel de la Démographie du Monde*, 1922–5, for births; female age groups from the same and from *Aperçu de la Démographie des divers Pays du Monde.*

above all, the tendencies that those movements will disclose. Has it been rising steadily and continuously to its present high level, or has it remained fairly constant around it, or has it been receding to it from an even higher level? The following tables will answer these pertinent questions:

CHANGES IN JAPANESE FECUNDITY. I[1]

Year	Births	Married Women aged 15 to 44	Average Births to Each
1898	1,494,000	5,381,000	·27
1908	1,824,000	5,839,000	·31
1918	1,934,000	6,586,000	·29
1925	2,210,000	8,397,000	·26

The number of births, the number of married women in the child-bearing ages, and the average number of children born to each in the year of the four census-takings between 1898 and 1925 are here given. It is seen that the average number of children born to married women has been declining since 1908. Up to 1908 fecundity was rising; but since then it has turned and has begun declining, especially since the end of the War.

The figures, to be satisfactory, should be further refined. The distribution of women over so large a group as that covering the ages 15 to 44 might vary, there being possibly a bigger proportion in the more highly reproductive years at one period than at another. That is to say, the number of births should be related, not merely to all the married women in the child-bearing ages, but to those between 15 and 29, the most

[1] Figures from same sources as in previous footnote, and from *Annuaire internationale de Statistique* 1920–1, Vol. V. Also *Japan Year Book*, and *Statistique internationale, Ministère du Travail*, Paris, 1907. It ought to be added that the figures are not strictly comparable since the census of 1925 was the first adequate census taken in Japan. The figures for the married women should be somewhat higher in each of the three previous census-years than as they stand here. But the tendency has no doubt been in the direction that the above calculations suggest.

reproductive years and those indeed which in Western Europe contribute about half of the annual quota of all births. Such a refinement is the more desirable in the case of Japan because the proportion of married women in the group 15–29 has not remained constant:

CHANGES IN JAPANESE FECUNDITY. II[1]

Year	Births	Married Women aged 15 to 29	Average Births to Each
1898	1,494,000	2,385,000	·62
1908	1,824,000	2,412,000	·76
1918	1,934,000	2,630,000	·73
1925	2,210,000	3,923,000	·56

Once again the essential truth is brought out: there is a decline in fecundity. Families are getting smaller. Up to 1908 fecundity was still rising, but since then it has fallen; and if the official statistics are anywhere near accurate it has fallen sharply. It is particularly interesting that the fall has been so pronounced in the seven years between 1918 and 1925. The census that is now (1930) being taken in Japan will be awaited with the keenest interest on the part of demographers to observe how far the decline has continued and to see whether between 1925 and 1930 it has been as sharp as between 1918 and 1925. It probably has been sharper.

Although the decline as is clearly shown by the tables is a decline actually in the fecundity of the married women and not merely an average decline which could be made to appear in the calculations because of a decline in the marriage rate, the following statistics as to the movement in the marriage rate have an interest on their own account:

[1] Same sources as before; also vide *Résultats statistiques du Recensement*, p. 35. For reasons pointed out above, the figures in 3rd column should be somewhat lower for years 1898 to 1918 than they are here; but whatever reduction may be necessary to get to the accurate ratio would not be great enough to reverse the trend revealed above.

MARRIAGES PER 1,000 INHABITANTS[1]

Year	Per 1,000	Year	Per 1,000
1920	9·76	1924	8·68
1921	9·14	1925	8·73
1922	8·95	1926	8·31
1923	8·77		

These are the crude rates and therefore ignore the changing age-composition of the Japanese population and the gradual swelling of the reproductive and therefore of the marriageable group. The decline in consequence is still sharper than these crude rates show. No statistics are available that would allow of a refining of the figures, but a further indication as to the decline and one which shows that it has been in process since 1908 at least is given in the following figures:

MARRIAGE RATE, 1908–25[2]

Year	Number of New Marriages	Women aged 15 to 29	Ratio per cent
1908	461,254	6,207,000	7·4
1918	500,580	6,972,000	7·1
1925	521,438	7,520,000	6·9

Not only are fewer of the Japanese who arrived at the marriageable age now entering into marriage than formerly but they are marrying somewhat later[3] (which may be the same thing

[1] *Annuaire internationale de Statistique*, 1920–1, Vol. V, p. 108; *Aperçu annuel de la Démographie du Monde*, 1922–5, p. 233.

[2] Sources same as in footnote [1], p. 82.

[3] The statistics of marriages show that those contracted at or before the age of 24 years have been declining somewhat since 1908 at least. There is a marked decline in the proportion of marriages contracted at or under the age of 20 years. Vide: *Ann. int. de Statistique*, 1920–1, Vol. V, p. 112; *Aperçu ann. de la Démog. du Monde*, Vol. I, p. 245; *Aperçu de la Démog. des divers Pays du Monde*, 1927, p. 103.

though not necessarily). The marriage rate indeed is lower than in France[1]—and Japan has an age-composition that is somewhat more favourable than that of France for the marriage rate, while also Japan has not the necessity of retaining a large number of women as spinsters because of the loss of men in the War. Moreover, the view on marriage in Japan is very different from that in Western Europe. In Western Europe the individual is practically free as to whom he or she marries, or as to whether he or she chooses to marry at all. In Japan the individual is not free, or at the best much less free, to choose his or her consort; and, more pertinent still, social conventions demand that people be married and regard the single state with disfavour. Here then is a significant movement under weigh. In order to bear down the obstacle of such a tradition forces of no ordinary power must be at work.

Such forces in fact are at work and the decline in the marriage rate is but one of several social changes that are being made in response to a changing social environment. The changes are yet in their beginnings, but already they are gaining pace, and the future which they promise is indeed far from what was known and approved in Old Japan. The changing conception of the standard of living and the new importance given to material comforts, above all, the infiltration of Western individualism, will at least among a considerable proportion of the people break down the old ideas on marriage as surely as they will make for smaller families. The rise of factory industries and the massing of large numbers of men into urban areas will accelerate the changes. For although industrialization is sometimes claimed to be followed by a higher birth rate, relevant historical evidence demonstrates the contrary in no ambiguous way. Chicago, to take one of many possible examples, though still growing in numbers cannot even renew itself, let alone increase itself by an excess of births over deaths. In point of

[1] Cf. *Annuaire Statistique de la France*, 1926, pp. 202–5. The marriage rate has been declining somewhat for all Western Europe.

fact the birth rate in Japan is higher in the country than in the cities.[1] All these factors will not only reduce the marriage rate and still more the birth rate, but they will retard the average age of marriage, and to retard the age of marriage is to introduce one of the most immediately depressing agencies on the birth rate that is known.[2] Were the age of marriage delayed by 5 or even by 2 or 3 years, it would almost certainly reduce the average size of Japanese families by one and probably by two children. The final factor that will operate to push down the birth rate further still is the spread of contraception, at least in the urban areas. What has been mostly a subterranean movement in other countries may assume a very different effectiveness when it is organized and, in a sense, encouraged by the authorities as one method of coping with the menace of surplus numbers.[3]

It is to be expected that the declining fecundity, and the forces making for that declining fecundity, which we have just seen to be at work over Japan as a whole, would be accentuated in the great urban areas like Tokyo, Osaka, or Nagoya. This in fact is happening. To illustrate the accentuation and to indicate the probable future movement of the Japanese population the author has made a study of the demography of Tokyo, from which the following summary tables are taken:

[1] Cf. Yamasaki, in *Proceedings Inst. Pacific Relations*, 1927 (ed. Condliffe), p. 36.

[2] Cf. C. T. Brunner, *Econ. Journal*, 1925, op. cit.

[3] The Deputy Mayor of Tokyo in his Report, Sept. 1929, urged that free information should be disseminated by the municipal authorities. Vide *Trans-Pacific*, 19.9.29; 6.3.30. A women's society with influential leaders, including Mrs. Miyazaki, a relative of the late Emperor Taisho, has also decided to launch a campaign propagating birth-control information in Tokyo. Vide *Trans-Pacific*, 14.2.29. Advertisements and articles on contraceptives appear in Women's magazines. Cf. Harada, *Labour Conditions in Japan*, pp. 97–8. The clinic, however, which was being conducted in Osaka by the Welfare Section of the Osaka Municipality, was raided and temporarily suppressed in August 1930. This clinic had been running for a short time only, but up to date had had over 3,000 applicants. Cf. *Osaka Mainichi*, 23.8.30.

CRUDE BIRTH RATE IN TOKYO[1]

Year	Tokyo	All Japan
1923	27·9	34·9
1924	27·8	33·8
1925	30·8	34·9
1926	27·8	34·8
1927	26·9	33·6

The crude rate for all Japan is added for purposes of comparison. It will be observed that the Tokyo figures are quite considerably lower than those for all Japan. But these are only the crude rates. Since the population of the big urban areas in Japan comprises a large emigrant stock from the country Tokyo, like the rest, will have a large proportion in the child-bearing ages. In point of fact the proportion of persons there who could become the parents of children was at the last census (1925) as much as 10 per cent. higher than for all Japan. The difference between the true birth rates is therefore still wider than that between the crude. The following table will bring this out:

FECUNDITY IN TOKYO (1925)[1]

Births	Married Women aged 15 to 29	Average Children Born to Each	Average Children Born to Married Women aged 15 to 29 in all Japan
61,498	133,507	·46	·56

The two final columns compare the fecundity. They show the fecundity of Tokyo to be about 20 per cent. lower than that of the country as a whole. Two other tests have been applied for ascertaining the comparative condition and they both show a similar result. It will be very interesting to see how the comparison has stood throughout the last 5 years when the census of 1930 has published its findings.

The decline in Tokyo fecundity is no doubt due to several

[1] The figures for Tokyo were supplied by the Statistical Bureau of Tokyo City.

factors. For example the sex-composition of the Tokyo population is abnormal in its unusual preponderance of males (55 males to 45 females). But it can be accepted that the decline in general is due to the well-known effects of urban environment upon the movement of population. One of these effects is the decline in the marriage rate of Tokyo, a decline that has been particularly marked during the last five years.

There has been no opportunity of studying Osaka, Kobe, or other urban groups; but it is not likely that these would be experiencing dissimilar changes from those of Tokyo.

Such are the forces, then, that are operating and will continue to operate against the present large annual increase. What of the forces that are operating in favour of it?

Of these the strongest comes from the peculiar age-composition of the Japanese population. The present reproductive group, as we have already seen, is still smaller than what might be regarded as the theoretically normal size and is much smaller than that of most Western European countries to-day. On the other hand, the pre-reproductive group is unusually large, and up to the 'Fifties and 'Sixties at least a larger and larger stream will be flowing from it into the reproductive group and so will be swelling the proportion of persons who can give birth to children to an abnormal size.[1] The following tables will make this clear:

INCREASE IN THE PRE-REPRODUCTIVE GROUP[2]

Year	Total Females	Aged 1 to 14	1 to 14 as a Percentage of Total Females
1898	21,689	7,102	32
1908	24,542	8,344	34
1918	28,042	9,827	35
1925	29,723	10,861	36

[1] Estimates of the working population (which is nearly identical with the reproductive group) of Japan and of the United Kingdom, made by Dr. A. L. Bowley for the League of Nations, indicate that the Japanese working population will have increased 35 per cent., the English 26 per cent. over the 1910 size. *Estimates of the Working Population, C.E.C.P.* 59 (1), p. 5.

[2] Same sources as in footnote [1], p. 82, plus *Japan As It Is*, p. 28, and *Statistique internationale Ministère du Travail*, Paris, 1905.

ABNORMAL SIZE OF THE PRE-REPRODUCTIVE GROUP[1]

Country	Total Females	Aged 1 to 14	1 to 14 as a Percentage of Total Females
Japan (1925)	29,273	10,861	36
Italy (1921)	19,621	5,895	30
Germany (1919)	31,632	8,527	26
France (1921)	20,352	4,379	21

The final columns in both tables contain the essential figures. An extraordinary and most striking characteristic of the Japanese population is thus revealed: the proportion in the pre-reproductive group in Japan is more than two-thirds as great again as that in France, that is to say two-thirds as great again as what would be the normal proportion in a stationary population and what no doubt will soon be the normal proportion in Western Europe. Such a characteristic has been brought about by the rapid growth of the Japanese population, a people of 30 millions in 1870 having grown to double that number by 1925; and in this doubling process the proportion in the pre-reproductive group has been steadily increasing to its present size. But the fact is not the less remarkable because we can see how it has come about. At all events the next two or three decades or so will see these children entering the child-bearing group, and they will in turn swell that group to an abnormal bigness. For the time being (as for the recent past) the Japanese population is still a very young population—one with an unusual percentage of its members in youth and early middle age, above all in childhood, so that the full effect of its reproductive forces is yet to come. Individuals may go on begetting, as they already are begetting, fewer and fewer children than did their fathers and grandfathers; but because there will be so many individuals in the begetting ages the aggregate number of children born in any one year is bound to be great throughout the next two or three decades or so.

[1] *Aperçu de la Démog. des divers Pays du Monde*, 1925, and *Aperçu annuel de la Démog.*, 1922–5.

The other force operating in favour of a high increase of population will come from the movement in the death rate. The crude death rate is now high—19·8 per 1,000 in 1928.[1] Judging from the average age of life in the pre-War years[2] and from the infantile mortality rate[3] and also partly from the smallness of the elderly group in the population there seems no doubt as to the true and not merely the crude rate being higher than in Western Europe and notably higher than in British colonies like Australia or New Zealand. From improved hygiene alone a decline may be expected. It is indeed already in operation.[4] And because less children will be born to any one family there will be an additional factor to diminish the present rate. Finally, the proportion of elderly persons will not increase notably during the next two or more decades.[5] That proportion, as might be assumed from the fact that the Japanese population has doubled its numbers during the last thirty years, is abnormally small, for the present group of elderly persons consists of survivors from a time when there were only half the present numbers in Japan. An idea of its smallness will be found in the table on page 92. Not only is the present elderly group small but the present reproductive group is small, so that it will take years before persons from the very large younger group can enter the elderly group in numbers sufficient to change the proportionate size. In brief, a diminution in the group at one end of the population (the children) and an unusually small group at the other end (the aged), both being the groups that contribute most heavily to the death rate, together

[1] Statistical Bureau of Ministry of Home Affairs, quoted in *Trans-Pacific*, 1.8.29.

[2] Cf. in *Diagram and Numerical Tables Showing Growth of Population and Vital Statistics of Japanese Empire*, 1915. So far as the author could discover the average age of life has not been worked out since then. The *Jap. Year Book*, 1928, p. 44, quotes an estimate worked out in 1911. (Later: there is a Life Table 1921–5, in *Résumé Statistique*, 1930, p. 22.)

[3] For infantile mortality, vide *Aperçu annuel*, 1925, op. cit., p. 273, and 1927, op. cit., p. 226; also *Annuaire internat.*, Vol. V, op. cit., p. 174. The rate is declining, notably since 1918.

[4] In 1920 the crude rate was 23·4 per 1,000, and has continued falling (with slight oscillations) up to the present.

[5] Cf. Bowley's estimates for League of Nations.

SIZE OF THE ELDERLY GROUP IN JAPAN

Country	Proportion of Population aged 50 and over	
	Millions	As a Percentage of Whole Population
		Per cent
Japan	9·031 out of 59·736	15
Italy	7·549 out of 38·710	19
France	9·833 out of 38·797	25

with the effects of a wider and better hygiene, will work an almost certain reduction in the Japanese death rate. For the next three decades it can be expected that a smaller proportion of the population will be removed by death each year.

Therefore, notwithstanding the factors that are operating for a lower birth rate like a spread of industrial and urban living conditions, fewer marriages and a later age of marrying, perhaps too a changing conception of marriage and of individual liberty and comfort, and contraception easily practised—all of these factors operating to accelerate a decline that has already been under weigh for a decade or two—yet the ever-increasing proportion of those in the child-bearing ages during the next thirty years or so, and a birth rate which even now as a crude rate must sink to more than half its present level before coming into line with the rate of Western Europe, and the smaller proportion of the total numbers removed by death each year, point to an obvious conclusion—a large annual increment to the population of Japan. How large? And for how long? Were more data available or accessible a safe workable prediction could be made for the next two decades, and it is probable that a competent statistician could make an acceptable prediction from the data that is already available. But in any case the substantial truth is clear and can hardly be in doubt: namely, within the next generation a very considerable addition to the present population is certain, probably not less than 15 to 20 million, not improbably more.

If 60 million inhabitants have strained Japanese agriculture into Diminishing Returns, how will it fare when the 80 millions have arrived?

CHAPTER V

ON GROWING THEIR OWN FOOD

I. DISTRESS AMONG THE PEASANTRY

We can spend little time in studying Japanese agriculture before we become aware that all is not well with it. At the outset we find the farmers in turmoil. The peasant in any country is not given to the game of riots and political demonstrations; in Japan, where his scheme of society revolves round the family and where obedience, loyalty, industriousness are ingrained in the very elements of his nature, this is especially so. To goad hundreds of thousands of such men into agitation requires sharp pricking indeed. Yet the "discontent and radical tendencies" that we usually associate with an urban proletariat are there "mainly confined to the rural population".[1]

Were we to glance through the files of Japanese newspapers during the last three years or so we should become familiar with paragraphs like the following:

> Five thousand men on Friday participated in the attack upon the houses of a number of landlords with whom the members of the local peasants' association had been in dispute for some months.[2]

> Determined to start a vigorous campaign to raise the price of rice and so save poor farmers from starvation more than 300 representatives arrived in Tokyo on February 15th from all parts of the country.[3]

> Messages from Nigata Prefecture on Saturday reported trouble brewing between 50 landlords and a group of more than 600 peasants there.... The men, after their failure to induce the landlords to agree to a reduction in rents addressed a petition to the local prefectural authorities.... In their petition they asserted that their incomes after payment of rent were utterly inadequate to provide for them and their families.[4]

[1] Cf. Dept. Overseas Trade reports on Japan for 1921–2, p. 66, and 1922–3, p. 5. Also *Trans-Pacific*, 24.12.27.
[2] *Trans-Pacific*, 3.12.27.
[3] Ibid., 15.2.29.
[4] Ibid., 3.12.27.

On the night of June 1st a party of some 300 farmers made a combined attack on the houses of their landlords.[1]

Eighty per cent. of the peasants in Isen-Mura . . . are being examined. . . . It is reported that they passed a resolution to expel six peasants from the village because they had not joined the Peasants Association. They forced the six to join finally under threat of violence.[2]

In some years the agitation is more marked than in others, but for the last fifteen years it has been widespread and it has been increasing.[3] Agrarian disputes in 1925 and 1926 covered more than 100,000 farmers, and in 1927 a larger number still. Peasant-Socialist parties have arisen—among a class notoriously difficult to organize for political action—embracing over half a million members, and they are running candidates for elections, national as well as local.[4] Tenant unions are increasing their membership at a notable pace. In some villages, as a gesture against the present order, they are withdrawing their children from the State schools and placing them in schools of their own founding, colliding heavily as a consequence with the authorities.

We are thus confronted with the spectacle of peasants—and those peasants disciplined with the immemorial traditions of Old Japan—forming radical parties and demanding socialist emancipation from the capitalist; and not less arresting is the spectacle of landlords in the House of Peers urging on the Government a nationalization of the land.[5] What is to explain this unusual, not to say unnatural, phenomenon?

One Japanese explains it as due to "the awakening of the peasant classes"; another says that "it shows how deeply young

[1] *Trans-Pacific*, 5.6.27.

[2] Ibid., 28.3.29.

[3] Cf. Dept. Overseas Trade reports on Japan, 1921–2, 1922–3 op. cit.; *Jap. Year Book*, 1929, p. 264, and 1927 Suppl. on Tenant Troubles; also *Trans-Pacific*, 18.6.27; 9.7.27, etc.

[4] Cf. *Trans-Pacific*, 1.10.27; Ayusawa, *Industrial and Labour Legislation in Japan*; Harada, 87; Y. Tsurumi, *Contemporary Japan*, p. 63.

[5] *Trans-Pacific*, June to Dec. 1927; *Journ. Pol. Ec.*, June 1929, p. 308 (D. J. Orchard).

men in the rural districts are influenced by modern ideas"; and a landowner informed the present writer that it was due to the spread of Bolshevist teachings among the village people.

Dr. King, however, an American Professor of Agriculture and an official of the U.S. Department of Agriculture, who wrote as long ago as 1912, has much to say from his skilled observations of "the tense strain and terrible burden to live" carried by the farmers, and he leaves us accounts all the more vivid for their naïveté....[1] In later years, Mr. Sugiyama, a social worker among the peasantry, tells of the bitter struggle for existence which is "the lot of the poor tillers of the soil".[2] And Dr. Kawada, a Japanese economist, writes that the tenant is given barely enough to keep body and soul together, and that in seasons of bad harvest he would not be able to live were not a reduction made in the amount of his rent.[3] And Dr. Nasu, another Japanese expert, says that a "further reduction of their standard of living will be impossible, for they cannot be worse off than they are at present". Every observer, as far as the present writer knows, agrees that the standard of living of the peasant is lower than that of the town wage-earner.[4]

Throughout the world to-day there is a depression in agriculture. Even in the United States, where until very recently an era of prosperity was being enjoyed unknown to any people at any time in the past, the problem has long been acute. And in France, the most prosperous country after the United States, the farming population is faced with economic adversity. In addition to local and subordinate factors the depression as a whole seems to be caused by a disequilibrium between agriculture and manufacturing industry: there are too many farms

[1] F. H. King, *Farmers of Forty Centuries*, cf. pp. 14, 261, 376, etc.

[2] In *Trans-Pacific*, 3.12.27.

[3] Kawada, *Kyoto Univ. Econ. Review*, Vol. III, No. 2, 138, Nasu, *Land Utilization in Japan*, p. 260.

[4] Cf. D. H. Buchanan, in *Quart. Journal Economics*, Aug. 1923, pp. 558–62; *Economic Journal*, 1918 and 1923; Dr. Washio, in *Trans-Pacific*, 20.8.27; Dr. D. J. Orchard, in *Journal Pol. Econ.*, April, June 1929; Mr. Kokura, in *Trans-Pacific*, 16.7.27; Tsurumi, op. cit.; and K. Takaoka, *Study of Immigration to Brazil*, Chap. I.

and too many farmers. Demand for agricultural produce, if not static, is incomparably less elastic than the demand for manufactures. It can move scarcely faster than the movement of population itself, if for no other reason than that there is a limit to the amount of bread or meat people can eat. The demand for industrial products, on the contrary, is as wide as man's conception of material life: there is scarcely a limit to the desire for new and different apparel, for motor-cars, radio sets, and the countless outpourings ot the industrial machine. Indeed the product of machinery is sometimes taking the place of the product of farms—perfumes and indigo dyes are now made in factories and not raised from the fields.[1] And once it is found that the same amount of agricultural produce can with new methods be grown by a smaller number of farmers, the drift to the cities will set in with triple force behind it. And thus bound, as it is, to set in in any case, the drift has been the greater because the abnormal expansion of agricultural demand during the War encouraged men to cultivate land that ordinarily could not yield profitable crops. With the disappearance of this temporary demand the land has returned to beyond the margin of profitable cultivation, and the men are having —or will have—to betake themselves to other occupations. England, for example, had on this account 3 million acres less under crop in 1927 than in 1918.[2] The United States show these factors—the permanent as well as the minor and transient —working on a vast scale. Nearly 20 million acres less are now under the plough than in 1918, and there are from 3 to 4 million

[1] The coming of the motor also eliminated the need for millions of horses. This is a considerable factor in the U.S. situation, for it means millions of less tons of hay, etc., are now needed.

Another element in the depression is that of the "uncontrollable surplus", which has an undue effect on agricultural price. Vide Sir D. Hall, in *Journal Roy. Inst. Internat. Affairs*, Jan. 1929. Also vide League Nations *World Ec. Conf. Reports*, *Literary Digest*, 15.8.29, Wheat's Menace to Prosperity; and Nourse, *Am. Agriculture and the European Market*. An interesting aspect of the disequilibrium is the discrepancy between prices of agricultural and manufactured commodities, the former being lower than the latter. Vide discussion on League of Nations' *Memo. on Production and Trade*, 1913, pp. 923–7, p. 58 et seq.

[2] *Statistical Abstract for the United Kingdom*, 1913–27. Board of Trade.

less men on the land.[1] But the same factors, on a less spectacular scale, are at work in many countries to-day.

Might we conclude, then, that the farmer's distress in Japan is due to a disequilibrium between agriculture and industrial production; in brief, to an overproduction of rice? That Japan is importing, even in years of most bountiful harvest, some 50 to 60 million bushels,[2] and in the future will be importing an increasing amount, sufficiently disposes of such a suggestion. The distress in Japanese agriculture is separate from and outside the general world-wide depression.

Farmers in Japan can be divided into three classes: tenants, owners, and those who at the same time are both tenants and owners. The following tables show the relative importance in which the classes stand to the whole:

FARMERS BY CLASSES[3]

Class	Percentage of all Farmers
Tenants	28
Owners	31
Tenant-owners	41

MODE OF TENURE OF THE FARM LAND[3]

Mode of Tenure	Percentage of the Total Farmland
Cultivated by Tenants	46
Cultivated by Owners	54

That is to say, approximately half the farmers are tenant and half *propriétaire*.[4]

As for the tenants, they are *métayers* or share-farmers rather than tenants in the English understanding of the term; some observers, indeed, regard their status as so much less

[1] *Report U.S. Sec. Commerce*, 1928, XIII–XXV; cf. *U.S. Agric. Year Book*, 1927, p. 413.

[2] Imports of Rice into Japan are given on p. 58; also p. 110.

[3] League of Nations, *Agricultural Problems*, from Internat. Inst. Agric., 1927, p. 403 et seq. Also cf. *Outlines of Agriculture*, 1910, Japanese Department of Agriculture and Industry, p. 9.

[4] This is not a very satisfactory way of stating the facts, for from one aspect nearly three-quarters of the farmers are *propriétaires*, at least in part, and from another two-thirds are tenants, at least in part. Tenants, like the tenant land, are less than a half of the whole.

favourable than that of the share-farmer that they prefer to classify them as labourers rather than as *métayers*. Provided due allowance be made for numerous diversities it may be said in general that the tenant provides the seed and fertilizers and other requirements as well as the labour of growing the crop, while the landlord provides the land and pays the taxes. Rent amounts to between 50 per cent. and 60 per cent. of the crop, varying from district to district and from year to year, and is usually paid in kind. It is not uncommon for the same family to cultivate the same parcel of land for generation after generation, holding and giving no documents, even the exact number of bushels being left for settlement at the planting or the harvesting of the grain. The system is personal and is based more on Status than on Contract.[1]

It is over the amount of rent to be paid each season that tenants have been disputing in recent years, agitating for a reduction greater than ever made before and claiming that they cannot pay what they undertook to pay.[2]

How much substance there may be in their claim is suggested in an account given of a farmer in the Yamanashi prefecture by an American student who studied the conditions in the field for some time.[3] This farmer was "better off than the average since the average farm in this prefecture is a little over 1¾ acres in area", and his farm covered 2¼ acres. The net income that the labour of himself, his wife, and children could earn from the 2¼ acres amounted, after paying rent, manures, etc., to a trifle over a third of the total yield, and from it "the cost of seeds and implements and incidental expenses" had yet to be deducted. The same writer gave an account of another tenant in the prefecture of Gifu. The second tenant's farm

[1] On rent, vide Dept. of Agric. and Forestry Report, 1925, as being 50–54 per cent. of crop, and Hypothec Bank's estimate as 22–3 bushels an acre, both quoted in Harada, p. 83; also Harada, p. 81; Orchard, p. 145; Kawada, in *Kyoto Univ. Ec. Review*, Vol. I, p. 1.

[2] It has been computed by the Dept. of Agric. that of the rent contracted for by the tenants in quinquennium ending 1920, only 90 per cent. was paid. Harada, p. 87.

[3] Dr. Dorothy J. Orchard, in *Journal Pol. Econ.*, April, June 1929.

was slightly smaller than the prefectural average, yet his income for the year amounted to about £51—and from that sum incidental farming expenses had to be subtracted, the remainder having to provide for his family for the whole year.

It might be concluded from these two accounts that here is a self-evident case of maldistribution of burdens and rewards: rents are too high. A family cannot be expected to subsist on from a third to a half of the produce of two acres of land or less: landlords surely should reduce rents and tenants should receive a higher proportion of the returns. The case is not so certain, however, as it may seem. Whether rents as a whole are higher or lower in Japan than in Europe or America is disputed;[1] but there is no dispute as to their being lower than elsewhere in the Far East. In Korea and Formosa and in China tenants get a smaller proportion still.[2] Nor is there any dispute as to the unprofitableness of the landlord's position. It is estimated that the owner after paying taxes receives only 3 to 5 per cent. on his capital,[3] a very low figure in a land of grossly over-capitalized values like Japan, where dividends are seldom below 10 per cent. and frequently above 30 per cent.[4] It is not likely that landlords would be advocating nationalization of land if they found their ownership profitable. But more pertinent still, it is when the condition of the *propriétaire* cultivating his own land is examined that one realizes that whatever part high rents may be playing in the peasant's distress it is not the only part nor is it the major part. The trouble lies deeper than mode of tenure.

The *propriétaire* cultivates a little more than half the farmland. The *propriétaire* class, moreover, has been diminishing,

[1] On one side cf. Buchanan, *Quart. Journ. of Econ.*, Aug. 1923, on other Kawada, in *Kyoto Univ. Econ. Review*. For China, vide *U.S. Labour Rev.*, Apr. 1928, p. 45.

[2] Vide Kawada, "Tenant Systems in Japan and Korea", in *Kyoto Univ. Econ. Review*, Vol. I, No. 1; "Tenant System of Formosa", ibid., Dec. 1928; *U.S. Monthly Labour Review*, April 1928, p. 45.

[3] Vide Nasu, *Land Utilization in Japan*, p. 171. The Imperial Agric. Assocn. has also made studies on this. Also see Orchard, who gives 3 per cent.; Harada gives 6 per cent., quoting Hypothec Bank.

[4] Vide statistics in Harada, pp. 48 et seq., 56 et seq.

absolute numbers as well as in proportion. The diminution is not considerable, but it may be significant. Between 1914 and 1924 the owner class has lost about 5,000 members a year; the tenant class has been gaining about 1,000 members and the mixed class of owner-tenant about 7,000 a year.[1] This looks—and it only looks, nothing is positive about it—that the smaller *propriétaires* are finding their holdings no longer adequate for supporting them and so are renting a strip or two additionally to their holdings, and in that way swelling the numbers of the mixed class.[2] And while touching on indications that may be significant, it is worth mentioning that Government projects for creating a proprietary peasantry have met with scant success.[3] This may imply that there is little to choose between being a tenant and being a small *propriétaire*. Not much could be claimed for this point, however, for the Government projects have carried at least an air of being singularly inept.[4]

That the basic trouble lies deeper than mode of tenure and that the difficulties of *propriétaires* and tenants are sufficiently similar is confirmed in a series of budgetary analyses that have been made by official or qualified investigators. The National Agricultural Society of Japan, for example, after a detailed investigation came to the conclusion that the "farmers cannot live on the income from their farms alone". Only by subsidiary occupations could they make both ends meet, and even then not always.[5] The Treasury also made an investigation and, it is reported, came to the conclusion that 30 per cent. of the farmers were in debt.[6] More convincing than either of these were the in-

[1] League of Nations, *Memo.*, op. cit.

[2] Also the pure tenants may be increasing as a result of *propriétaires* losing their holdings through debt and so becoming obliged to rent land, or again by new land brought under the plough being thrown open to tenancy.

[3] Cf. *Trans-Pacific*, 26.11.27.

[4] For Government Projects, vide Kawada, in *Kyoto Univ. Ec. Rev.*, Vol. III, No. 1, and *Trans-Pacific* during 1927.

[5] Vide Takaoka, *Study on Immigration to Brazil*, pp. 4–10. It is in Japanese. The author is indebted to Professor Yoshida for kindly translating several chapters of the book and for discussing them with him.

[6] Ibid. Also cf. King, 429; *Trans-Pacific*, 20.8.27.

quiries conducted by the Department of Agriculture and Commerce. In 1920 it took at random 120 families from 40 villages and constructed, from data supplied by them, what it regarded as average budgets for each of the three classes—tenant, landowner, and owner-tenant. The budgets are not entirely satisfactory and can be criticized on a number of points, but on the most conservative valuation the results may be accepted as pointing the broad truth. The tenant finished the year with an average deficit of about £4 10s 0d., the landowner with a surplus of about £2, and the owner-tenant with a deficit of £18. Between 1921 and 1922 a further inquiry was made, this time a hundred farmers being taken from 21 prefectures, again covering all three classes. It was found that while all three classes on average figures scraped through, they scraped through only by earning income outside of farming proper. In all three classes the income from farming alone did not suffice, and the deficiency which had to be made up by subsidiary work averaged a little less than a quarter of the total income. It ought to be added that the addition from the subsidiary occupation left them with a surplus over all expenses that averaged about £3 10s. 0d. for the tenant and about £12 10s. 0d. for the owner; but it ought also to be added that these figures are an *average* which might disguise the serious fact that 37 of the 100 farmers studied ended the year with a deficit, and also that both the owners and the tenants studied were occupying farms of bigger area than usual.[1]

Other studies were made five years later (in 1926–7) by the Bureau of Statistics and the results obtained were similar to those published here.[2]

Undue claims would not be made for these budgetary studies; nor is it urged that they prove anything; but one or two inferences from them can hardly be resisted. They confirm the impressions of men in close contact with rural Japan as to the distress and poverty being very widespread among the farming

[1] For accounts of these studies, see K. Takaoka. Also Harada, p. 83.

[2] In Nasu, *Land Utilization in Japan*, p. 196 et seq.

class; and that the distress is not confined to tenants alone. The owners, too, are struggling with debt or unprofitableness.

A study of the size of properties held by the owners makes it difficult to see how they could escape distress:

DISTRIBUTION OF OWNERS ACCORDING TO AREA OF PROPERTIES[1] (1924)

Size of Property	Number of Owners	Percentage of all Owners
Under 0·5 hectare	2,470,162	49·6
From 0·5 to 1·0 hectare	1,207,052	24·3
From 1·0 to 3·0 hectares	890,874	17·9
From 3·0 to 5·0 hectares	232,923	4·7
From 5·0 to 10·0 hectares	117,088	2·4
From 10·0 to 50·0 hectares	47,695	1·0
Above 50·0 hectares	4,950	0·1

It will be seen from the figures that a half of the entire *propriétaires* are owning farms of less than 1½ acres in extent, and that three-quarters of them are owning farms of less than 2½ acres.[2] None but a few—a tiny fraction of all—the land-owners can under these circumstances be better off than the tenants. For if the tenant has to hand over half his crop to the landlord in rent, the proprietory peasant has to bear the burden of rates and taxes, a burden agreed by students to be very high and according to the budgets constructed by the Government itself amounting to one-fifth of the land-owner's income.[3] It is probably higher still. What the petit *propriétaire* saves in rent he pays out in rates and taxes.

[1] League of Nations, *Memo.* from Internat. Inst. Agric., 1927.

[2] Of course not all the owners are cultivating their land. Some are absentee. But this does not affect the main point. Also cf. *Outlines of Agriculture*, 1910, p. 11.

[3] 24 per cent. according to the budget, but this included charity expenditure with tax expenditure. This owner is bigger than most, so that his proportion is probably higher. But it would not be twice as high. Vide Orchard, p. 133. Also Takaoka, op. cit.; Harada, op. cit.; *Trans-Pacific*, 7.8.28; and *Outlines of Agriculture*, 1910, p. 12. The Imp. Agric. Asscn. has given the author figures showing a combined central and local tax rate as high as 34·5 per cent.

It is evident that the land system of Japan is essentially one of smallholders. There are, for example, less than 5,000 owners whose farms are 125 or more acres in extent, and they constitute the merest fraction of the whole. Even when not farming themselves, but living on the rents of their tenants, the landlords are small men with small incomes. The forests, too, are similarly parcelled out among smallholders—there are nearly 3 million who own 1¼ acres or less. And regarded from the Japanese point of view their capital is employed unprofitably: estimates of interest earned by the capital value of their land range from 3 to 6 per cent., not a high figure anywhere; in Japan, where interests on mercantile or industrial capital are at least twice as high, a very small figure indeed. For men in such conditions to reduce rent would be to declare themselves bankrupt.

The system of tenure may be exacerbating the malaise of Japanese farming, but it is not the malaise itself: at the most it is a case of the tenants being in a somewhat more evil plight than the evil plight of the farming class as a whole. The cause of the malaise has already been implied. The following table can leave little doubt:

DISTRIBUTION OF FARM HOLDINGS IN JAPAN[1]
(1924)

Area	Number of such Holdings	Percentage of all Holdings
Under 0·5 hectare	1,944,663	35·2
From 0·5 to 1·0 hectare	1,868,794	33·7
From 1·0 to 2·0 hectares	1,181,133	21·3
From 2·0 to 3·0 hectares	323,666	5·9
From 3·0 to 5·0 hectares	138,011	2·5
Above 5·0 hectares	76,162	1·4

That is to say nearly two million farmers are occupying holdings of less than 1¼ acres in size, and more than two-thirds of all the farmers—irrespective of their class, whether *propriétaire* or

[1] League of Nations, *Memo.*, p. 403 et seq.

tenant—are occupying holdings of less than 2½ acres. There are too many farmers for the farmland: that is the source of Japan's agricultural problem. The produce that can be wrung from one or two acres of land even when cultivated with the intensiveness and cunning of Japanese farmers cannot, after the deductions have been made from it, in the case of the tenant for rent and in the case of the *propriétaire* for taxes, provide an adequate living for the farmer and the five or six or more members of his household.[1]

In order to give a sense of the relative as well as the actual tinyness of Japanese farms figures are given below comparing the number of acres to each person working on the land in five different countries:

ARABLE LAND TO ONE FARMER[2]

	Acres
U.S.A.	31·7
Denmark	16·2
France	6·1
Italy	3·1
Japan	0·9

It is seen that the Japanese farmer has less than one-sixth of the land that the French peasant has. Were the figures strictly

[1] A great deal of corroborative evidence can be adduced as to this basic cause, among which Harada's calculation dividing total farm produce by total number of farmers is interesting. Probably there is some significance too in the decline in numbers of the holdings under 0·5 hectare since 1914. The general distress is illustrated in instances like the village having to postpone paying the local schoolmaster's salary. Also vide Kagawa, quoted in Tsurumi, p. 61.

[2] Such figures, of course, are offered only as an exceedingly approximate indication, and even then proportions rather than absolute facts. They are arrived at by dividing the gainfully employed farm population—i.e. excluding dependents—into the total arable land, the statistics for the former coming from the *Internat. Statis. Year Bk.*, 1927, p. 34 et seq., and the latter from the *Internat. Year Bk. Agric.*, 1927–8. The former include fishermen with farmers, but this would not invalidate the approximate proportions, and that is all that is sought here. It ought to be added that "farmer" here includes all breadwinners working at any kind of agriculture—dairy-farming, market gardens, etc. The figures for Japan were arrived at by dividing the total farm workers plus total fishermen into total arable land for 1925, the figures for farm-workers and fishery workers being taken from Nasu, *Foreign Affairs*, July 1930.

accurate and comparable the proportion would probably be smaller still. For anyone acquainted with French peasants the comparison need be carried no further. Not only has he less than one-sixth of the French peasant's land, but he has a bigger family, a considerably bigger family, to support from it,[1] and he has not the same access to woodlands, and no poultry, and no cows and swine, no co-operative *laiterie* or *crêmerie*, and no walnut- or apple-trees along the roadside, to swell out his earnings as the French peasant has.

Yet, necessary as it is to etch in this urgent pressure on the land with clear, dark lines, it must not be thought that pressure itself is a new experience for the Japanese people. The history of Japan, at all events in the last two hundred years, leaves no doubt as to a persistent embarrassment from the ratio between numbers and food.

The *Shi No Ko Sho* division of society into four grades, in the descending order of nobility, farmers, craftsmen, and merchants, and the high social status accorded to farmers, was itself the outcome of economic necessity. A diminution or a hindrance in the production of rice, when rice held the importance that it held in Japan, shook society to its foundations. And if the farmers were accorded a high status it was seen that sumptuary edicts and continuous poverty kept them close to their fields. More important still, for a century and a half the population maintained itself at a stationary level. Stabilization was achieved in part by codes like that which made it shameful for a gentleman to have more than three children, and in part by the practice of Mabiki—Mabiki means thinning out, and is used particularly in reference to thinning out surplus plants—that is to say, the practice of exposure and infanticide.[2] These rough checks to population growth were practised on a striking scale until the Meiji regime made them

[1] The birth rate in France is lower in the rural districts than in the towns. In Japan the contrary is the case.

[2] Cf. Honjo, *Kyoto Univ. Ec. Rev.*, Vol. III, No. 2; ibid., Vol. III, No. 1, esp. Dec. 1927; Droppers, in *Transactions Asiatic Society of Japan*, Vols. XXI–II, p. 252; T. Kayahara, in *Trans-Pacific*, 22.10.27.

illegal.[1] If positive increase of numbers could be countered in such a way failures in the rice crop, however, could not. Nature did not always stay her hand: droughts and floods and typhoons descended on the countryside, and then the patient peasantry was at last maddened into a frenzy of hunger and rioting.[2]

Yet though the pressure of numbers on the arable land is not new, there have entered into the situation in latter years elements that are new. These are throwing a new weight upon the old problem.

In the first place it is clear that the pressure now is somewhat more urgent than one or two generations ago. This is clear from the simple fact that although the population has doubled itself in the last fifty years the area of arable land has increased less than 25 per cent. More men are now seeking to draw their living from a given acre of land than in, say, 1890, and still more men when compared with twenty years earlier. Not only is this so, but in the last decade (1919–29) the area per farming family has decreased. Were Hokkaido (the north island) eliminated from the calculations a still more marked decrease would be revealed.

This condition in itself—especially as we now know that through the farmer thus making an acre grow more produce it is resulting in Diminishing Returns—is so serious that it is scarcely necessary to pass on to other deranging factors. We shall, however, pass on.

In the second place, although the standard of living of all classes has risen during the last twenty years, it has risen higher among the urban than among the rural classes.[3] Wage-earners in the town are better off than the tillers of the fields. This is a disparity that would foment discontent and unrest at any time: to-day, when another conception of life from that of

[1] Cf. Honjo, *Kyoto Univ. Ec. Rev.*, Vol. III, No. 2.

[2] Their hard lot "found violent expression in the form of subordination, revolt against their feudal lords and government officials. . . . They sometimes reached tens of thousands. They beat drums, blew horns, and rang bells as they proceeded, flying straw mat banners and carrying weapons in the shape of bamboo spears, sickles, hoes. . . ." Honjo, op. cit. Farmers' riots became frequent in the latter days of the Tokugawa Shogunate.

[3] Cf. Takaoka.

former times and another conception of the standard of living are abroad in Japan, it is a disparity that rankles deeply. The peasants are literate and are open to the appeal of the written word; they command a vote in both central and local assemblies and are therefore canvassed by candidates and themselves the canvassers of a policy; and they are in contact with the cities, where few villages have not some of their sons and daughters working in the factories. They are breathing in the subtle air of new standards and at the same time are self-conscious spectators of their own inferior conditions. Under these circumstances it is irrelevant to urge that they are not worse fortuned than their forefathers, or that in olden times Nature scourged them with catastrophes, and the starvation begotten of such catastrophes, no longer known in these days. For, as always, men fight and found causes not to ward off discomforts or to make their material lot easy so much as to attain to what they conceive to be their rights; and nothing breeds a wider conception of rights than the sight of neighbours in better fare.

A third new element is the change that has been coming over the everyday economy of the peasantry. The days of subsistence farming when each household was nearly self-contained have retreated before the spread of Money and before the loss of the early domestic crafts. The farmer's household no longer produces all that it consumes: clothing especially it must buy. And just as his family no longer spins its yarn or weaves all its cloth, so, too, it no longer spins and rarely weaves a surplus that could be exchanged for necessaries not produced within the household: more and more are former spare-time occupations going into the factories, and with the cheaper products of these the farmer's hand-made goods cannot compete.[1] And since after paying rent or taxes he has little or

[1] At farming alone the peasant has a good deal of spare time on his hands at certain seasons—Dr. Kawada, a Japanese economist, says that he is idle from a third to a half of his time; that is, unless he has some other occupation. Most of the farmers have this, sericulture being the most common. Also cf. *Outlines of Agric.*, 1910, p. 34.

The problem of economically distributing the farmer's labour, and of

no rice to spare beyond what his family must keep as food, he has been forced to earn the money needed for outside necessaries (principally for fertilizer) by some new method. This brings us back to sericulture.

Silk indeed is second to rice alone, in the national economy no less than in the farmer's economy. The extension of its culture during the last thirty years has been as remarkable for its scale as for its postponing the disastrous effects of overabundant numbers. The subsidiary income that hitherto was drawn from old village crafts is now drawn more and more from cocoon-raising. That the Japanese farmer has not been overwhelmed, working at a task like that of Sisyphus in striving to wring what he required from his tiny farm, while at the same time often losing his former subsidiary industries, is due to Silk.

The newness of sericulture as a widespread common occupation—hitherto it was a highly specialized craft concentrated in a few localities and producing wares for the aristocracy—is suggested in the following figures:

PROGRESS OF SERICULTURE[1]

Cocoons	(average)	for 1895–9	21·5 million kamme
		for 1927	90·0 million kamme
Exports of Raw Silk	(average)	for 1909–13	21·9 million lb.
		for 1927	70·7 million lb.

That is to say, the production of silk cocoons has more than quadrupled in thirty years, and the exports of raw silk have more than trebled since only the pre-War quinquennium. More than a third of the farming families are now raising silk cocoons, and a still larger proportion if we include other sericultural

terminating a condition of virtual unemployment throughout a part of every year is as insistent in Japan as in U.S.A. or other farming countries.

As for the older industries, handloom weaving is still to be found, and so, too, straw-plaiting, hat-making, charcoal-burning. Cf. *Outlines of Agric.*, 1910, p. 79. A good deal of domestic industry can still be seen in the villages.

[1] Figures for cocoons are from *Jap. Year Book*, 1929, pp. 506–8; for exports of raw silk from *U.S. Commerce Year Book*, Vol. II, 1928. The acreage under mulberry has doubled in the quarter-century and now covers about 1½ million acres. Also vide *Annuaire Statistique de la France*, 1926, p. 305; *Outlines of Agric. in Japan*, 1910, p. 63; and ibid., 1914, p. 15.

processes.[1] In few parts of the country is it now possible to travel without seeing on all sides the fresh green of the meticulously cultivated mulberry bushes.

The rise of the silk industry then has saved the situation; or at least it has postponed the day of reckoning. For without question had Japanese farmers not been able to fall back on the profits gained from raising this and selling it to America the increasing costs of producing a bushel of rice would have brought about a great social collapse. Sericulture has staved off the effects of overpopulating the farmlands.

The most convincing evidence in corroboration of the conclusion that there are too many farmers pressing on the available farm land is yet to be given. It is given by a study of the price of rice. During the decade since the Armistice the price of rice has moved—and remained—higher than the general price level in Japan.[2] Not only are the farmers in spite of *really* higher prices for their grain still in distress, but furthermore they are on the horns of a curious dilemma. A poor harvest is disastrous if only because it leaves them with insufficient rice

[1] Figures in available official publications give about 2,200,000 families in cocoon-raising in 1927. These are not entirely satisfactory. Ogata gives over five million for 1918. Ogata, p. 86.

[2] Cf. *Comparison between General Price Level and Price of Rice, 1920–7 (Wholesale)*:

Year	General Price	Rice
1920	100·0	100·0
1921	91·2	84·8
1922	90·8	89·5
1923	91·2	85·4
1924	95·0	103·1
1925	93·8	111·7
1926	84·4	94·9
1927	79·8	87·6

Both columns are taken from the *Statistical Report of Tokyo Chamber of Commerce* (1928). According to a communication from U.S. Dept. of Agric., while General Prices in Japan had increased 230 per cent. since 1910 rice prices had increased 250 per cent. Also vide *World Ec. Conf. Memo. on Agric. Prod.* from Internat. Inst. Agric. This discrepancy in the two price levels continued throughout 1928 and 1929. Cf. *Trans-Pacific*, 13.2.30.

for their own needs, but a very good harvest is equally disastrous because it lowers the price of rice.[1] During 1927, 1928 (two years of bumper crops), and part of 1929, the Government was harassed with efforts to keep up the price, and we find a tariff system in operation ominously reminiscent of the English Corn Laws.[2] In the newspapers we read passages like the following: "The authorities of the Ministry of Agriculture and Forestry are worried as to the rice price in connection with the bumper crops for the preceding two years. Despite the Government's measure of buying 500,000 koku (i.e. 2½ million bushels) recently, the price has shown no improvement."[3] Ordinarily one would conclude that the price was falling because production had outstripped consuming capacity and that the market was glutted. But this will not fit the case in Japan: the most abundant harvest is still insufficient for her needs and millions of bushels are imported in the best years.[4]

[1] It is not denied that the factor of the "uncontrollable surplus" accentuates the price depression; but the fundamental significance of the phenomenon noted here is that rice production in Japan has gone into the state of Diminishing Returns. Its cost is uneconomically high. It is worth remarking that the movement in the price level of wheat (which of course has a world price) has been lower than the movement of general prices—the exact contrary to Japanese rice.

[2] The tariff is a sliding rate and may be raised, as in the Spring of 1928, to a point that amounts to embargo. Also the Government purchases large parcels. Cf. *Annual Report Bank of Japan*, 1928, Governor's address.

[3] *Trans-Pacific*, 26.1.29. Cf., too, ibid., 15.2.29. There has even been an agitation for discontinuing the programme of increasing rice acreage in Korea. In reply to this the Minister of Agric. of the day replied that he believed that imports of rice should be restricted for the time being, but pointed out the obvious necessity of Korean imports to Japan.

[4] IMPORT OF RICE

(*Million Koku*)

Year	Production in Japan	Total Imports	Imports from Korea
1924	57·1	11·3	4·5
1925	59·7	11·6	5·2
1926	55·6	11·9	5·9
1927	62·1	—	6·1
1928	60·3	12·6	7·0

1 koku = 4·96 bushels. The imports should be reduced slightly by subtracting the volume of rice exported from Japan each year; but the exports

No other conclusion can be drawn, it would seem, than the one which the preceding pages have prepared us for, namely, that the rice is being produced at too high a cost. Whether it be due to the intensiveness of the farming or to a shifting on to poorer land, the rice harvest is no longer grown on an economic basis. The high yield per acre draws our attention from the low yield per man. It is cheaper to import foreign rice—as much as 50 per cent. to 100 per cent. cheaper, a discrepancy far too wide to be explained by the superior quality of the Japanese article.[1] In this we see the first small shadow of Diminishing Returns falling across Japanese agriculture.

II. The Capacity of Japan to Produce her own Food

With this background in mind we are the better prepared for proceeding to the central inquiry of the chapter, namely, can Japan continue to grow her own food? Or is she to be confronted with a population that can no longer subsist on what it produces?

It has already been shown that the Japanese population is bound to increase, and on the most conservative estimates to

are not great enough to affect the figures much. In the following table the imports are given minus the exports. It will be observed that Japan in recent years has been importing about 60 million bushels of rice annually, or between 15 and 20 per cent. of what she consumed. (In addition she imports more than 20 million bushels of wheat and more than 4 million quintals of soya beans, vide footnote, p. 173.)

IMPORT OF RICE INTO JAPAN

(Millions of Quintals)

Year	Production	Imports (– Exports to) from Korea	Imports from Formosa	All Imports
1909–13	90·87	0·612	1·129	4·237
1925	107·96	5·287	2·396	14·983
1926	100·53	7·633	3·338	14·361
1927	112·3	7·547	4·040	16·945

[1] On foreign rice being cheaper, vide Nasu (ed. Condliffe), p. 358; also Harada, p. 152.

increase by many millions before a stationary condition is likely to be reached. For the next twenty or thirty years the increment—in so far as any prediction can be reasonably offered—will be around a million a year.

It has been shown, too, that Japan at this moment is importing food for her present population—about 60 million bushels of rice and upwards annually or nearly one-fifth of what she consumes, besides wheat, flour, meats, and other foods. Can she enhance her output not only by the 15 to 20 per cent. required to relieve herself of the present deficit, but by the further amount that will be required each year to sustain the new increase in her population? Between 1880 and 1925 the rice crop was raised from 150 to 300 million bushels—a doubling that more than kept pace with the growth of population. Can it be repeated?

The total harvest will be increased either by increasing the yield per acre, or by increasing the area under cultivation, or by both.

As for increasing the yield per acre, Japan has already accomplished very much along the line of intensive culture. The vast augmentation of the world's food supply in the nineteenth century was for the most part due to extending the world's arable land—to bringing the new areas of America and Australia and Russia beneath the plough; but in Japan the equally vast augmentation of her food supply was mostly due to better and more intensive cultivation. While the area under rice increased by only 18 per cent. the yield per acre increased by 48 per cent., that is by nearly three times as much.[1] What hopes do reorganizing present practices and employing modern machinery offer of increasing the yield? Experts have pointed out defects which are doubtless diminishing the acreage yield and yet could be remedied. According to a Government Report in 1924 nearly one-fifth of the irrigated land was still without sufficient water, and a similar proportion

[1] Cf. Nasu, *Population and Food Supply in Japan*, *Inst. Pacific Relations*, p. 341.

was inadequately drained.[1] And an American engineer with first-hand knowledge of the country has expressed the opinion that by a series of engineering improvements two crops could be grown yearly on most of the land now producing one.[2] There seems little doubt that improvements of this nature are needed; indeed they are already being made, and when completed they can be expected to result in a higher yield on the land now disadvantageously affected.

And mechanization, judged by the recent records of the United States, would appear no less hopeful. Officials of the United States Government estimate that between 1919 and 1927 agricultural production in that country had increased approximately 18 per cent.—that is by nearly one-fifth—and yet in the same period the number of men on farms had decreased by 3 to 4 million and the acreage under cultivation had decreased by 15 to 20 million.[3] Can any part of this spectacular transformation be repeated in Japan? A system of farming where nearly all the motive power comes from human muscle, the soil being turned with spade and the water raised in pails or by tread-wheels and the grain threshed by flails, the aid of animals so seldom used that one can travel hundreds of miles without seeing a beast and that only one farmer in five or ten can boast a horse and cow[4]—this would seem the very condition for calling upon the services of mechanization and modern "efficiency methods". Tractors and American implements, steam pumps, motor threshing and

[1] Cf. *Japan Year Book*, 1927, p. 693; U.S. *T.P.S.* 73, p. 89; *Trans-Pacific*, 8.8.29, shows a typical instance of what lack of irrigation results in.

[2] Two crops are generally grown on a third to a half of the uplands and two on about a third of the wet land (i.e. rice paddies). Vide *Outlines*, op. cit., p. 18, 1910. Also Nasu, *Land Utilization.*

[3] *U.S. Agric. Year Book*, 1927, p. 413; *U.S. Sec. of Commerce Report*, 1928, Vols. XIII–XXX.

[4] According to the *Japan Year Book* there are just over a million horses and slightly more cattle used in farming. To divide these by all the farms, however, gives a false sense of the true condition insomuch as many of these animals would be in Hokkaido, where the farming is essentially on the American and not on the Japanese system and scale. Cf. Copeland, *Rice*, op. cit.; also W. Weston, in *Transactions Japan Soc., London*, Vol. XIX, "Some Aspects of Rural Japan".

hulling machines, and large-scale production on consolidated holdings would surely work some much-needed changes here. And California demonstrates that rice can be grown by such methods.[1]

The American example on investigation, however, turns out to have little relevance for Japan. The increase in the volume of agricultural production there was due mostly to a shift from "less productive crops . . . to more productive crops"—from cereals to fruits and vegetables—and to a shift in the area of production from East towards West, while the decrease in the area cultivated and the men cultivating it was due to the disappearance of the horse and mule before the rise of motor-cars and tractors. There are now millions fewer horses and mules to be fed, and as a consequence millions fewer acres of land to be tilled for their hay and fodder.[2] Japan cannot shift her production from cereals to fruit and vegetables—she needs more and more cereals; or from one area to another—she needs more land than all she can now command. Nor can she supplant millions of horses and mules by motor traction: she has scarcely any mules and horses to supplant. And if the American example has little significance for her case, mechanization in itself would present peculiar difficulties for her. There are the difficulties of raising capital among so poor a people for so vast an undertaking—the reclamation projects alone are estimated to require £200 million.[3] There are the greater difficulties that would come from the physiography of a country that is crumpled and riven into mountain and valley even more than Greece, and from the nature of her staple crop which, requiring as it does a level area for irrigation, is frequently grown on fields too small to allow a plough to turn round in them. The triumphs of American machinery and American methods were won with other

[1] For Rice cultivation in Calif., vide *U.S. Agric. Year Books*, e.g. 1927, p. 555; also Copeland, *Rice*, p. 165, et seq., and p. 205 *re* smaller holdings.

[2] In fact the change from one sort of agricultural product to another gives a somewhat spurious magnitude to the increase in total production. Two-thirds of it, e.g., are due to increase in cattle, etc., which are taking the place of some of the horses that have been destroyed.

[3] According to S. K. Inoui, in *Trans-Pacific*, 12.9.29.

crops and in other country. But far more important than these obstacles is a consideration that must make any Government of Japan hesitate before embarking upon a widespread project of mechanization: mechanization could scarcely increase the acreage yields, while it would displace millions of men from employment in agriculture.[1] Many of the men driven from the farms would in time, no doubt, be absorbed in new industries like implement-making, in transport, and in distributing and financial agencies and the like; whether most of them would be so absorbed, however, is uncertain and cannot be known until statistical analyses of an extremely painstaking kind and over a long period have been made on the whole question of displacement from employment through technical changes. In any case the country would be confronted with unemployment on so serious a scale as to hazard social peace. Mechanization of Japanese agriculture, in brief, would mean not more rice—since no culture is so intensive as that of unmechanized hand labour—but less men needed to grow it, and almost certainly less rice from the same area of land.[2]

This is not to say, of course, that there is no scope whatever for mechanical processes in Japanese agriculture. Hulling and milling could be done by machine. There is a not insignificant area on the level valley floors that could be cultivated by implements and traction. Indeed until some measure of mechanical help is introduced there is no way whereby the Japanese farmer, now wallowing in mud and with his back bent beneath

[1] For the effects of mechanization in displacing labour, vide account of a 95,000-acre farm in Montana, U.S.A., run on mass-production methods, in N.Y. *New Republic*, 17.8.29. Also cf. the cotton sled which picks as much cotton as 8 or 10 men, but more wastefully.

[2] For some interesting opinions, and some with statistical proof, as to the higher productivity of land cultivated on small peasant system, including peasant ownership or part ownership, vide Thompson, in *Journ. Roy. Stat. Soc.*, 1926; vide Faber, ibid., Vol. LXXXVII, p. 22; vide ibid., Lord Bledisloe; and Mitrany, in *London Essays in Econ.* (to Prof. Cannan), p. 324. The U.S. Chamber of Commerce, after an investigation, concluded that the "little" farmer was making as much profit acre for acre as the "big" farmer, according to report in *Lit. Digest*, 24.8.29. For instance of wastefulness of mechanical devices, vide Copeland, *Rice*, p. 192; and for their inferior cultivation, ibid., p. 251.

the rays of the sun, can be relieved of the grinding toil exacted by rice culture. The upward trend in his standard of living cannot go far without the use of machinery. Also, as will be seen later, mechanization may have some scope in extending the arable area. But for Japanese agriculture as a whole it can have little scope, and less scope still as a solution to the pressure of numbers.[1]

Perhaps the most pertinent comment—if any be needed after what we know of the working of Diminishing Returns—on projects for increasing the acreage yield in Japan is the following table:

POUNDS OF RICE PRODUCED PER ACRE[2]

Country	1909–13	1921–5	1926	1927
U.S.A.	922	1,076	1,121	1,130
British India	957	864	834	805
Java	932	881	918	970
Japan	2,163	2,350	2,256	2,510

That is to say, the yield per acre in Japan is the highest among the notable rice-growing countries of the world. It is more than twice as high as that of any country on the above table, including the United States. And to get to this figure it has risen

[1] Cf. Kawada: "Japanese Agriculture . . . is bound to remain a handicraft industry," *Kyoto Univ. Ec. Rev.*, Vol. I, No. 1, p. 171. The position recalls that which has been found to exist in the American bread-making industry, in which the difficulties of large-scale production are so great as to save the small baker. Vide C. L. Alsberg, *Combination in the American Bread-Baking Industry*, 1926.

[2] Calculated by U.S. Dept. of Agric. and published in *U.S. Commerce Year Book*, Vol. II, 1928, p. 689. China is omitted—of course a big omission —because no statistical data are available, but it is believed that the yield there is not as high as in Japan. Cf. Copeland, p. 295. The only countries with a bigger yield per acre than Japan are Spain and Italy; but in both cases the area cultivated is small—about one-thirtieth of the Japanese area. It is likely that Japan has an equal area—200 to 300,000 acres—that is producing as high a yield, probably a much higher in fact. The high yield from the small selected acreage in Spain and Italy does not invalidate the above point. On rice yields in Spain and Italy, vide Copeland, *Rice*, pp. 301, 308, et seq.

twice the height it was fifty years ago. Also the ascent has been markedly retarded in the last decade or two. These facts suggest not only the effort that is being put into extracting the utmost from the soil, but they suggest too the unlikelihood of pushing intensiveness much farther. Improved irrigation and drainage, better rice seed, and better fertilizers[1] will all help to heighten the yield, some increase in which can be expected. But there is no ground whatever for believing that it will amount to the extra volume needed to support the extra population added every year. Indeed it is probable, in view of the peasants' demands for a higher standard of living, that the improvements mentioned above will be used not for increasing the present yield, but for reducing the present number of farmers and the present number of hours they work in order to produce it.

If intensification offers no solution of the problem, will an expansion of the arable area provide for the new needs? The huge increase in the population of European stock in the nineteenth century was made possible by extending the area of land cultivated by it. Since less than one-sixth of the area of Japan is now cultivated there would appear to be room for extending the proportion. Visitors to Japan are impressed with the minute particularity with which the land in use is cultivated, not a foot being wasted; but they are equally impressed when pushing beyond the cultivated regions to find miles and miles of country still in a natural state. Cannot some of this be turned into crop fields?

Students of Population are familiar with a curious congestion that is sometimes to be found at the centre of regions the outer areas of which are but sparsely settled. In the Netherlands East Indies, for example, Java is densely populated—a narrow and mountainous strip only 700 miles long sustains 40 million people—while the outer islands are thinly inhabited. Again,

[1] Professor Copeland, however, says that Japan already leads the world in knowledge of rice-fertilization. Copeland, op. cit., p. 299. This same opinion expressed in 1913 by an expert: J. G. Struthers, *T. Asiatic Society, Japan*, 1913, p. 351.

in the Philippines the main island, Luzon, and especially parts of it, are densely populated while other islands including the rich Mindãnao have relatively few inhabitants.[1] It is in order to correct such "spotty" conditions that schemes for "internal colonization" are worked out. Signor Mussolini, it is well known, has been working on such a scheme, among others in his programme of *Bonifica integrale*, and the *battle for grain* in Italy over the last two or three years, and it is claimed that there are over 3 million acres there that may thus be brought beneath the plough.[2]

An examination of the density of population in various prefectures in Japan certainly gives a strong appearance of the need of redistributing population. In the main island—Hondo—the density is 157 to the square kilometre, in Hokkaido only 28. And within Hondo itself there are some surprising disparities: in the Kwanto district, for example, it is 560, in the North-East only 91.[3] Over half the area of Japan, in fact, is under forest. The Government would appear to have ample reason for proclaiming a policy of internal colonization and a project for reclaiming 5 million or more acres of land.[4]

Yet to cut down the forests (even assuming such forest land is fit for tillage) when the country is so mountainous and the rainfall so heavy would bring about erosion on a disastrous scale.[5] And the small area of unused land that does not come

[1] On the one island there is still unused land, while on other parts are such scarcely believable rice terraces as those of the Igorots. Cf. Copeland, *Rice*, p. 242 and photograph.

[2] Cf. *Giornale degli Economisti*, Agosto, 1929: Lo Svoglimento ed il Sistema della Bonifica Integrale, M. R. Bucella.

[3] Yamasaki, *Inst. Pacific Relations*, p. 361.

[4] Vide Toynbee, *Surv. Internat. Affairs*, 1926, p. 390; Yamamoto, in *Kyoto Univ. Ec. Rev.*, 1927, p. 55; Nasu, op. cit., p. 343; *Jap. Year Book*, 1927, p. 481.

[5] Deforestation has had this result in Manchuria (vide *Progress in Manchuria*, p. 35) and Korea, where its disastrous effects are very evident. Parts of Greek mountains, notably in Boeotia and Thessaly, that are now bare and useless were covered with forest in some cases even down to a century ago. Also cf. Mallory, *China, Land of Famine*, pp. 28, 37. It ought to be recorded, however, that an expert of Dr. S. Sato's standing is of the opinion that some part of the land now under forest can be cultivated. Cf. *Econ. Journal*, 1918.

under this category is rocky or thin in soil. No greater error could be made than to assume that because there is land it can be turned to growing things—an error universally made by the critics of Australia, whose dominion they fail to perceive is mostly over unused and unusable deserts. That a people so long pressed for arable land and so industrious as the Japanese should not have already reclaimed these waste stretches is a strong presumption against their value for cultivation, the more so as land utilization has been the dominant note in Japanese economic history and the constant preoccupation of Japanese rulers for centuries. It is true of course that an undertaking which would be impossible to a spade-farming people living in a feudal society might be made both possible and economic with the resources of a twentieth-century State behind it. But it is in the history of the recent past that we find the least encouragement. Japan has doubled her rice crop since 1880, yet she has increased her rice land by less than one-fifth; in other words, the bulk of her additional crop has come from a higher yield to the acre, not from an extension of the area cropped. A concentration on intensiveness like this, costly as it is, has probably been chosen because no alternative was available. Moreover, in the decade 1915–25 the arable land was increased only 3·5 per cent., and of this land nearly one-half was in Hokkaido, and nearly one-half (which almost amounts to saying the other half) went into mulberry orchards.[1]

Indeed, while during the last fifty years the arable land has increased in round figures from 11 million acres to 15 million acres, of the 4 million new acres thus added only about one-third or less were added in the last twenty years, and the rate at which the increases have been made show a significant retardation in the second half of the period.[2] There is reason for believing that scarcely anything has been added to the

[1] Harada, p. 79; cf. J. E. Orchard, in *Geographical Review*, 1928.

[2] Cf. figures given by Secretary to Ministry of Agriculture in Supplement to *Japan Year Book*, 1927, and also vols. of *Statist. Abstract Min. Agric. and Forestry*.

total arable area since 1923.[1] There is reason for believing, too, that much, perhaps most, of the land added in the second half of the fifty years under review has come not from reclaimed waste land but from land saved through readjusting the fields (a movement similar to the abolition of the strip system and the consequent utilizing of "baulks" during the English Enclosure Movement). Though the area under rice has not ceased from gradually extending itself, its extension has not kept pace (unless it be in latter years, when it probably has kept pace) with the extension of arable land as a whole. Much of the new land has been going into industrial crops like mulberry, sugar, and hemp, especially mulberry, the area under which has risen from about ¾ million acres to over 1½ million acres in the last twenty-five years. Not only is this so, but with the exception of rice and wheat (and to a trifling extent of oats), every other food crop—barley, rye, millet, maize, and even beans and potatoes—shows a smaller and smaller area for the last decade or so. Even the total area under cereals has steadily declined since 1922–3 at least.[2] This is a phenomenon that may have several causes behind it, but it seems clear that one among these is that the limit of economically expanding the rice land in Japan is moving within sight. One is led to this belief either by balancing up such quantitative information as is available or by what one can see for oneself. To one travelling over the country it seems that very few acres might be utilized which are still left unutilized, even though the utilized land is less than 16 per cent. of the whole. Nothing could be more unlike the gently swelling landscape of England than the sharp volcanic landscape

[1] The figures in the *International Year Book of Agric.* show a total increase between 1924 and 1927 of about 50,000 acres to the arable land—i.e. about 12,500 acres per annum. Although these are the most acceptable figures available, their accuracy is very questionable. The International Institute of Agric. apparently recognizes this, for in some of the Year Books the figures for arable land in Japan are omitted. Also among some of those given there are contradictions. Figures also given in *Statistical Abstract Ministry Agric. and Forestry.*

[2] Figures will be found in *International Year Book of Agric.*, years 1922–3 to 1927–8.

of Japan: its contours are those of most of the Pacific Islands—Tahiti or American Samoa, for example—small flats or shallow basins around which mountains arise abruptly and generally at too steep an incline for much cultivation on their sides. The vast bulk of the land is useless for tillage. As it is, one sees terraces on the hill-sides that could scarcely be worth the enormous labour that went into the making of them.

At all events the member of the Japanese Government who writes that "the actual results (of extending the arable area) have been disappointing up to date" is stating the fact moderately.[1] Those best qualified to judge, are indeed unanimous as to the unlikelihood of securing much relief by reclaiming the vast areas of waste land.[2]

This again, however, is not to say that there will be no extension of the present arable area and no relief from the extension. The proposals contemplated by the Government will probably add in some measure to the cultivable land: the one project of eliminating the borderways, a foot or so in width lying between the numberless fields, will continue to turn land now idle into productive areas.[3] And some part of the land lying in waste has probably been left uncultivated because it was not good enough to repay the meticulous tillage of spade-farming, but which if cultivated in areas large enough to repay machine farming, and perhaps for less troublesome cereals than rice, would well repay the effort. The mallee wheat

[1] Inouye, in Suppl. to *Japan Year Book*, 1928, p. 13. It must be understood of course that though the total area has scarcely been increasing recently the area of rice fields has continued gradually to increase. Figures can be found in *Statistic. Abstract Min. Agric. and Forestry*, 1928, p. 2.

[2] Cf. Secretary to the Ministry of Agriculture: "As things stand it is almost impossible to expect any larger expansion in this direction in Japan Proper," etc., in Suppl. to *Jap. Year Book*, 1927, p. 13. Also Consul-General Saito: "Any increase of acreage will only be at a high cost of production." *Anns. Am. Acad.*, 1925; also cf. Nasu, *Land Utilization*, pp. 68, 107, 109, 140, 260–1. It is worth noticing that the wheat land in Japan—and there are over a million acres of it—has a low acre yield—only 20 bushels. Germany, e.g. where the wheat area is more than four times as big, has 30 bushels; Denmark has 45.

[3] On eliminating borderways, vide *Outlines of Agric. in Japan*, 1910, p. 22; 1914, p. 4; and the photographs. King, op. cit., 30–1.

lands in Australia, producing from 10 to 12 bushels to the acre, could never be cultivated by spade if for no other reason than because a farmer using his utmost physical strength could spade only a few acres of it annually, and the harvest from a few acres of such land would yield him less cereal than he consumes. But by the aid of machinery one farmer can cultivate 500 or 1,000 acres of such land and reap a harvest eminently worth his efforts. The same observation can be applied to much of the land now cultivated in South Africa, Canada, and the Americas.[1]

The author could wish at this point that a statistically acceptable estimate of the new land that might be added to the arable area in Japan could be given here; but assiduous efforts have not succeeded in collecting adequate data. Nothing more definite can be given than what is given above.

Yet before leaving the subject some reference should be made to the Japanese colonies—Chosen, Taiwan, and Karafuto—and to Hokkaido and the Royal Demesne, as sources of further rice land.

In recent years about two-thirds of all the rice imported into Japan has come from her own colonies of Chosen (Korea) and Taiwan (Formosa). About one-third of the entire Chosen crop and about two-fifths of the Taiwan is sent to Japan.[2] Some of the more sanguine of colonial administrators have held that by a properly conceived and properly executed programme Japan's future rice deficit could be made good from these sources. A wide programme, in fact, has been in adoption for Chosen (much the more important colony) since 1920. Nor is there any doubt as to the practicability of increasing the rice crop in Chosen and Taiwan alike, both by extending the area cultivated and by intensifying the yield per acre. Chosen, for example, has about 4 million acres under rice as compared with Japan's 8 million, and the yield per acre is less than half of that in

[1] Vide interesting idea of an economist in the U.S. Dept. of Agric., Dr. O. E. Baker, in Inst. Pacific Relations on developing unused land in China. *Land Utilization in China*; and in *For. Affairs* (U.S,A.), April 1928.

[2] Vide *Japan Year Book*.

Japan. According to the Government, two thirds of the rice fields are without any system of irrigation, and 2 million acres are fit for first-class paddy land. The first programme for Chosen having been rather unsuccessful, was revised in 1926. It envisages increasing the rice crop by 40 million bushels.[1] The area of cultivated land has already increased 60 per cent. since 1910. Improvements are equally practicable in Taiwan. Nevertheless it seems certain that Japan can find no solution to her food shortage from her colonies. The present imports will probably continue at least for a long time: they may even increase considerably. But they can hardly increase to the figure necessary to supply Japan to the amount of the deficit which her present rate of consumption will leave her in a couple of decades hence. For the final objection to all such hopes, even assuming that the colonial crops will be greatly increased, is what of the Koreans and the Formosans themselves? While they export rice they also import millions of bushels of the cheap, coarser grains like millet.[2] They are now too poor to retain at home the rice they grow. But as soon as their standard of living begins to rise it will take the form that it has taken in Japan—eating less coarse grain and more rice. Nor must it be forgotten that the colonial populations are also rapidly growing. Chosen, for example, already with a population of 20 millions, has even a higher birth-rate than Japan. But, above all, what difference is there ultimately between importing food that cannot be grown at home from colonies and importing it from the foreigner?

Hokkaido, it is true, is not a colony, but a part of Japan proper. It is a large island (in area somewhat larger than Scotland) lying to the north of the main Japanese island. Until fifty years ago the Japanese left it fairly undisturbed to the

[1] For Chosen, vide *Annual Report on Administration of Chosen*; M. Inouye, in *Japan Year Book* Suppl., 1928, p. 16; and *U.S. Commerce Reports*, 8.4.29. The Oriental Development Coy., a semi-Government corporation, is playing a big part in opening up land and placing Japanese settlers on it. For Taiwan, vide *Japan Year Book*; C. M. Sawley, *Island Dependencies of Japan*; Nasu, *Land Utilization*.

[2] Cf. *Report on Progress in Manchuria*, 1907–28, pp. 4, 110.

few Ainu aborigines. Since then, and especially since the beginning of the twentieth century, serious efforts have been made to settle it. The Japanese there now number nearly 3 million. The condition of the country and the life it demands is most easily understood by recalling the opening-up of Western Canada.[1] The holdings are bigger than in Japan, machinery is used, and live-stock are common. It is claimed that from 500,000 to 700,000 acres of land may still be utilized for rice culture,[2] and that it has a great future for stock raising. Much of these claims can be believed. At the same time the serious limitations imposed upon the country's development by its climate must be recognized. Persons familiar with both say that Hokkaido is colder than Manitoba.[3] Excepting in the south apples will not grow there. The rice that is sown has to be of a specially bred variety. Snow is said to lie on the ground for about five months of the year.[4] These elementary facts seem to make it clear that Hokkaido, develop though it certainly will in the future, can be but a small factor in providing either settlement or food for Japan's rising millions.[5]

From what is known of the history of the land-holdings of royal families in Europe one would be inclined to expect that there might be a considerable area of valuable land in Japan now lying waste as Imperial demesne. This would appear the more probable because of the unusually exalted status of the Japanese Imperial Family. No positive information could be obtained on the matter; but there seems no reason for discrediting the virtual accuracy of the estimate made by the Department of Agriculture in 1918. The total area in the hands of the royal family, it was then announced,

[1] Cf. H. Molisch, *Im Lande der aufgehenden Sonne*, p. 226.

[2] S. Nasu, *Land Utilization in Japan*, p. 112, gives a higher figure.

[3] Cf. J. W. Scott Robertson, *Foundations of Japan*, p. 335. It is a matter of regret to the author that he did not come upon this interesting book by the editor of *The Countryman* until the MS. was nearly completed.

[4] *Im Lande der aufgehenden Sonne*, op. cit.

[5] Karafuto, as the Japanese call South Saghalien, is omitted from the above discussion because, whatever its future may be in Forestry or Fisheries or Oil mining, it has no relevance agriculturally.

amounted to 3½ million acres, of which over 3 million acres were forest land and less than 25,000 acres were land that could be used for rice cultivation. Small as the last figure seems it is probably near the truth: the pressure on the land has been so acute in Japan, the consciousness of that pressure so lively, and the Imperial Family itself so solicitous of the national welfare, that it is difficult to believe that large tracts of valuable land could still be lying unused.

III. Changing the Diet

If Japan cannot produce all the rice she now consumes might she not produce some other foods that will make up for the deficiency? Might she not indeed substitute some other staple or staples for the single one of rice? Rice is a costly cereal, not only costly in the kind of land it requires (which must have access to abundant water and favourable topographical conditions for irrigating) and costly in human labour, but costly in actual price. Its market price in Japan is from two to three times that of wheat.[1] And for all this expensiveness it is inferior in food value. Dr. Egerton Charles Grey, who was sent on a mission of research to Japan by the Health Section of the League of Nations, concluded that the intestinal diseases, which form the highest single death factor in Japan, were due to an excessive carbo-hydrate and an insufficient protein and vitamin diet, for which rice, especially polished rice, must be blamed.[2] He recommended a gradual widening of the diet so as to reduce the very high proportion of rice in it, using milk and meat and above all fish, which are very plentiful in Japanese waters. It is not easy for one who has not lived in Japan to realize how much the people depend on rice and how little

[1] Cf. League of Nations, *C.E.I.* 36, *Agricultural Problems in their International Aspect*, p. 304; Grey, op. cit.; Sec. to Ministry of Agric. and Forestry in Suppl. 1927 *Jap. Year Book*, p. 20; *Jap. Year Book*, 1929, pp. 595–6; *Trans-Pacific*, 27.8.27. Barley costs 40–50 per cent. of rice—*Outlines*, op. cit., 1910, p. 49.

[2] *The Food of Japan*, E. C. Grey, M.A., D.Sc., M.R.C.P., etc. League of Nations, Geneva.

they use common European protein foods: the per capita consumption of milk, for example, is not half a gallon per year—in the United States it is 111 gallons, that is to say, about 230 times higher; so, too, the per capita consumption of meat and of eggs is many times higher. In 1925 there was an average of only one milch cow to a thousand persons; and more seaweed is eaten than meat.

Apart from the natural reluctance of a people to forgo a staple food which has the habit of centuries behind it, the change in Japan will be the harder because of the association of rice with social status: the less expensive but more wholesome cereals are the badge of menial rank. As already pointed out, the most convincing evidence that can be adduced as to the rise in the Japanese standard of living is the fact that rice has been encroaching more and more on "muji" foods—barley, rye, and buckwheat. There are, moreover, very stringent economic limitations in the way of a considerable change in the direction that Dr. Grey recommends. The rice land, which is now yielding around 70 bushels to the acre, will certainly not yield 70 bushels of wheat: land that is suited—and it has been made suited by generations of effort—for rice is not suited for wheat.[1] The small and selected area of land already growing wheat has an acreage yield 50 per cent. lower than the average yield for all Germany. And as for raising milk and beef and pork, this will be an economic gain only in so far as the foods are raised on lands now lying waste. To turn land hitherto used for raising crops into fodder sources for cattle and swine is a luxury that Japan cannot afford. The Animal Nutrition Institute at Cambridge has estimated that "a pig consumes 12 lb. of vegetable food to produce 1 lb. of human food"; and Denmark, during the exigencies of the War, when corn could no longer be imported, was compelled to "reduce her pig population from 2½ to below ½ a million" in order to economize her food

[1] On the other hand there are other grains than rice that yield even higher output from a given unit of land—e.g. manioc in Java. This of course has no relevance for Japan.

resources.[1] To turn 12 lb. of plant produce into 1 lb. of meat will be to lessen vastly her capacity to sustain the population she now sustains. And, although there are highly successful instances, notably in New Zealand, of animal husbandry on a small scale, to raise cattle and sheep on pastoral ranches generally requires wide tracts of land so that efforts in that direction will also be severely curtailed.

For all that, the national diet is changing in no uncertain way, especially in the cities.[2] Pork and eggs are consumed in increasing quantities. Most striking of all is the rising consumption of flour and wheat—either in bread or macaroni—as revealed in the foreign trade statistics. (Not only does Japan cultivate more than a million acres of wheat, but she imports about 20 million bushels a year.[3]) Japanese and foreign observers alike are insistent, and rightly insistent, as to such trends. There is adequate reason for believing that the exclusive position of rice is beginning to give way to other cereals and to protein foods. Diets, for all the weight of custom to retain them, have changed in the past. So characteristically national a habit among Englishmen as drinking port is only two centuries old and was forced upon an unwilling people by considerations of State—relations with Portugal instead of with France. Scotsmen, who in Dr. Johnson's time were classified with horses as being supported by oats, have in these days no distinction whatever on that account. And much can be done to further the trend towards a cheaper and more wholesome diet. Merely to desist from polishing the rice would not only heighten its food value

[1] Harald Faber, in *Journ. Roy. Statistical Soc.*, Vol. LXXXVII, p. 22. The Chinese, however, use swine to an extent as "transformers of coarse food-stuffs." Cf. King, op. cit., p. 135. But King also points out that for the Chinese to change their vegetarian diet for meat and milk would leave them with much less food.

[2] Cf. Dept. Overseas Trade report on Japan, 1923–4. Also U.S. *Trade Information Bulletin*, p. 642. A great difficulty in the way of changing the diet is the absence of stoves as required for cooking western foods, notably meat. The unpopularity of Taiwan and Indo-Chine rice is partly due to an absence of adequate facilities for cooking it. Cf. Harada, p. 154.

[3] Cf., e.g., *U.S. Commerce Year Book*, 1929, Vol. II, p. 704. In addition to importing 20 million bushels of wheat she also imports about 200,000 tons of wheat bran. Cf. ibid., p. 401.

but would save perhaps 5 per cent. or more of the grain that is now wasted in the polishing process. Another economy is at the moment being advocated by a group that points out the considerable portion of the rice crop that goes to making Saké, a rice wine that is the national beverage: Saké takes about 7 per cent. of the rice consumed. To say that, however, is to reveal how small a proportion of the rice crop goes into Saké. And the proportion has diminished in recent years. Nor are any reasons advanced for regarding Saké as less a food than rice potage; and although an American writer informs us that "intemperance is a more prevalent vice in Japan than the casual visitor realizes, as drinking is usually done in the home at night where the effects are quietly slept off before the next day", travellers in general are agreed as to there being no great problem of alcoholism among the people.[1]

If the Imperial Family and the aristocracy were to use the new foods, above all to have it announced that they were using the new foods, a sanction would be given to them far stronger than the sanction which Queen Elizabeth gave to potatoes. As with every aspect of Japan's population problem, much is being done here too. Unpolished rice has been announced as an Imperial dish. During the spring of 1929 a Foodstuffs Exhibition was held at Tokyo for a month, disseminating in an effective way the information that the ordinary Japanese needs on such matters.[2] And in the Imperial Nutrition Institute is a group of experts devoting themselves to studying Dietetics and to propagating advice on it.[3] As in China and Java, so too in Japan, the water-covered rice fields are being made to nourish eels and fish, as well as to grow grain, and are therefore now yielding both bread and meat.

Among such resourcefulness it is to be expected that a few projects will be less happily advised than the general, but since these are so few we may welcome them as a little comic relief

[1] Arthur G. Brown, *Japan of To-day*, p. 125.
[2] Vide *Trans-Pacific*, 28.3.29.
[3] Ibid., 11.4.29.

amid the direness of the struggle. A Japanese newspaper has announced that: "Japan proposes to export bull frogs to America to relieve the situation caused by over-production in the frog-raising industry. It is reported that the Association of Frog-Growers in Miei Prefecture recently shipped about 50 lb. of live frogs as samples . . . and is prepared to accept large orders from American dealers. Frog-raising in Japan was started several years ago by the Ministry of Agriculture. The present over-production is due to the fact that the frog as a food is not yet in great demand although the Government has been encouraging it as a factor in the solution of the population problem."[1] The international charities of America are indeed spectacular, and the interest of her citizens in all things new justly famous, but it is perhaps hoping for rather much that these will extend to eating Japanese frogs.

IV. The Deductions

It seems fairly certain that unless Japan reduces her present rate of per capita consumption she will not be able to produce all the rice her population will consume. She is already importing nearly one-fifth. At the opening of the century her imports were trifling, but since then they have steadily risen until the last decade when their rate of increase has been too quick to be described as steady. And as her numbers will be increasing by a million or more annually for the next twenty or thirty years at least, and as schemes for extending the arable area, even if successful, will provide for but a moiety of the new demands, while schemes for intensifying the acre yield can contribute less still, this imported proportion is bound to rise further and yet further. The only condition under which it will not rise is that of reducing the per capita consumption.

The basic fact about Japanese rice is that it is costing too much to grow. According to a Japanese expert it is twice as expensive as Chinese rice. Japanese agriculture is thus resting

[1] Vide *Trans-Pacific*, 14.3.27.

on an uneconomical foundation. So far from not producing enough from a given area of land it is producing too much. The acre yield is extraordinarily high—twice as high as in any other known country that grows rice to any extent. But on looking more closely we find that the yield is not strikingly high per man. A very large quantity is wrung from an acre, but it is not so much when shared round among the many farmers who are wringing it: while the yield amounts to 70 bushels to an acre it averages only 50 bushels to a farming family. The high acre yield which looks so impressive on a diagram of comparative statistics is more than an indication of technical efficiency: it is a symptom of social illness. The figure is inflated to its unwholesome size by the pressure of too many farmers on the soil.

The agricultural system of Japan is for this reason on the threshold of a crisis. That it has been arrested on the threshold is due to the growth of Silk Culture. But the ameliorating influence of that windfall is within sight. A far-reaching reorganization can hardly longer be delayed. The cost of production clearly must be reduced; and in the long run it can be reduced only by reducing the yield per acre—by deflating that spurious figure—and that in turn means reducing the number of farmers. Their numbers in any case must be reduced if any part of their demands for a better standard of living are to be satisfied. And in order to save the present wastage of human effort in Japanese agriculture a long series of changes are envisaged. Farms on the levels and valley floors at least must be combined and cultivated as larger units. Machinery can then be used for much of the work. For this, no less than for satisfying the conflicting demands of tenant and owner, the land will before the end probably have to be nationalized or semi-nationalized in some form or other and then a redistribution effected. Not less necessary is joint action among the farmers for economic purposes. Co-operation is urgently needed, in the buying and selling of produce and in many stages of its cultivation: the example of Denmark, no less than the heritage of their own co-operative experience in *Mujins* and *Hokokusha*,[1] points the way to eliminating unnecessary middlemen and anti-social grain speculators. Until some such far-reaching reorganization is effected Japanese rice will continue to be more expensive than other rice, while the demand of the peasants for a better standard of living will become exasperated because unsatisfied. Economic and social considerations alike demand a drastic treatment.

This point grasped we can revert to the proviso mentioned just now: Japan's future will be one of increasing rice imports unless the per capita rate of consuming it declines. Actually there is not a little prospect of the present rate declining. The old dependence on rice as the single staple shows unmistakable signs of diminishing: fish, always a common food among certain classes, is now eaten in double the quantity per capita of a decade ago, and indications point to no abatement of this steep upward trend; while wheat and wheaten flour are also manifesting no uncertain tendencies. The importance of these signs is much greater, in our judgment, than might appear on the surface. In the first place it is conceivable that the proportion of rice in the total diet will diminish to the extent that Japan will be able, with the help of her colonies, to produce all, or nearly all, the rice she will consume. In the second place her protein needs will be supplied not from uneconomical pork or beef, but from fish, with which her waters are richly endowed. In the third place the other cereals she will need, wheat for the most part, can be drawn from the available surplus of countries like Siberia or Russia or Australia or the Americas, and at a considerably cheaper price than she could grow it herself. The change in diet, the significant beginnings of which are already evident, will have behind it not only the force of a sounder knowledge of hygiene, but the greater force of urgent economic interests.

[1] On Mujins and Hokokusha and co-operation generally in Japan, vide K. Ogata, *Co-operation in Japan*. Also International Institute of Agriculture, *Japanese Agricultural Co-operation*, p. 353, etc., in *Bull. du Bureau des Institutions économiques et sociales*, 1910.

The future of agriculture in Japan is interwoven with a change in diet; with greater imports of wheat and possibly a decline in the amount of cereal especially in the amount of rice grown at home; a reduction in the number of farmers and accompanying this reduction a reorganization in the scale and technique of farming. These changes made, the menace of numbers that is now darkening the life of the country can be exorcised. Can the changes be made? To answer that question it must first be known whether Japan can buy and pay for the wheat and the other foods she will be needing from abroad.

CHAPTER VI

THE WAY OF INDUSTRIALIZATION

In former times communities finding themselves with a greater population than their fields could feed have taken to making goods and exchanging them abroad for foodstuffs. The part which this arrangement played in the economy of the Attic Greeks and the part which that economy played in their general history in the sixth and fifth centuries B.C. is a famous example. The *locus classicus* in modern times is our own country. A population that at 1700 numbered about 5 millions grew to about 8 millions in 1800. The series of changes generally summed up as the Agricultural Revolution enabled English farmers to grow the extra food. By 1900, however, the 5 millions of 1700 had become over 32 millions. To sustain so many people on the island was made possible only because we exported manufactures in larger and larger amounts in return for grain and meat and textile fibres.

The evidence brought forth in the former chapter can leave little doubt that the problem of numbers in Japan revolves around whether she can repeat the example of England. Is it possible for a considerable proportion of the sons of the farmers to come into factories and there make goods which the foreigner will buy?

It is the course on which the Government of Japan has elected. A spokesman of the Foreign Office (of Japan) is reported as saying that "A more intensive industrialization of this country will be the positive remedy to cope with the situation. . . . Building up trade and industry will furnish the only solution".[1] This is the typical utterance of official opinion. Further industrialization, is the cry.

I. FOREIGN TRADE: THE CHANGING RATIO BETWEEN WORLD PRODUCTION AND WORLD COMMERCE

Further industrialization, however, apart from all consideration of assured supplies of raw materials and of energy resources,

[1] *Trans-Pacific*, 28.5.27.

which in themselves are problems of the first import, involves finding and keeping markets in which to sell the goods. Until recently most men held the belief, systematized and held so earnestly by Englishmen of two and three generations ago, that in the future countries would specialize or tend to specialize in producing what they could most profitably produce, one country naturally devoting itself to raising wheat and another to making cotton garments, according as the Law of Comparative Costs should decide; so that Foreign Trade was bound to grow immeasurably greater and yet greater. Let men see the light as Cobden saw it and embrace the truth of Free Trade. Nature would do the rest.

The reasonableness of the opinion seemed so far beyond dispute that not until recently have authoritative doubts been entertained.[1] Contemporary statistics no less than general considerations now make it clear that a stringent modification is needed if the belief is to square with the facts. When it is found that but one-quarter of the Australian people are working on the land; or that Brazil is manufacturing over 90 per cent. of the cotton goods it consumes; or that the Belgian Congo is operating a textile equipment ranging from spinning to dying, a re-examination of the fundamentals of foreign trade becomes desirable. It is at least suggested that the position of England, a country buying the food it cannot raise itself with the exports of its manufactures—or conversely the condition of an agricultural country buying its clothes with the food it exports—will never be general The question for Japan is whether the course of England can even be repeated.

The survey of American economic life recently made by the Committee of Experts presided over by Mr. Hoover (then Secretary of Commerce) found that in the United States

[1] Vide article by Mr. J. M. Keynes in the *Economic Journal*, Dec. 1923; also a valuable statement of some recent facts in *Econ. Journal*, 1926, p. 177 et seq., by Professor Warren S. Thompson. An epitome of one part of the new movement is provided by a study of U.S. foreign trade in the last twenty years. Exports of crude materials and foodstuffs are declining, while those of manufactures are rising both absolutely and proportionately.

there is "a breaking down of local concentration", "a tendency for industry to shift from the city to the country", and "a trend to the more equal distribution of manufacturing activity throughout the country. The old areas have lost their supremacy and the greatest gains are being made by those States in which manufacturing has not been relatively important".[1] The same tendency, though on not so spectacular a scale, is to be seen in Europe; and it is permissible to wonder whether the experts at the World Economic Conference have not ascribed too much influence to Tariffs[2] in this matter, regarding them too exclusively as an economic perversion (which up to a point they no doubt are) rather than as a manifestation or a concomitant of some deeper and permanent urge to economic devolution.

For the rise of new industries in hitherto unindustrial regions is to be seen throughout the world to-day. The movement that the American experts found to be among the most striking of the recent economic changes in their country is but a miniature, somewhat heightened of course, of an international phenomenon. Statistics of Foreign Trade clearly manifest this. The cargoes borne by 70 per cent. of the world's shipping were, according to Mr. G. C. Layton,[3] in 1928, only 10 per cent. above those of 1913: an increase that is surprisingly low in view of the great increase in production. Still more striking, the estimates of the Economic and Financial Section of the League show, up to 1926, a wide gap between the increase of world production (also the increase of world population) and the increase of world commerce. Up to 1924 world trade was even less than it was in 1913.[4] Such estimates cannot and

[1] *Recent Economic Changes*, Vol. I, pp. 210–18.

[2] Just as the absence of customs barriers in the U.S. market is greatly exaggerated as a factor in U.S. prosperity.

[3] G. C. Layton, in *Trans-Pacific*, 12.9.29.

[4] *Memo. on Production and Trade*, 1913–1923–6. The actual volume of foreign trade must be smaller still than the statistics show for the Post-War period, because the creation of new frontiers in Eastern and Central Europe (e.g. Czecho-Slovakia, Esthonia, etc.) is causing trade figures now to appear as exports and imports which before the war were merely internal trade within Austria, Russia, etc.

do not claim absolute statistical veracity: but they are approximate enough to indicate the trends. Descending to individual countries we see why the movement is in this direction; while a country like China is importing less manufactures and more raw materials than formerly, even standing in the front rank of cotton manufacturers to-day, a country like the United Kingdom is losing markets on every side. Not only is England's share of world trade smaller than before the War, but the share of Europe as a whole is smaller; and as more than half the world's trade still belongs to Europe there is reason to believe, in view of this disproportion, that it will shrink further yet. It is conceivable—though only a detail it is mentioned because of its significance—that some part of the agricultural or semi-agricultural products like wool, or rubber, or hemp, which now form so large a share of international commerce, will give way to artificial substitutes manufactured in the countries needing or consuming them. The striking development of artificial silk is a reminder that the huge commerce in natural silk now conducted between the Far East and America may disappear before the rise of rayon factories in the latter area. That the amount of wool grown in recent years is scarcely greater than the amount grown before the War is a suggestive fact. It reminds us that indigo is no longer cultivated from plants but is a product of machines. At all events, in one staple commodity—cotton yarn—the volume of international trade is, and for some time has been, actually smaller than before the War, though the total production of it is considerably greater—wherein is the root of Lancashire's troubles.[1]

This tendency, of course, must not be overestimated. The gap between production and commerce, mentioned above as a significant fact, shows a progressive tendency to close up. Further, the inequality in the distribution of iron, coal, and

[1] Not only are hitherto unindustrial countries building factories, but conversely Europe is increasing its agricultural output. Thus an American authority characterizes it as "folly" for U.S. farmers to count upon exporting agricultural products to Europe. Cf. E. G. Nourse, *American Agriculture and the European Market*.

energy resources over the surface of the earth promises a permanent disparity in the degree of industrialization between one country and another. It is possible that Applied Science may utilize sources of energy now unknown, but, taking things as they are, China and the Far East in general will not be able to industrialize on the scale of North America or Western Europe; and a similar dearth (or relative dearth) elsewhere in minerals and petroleum and water resources will impose a similar restriction. Some degree of specialization will probably follow from this disparity, and Foreign Trade from the specialization. The very insatiability of human economic wants will further add to this trading incentive.

There is no prospect of the disappearance of Foreign Trade. On the contrary, there is a prospect of its augmentation. But it will not be so great as is sometimes believed. The disparities of Nature will be partially countered by the ingenuities of applied science and the yet greater ingenuities with which the urge to profit endows men. The "breaking down of local concentration" will extend farther and farther, not only within the State as from one district of the United States to another, but from one State to another, and from one continent to another. Economic activities in countries will be less specialized and more balanced.

Proceeding from these contemporary facts to seek an explanation for them we seem to find it in the recent economic history of the Argentine and Australia. It is there shown that countries are not likely to remain communities of wool growers or cattle breeders or palm oil planters, buying from other countries the manufactured goods they need. In addition to the purely economic forces driving men off the land that have been indicated elsewhere in this book,[1] the adventure of industry and commerce, the more exciting life and the greater proportionate returns to human effort in them, will draw some part of the farmers away from the fields to found cities and to reap the profits of exploiting an economic want. Thus textiles

[1] Chapter V supra.

that were once imported from England will be manufactured within the erstwhile importing country; and this movement will be gradually carried over the whole gamut of economic wants, at least so far as the local possession of natural resources will allow it. The reports of the Department of Overseas Trade, already plaintive of the development of industries in this or that country, will chant the refrain still more loudly. And experts co-ordinating and studying international statistics, like the experts of the Economic Section of the League Secretariat, will continue to observe that "Europe is more dependent on foreign countries for the disposal of her goods than formerly, while the foreign countries are less dependent on Europe for the satisfaction of their needs".[1] The rise of a steel industry in South Africa or of a railway-material industry in India, which European exporters are finding so much to their discomfiture, is but the beginning of a process that is certain to develop.

As for the foreign trade of the future, it will arise as the foreign trade of the past has arisen; that is, when the importing country experiences a *demand* that cannot be adequately met by itself, but which the exporting country can not only meet but can meet on terms more advantageous than those of rival exporting countries. The new element, however, will be that the ratio between the total production and the total commerce of the world is changed: the former will be greater than the latter; the aggregate output will be much greater than aggregate imports; because economic balance and economic devolution will be the trend, not concentration and geographical specialization. In consequence the competition for the markets which still remain or are to be opened will be more and more strenuous.[2]

At this point it may be objected that the victory of one

[1] Cf. *Memorandum on Balance of Payments*, 1912–26, p. 51. What this means to Europe, or to any individual country which is in the position that it *must* export so as to pay for necessary imports, is illustrated in the case of Japanese silk, vide infra.

[2] The rivalry now in progress between British and U.S. business in South America is perhaps a promise of what will become more pronounced and more general. For this S. American rivalry, cf. Haring, *South America Looks at the United States*, p. 122, etc.

country in foreign markets is not the defeat of another; that an increase in the foreign trade of any given country does not entail a curtailment in the foreign trade of another country; that, in short, such an argument is but a form of the old "mercantilist fallacy" against which Professor Cassel spoke at the World Economic Conference.[1] In the annual report of the United States Secretary of Commerce for 1928 the case is stated with vigour:[2] it is insisted that the United States' great volume of exports had not harmed Europe; on the contrary it had benefited Europe because American imports from Europe had increased. This expansion, the official report proceeds picturesquely, "should be judged . . . not simply in terms of cold values of goods sent abroad but in the larger aspects of the human equation". The larger aspects of the human equation, unfortunately for the European, turn out on analysis to be large only for the American. In any case the instance brought forward in the report is a special instance, for since Europe is obliged by reason of subsistence to import goods from America, to the extent that she does so she must send exports back in payment for them. But the choice as to what exports she send rests with the United States, if for no other reason than that the United States is economically less incomplete and can secure its choice through its tariff. It may, for example, have been more advantageous for Europe to send Textiles or Wines, but instead the United States has required her to send amongst other things her Art Masterpieces to the houses of American millionaires, her old maps and manuscripts to their new galleries and libraries, or to exile her musicians and scholars and scientists in American seats of culture for a period. The point to be stressed is that Europe needs to sell to the United States more than the United States needs to buy,[3] and the United States therefore decides on what she will take in payment for European imports. It is scarcely necessary to

[1] May 1927, opening address.

[2] *Report of the Sec. of Commerce*, 1928, p. 93 et seq. Also cf. Prof. Taussig in *Foreign Affairs*, Oct. 1929.

[3] Cf. *Memorandum on Balance of Payments*, 1912–26, p. 51.

remark that no sort of criticism can attach to her for this: it is her good fortune. It is necessary to remark, however, that the official document in question sees the larger aspects of the human equation from a somewhat restricted point of view. And reference to the prohibitiveness of the U.S. Tariff would not have been irrelevant—it levied about £120 million in 1927, and will levy even more now that the new Tariff has been passed. The report omits too the obligation of Europe to send goods to the United States annually in redemption of the War Debts, an obligation entailing exports of from £43 million rising to £80 million annually[1]—and exports again in the form that the United States chooses by means of her Tariff to accept—even if the United States never shipped a single article throughout the year to Europe. That exports to the United States are rising in volume is thus no evidence whatever that Europe is benefiting from the expansion of the United States' foreign trade.

Such evidence as there is implies the contrary. The United States is sending not only a bigger proportion of her total exports to non-European markets, but considerably bigger amounts.[2] She now has to find foreign consumers for more than one-tenth of her huge output, a proportion, moreover, that seems destined to rise in the early future, and the deliberation and imagination and energy with which the United States Government is seeking these markets must command the admiration no less than the misgivings of her rivals.[3] The

[1] Cf. Hon. R. H. Brand, in *Journal Royal Institute International Affairs*, May 1929, p. 209. The Reparation Problem is really the American War Debt problem, in so far as Reparations eventually go to U.S.A. to pay War Debts. Vide article by Right Hon. Philip Snowden, in *Manchester Guardian Weekly*, 24.5.29.

[2] Cf. *International Trade and Balance of Payments*, 1913–27, Vols. I and II; also *U.S. Report of Sec. of Commerce*, 1928, Vol. XXII. U.S. Foreign Trade is singular for its large "favourable" balance, exports exceeding imports by 340 million dollars in 1929. Vide Dept. Overseas Trade, *Review of External Trade of U.S.A. in 1928*.

[3] The Bureau of For. and Domestic Commerce, a bureau in the Dept. of Commerce, has a grant of about £1 million a year. Its thoroughness and efficiency, as is known to all with any acquaintance with its numerous publications and bulletins, cannot be too highly praised.

official report might justifiably have been more exuberant than to write merely that "the results of . . . Government officials to expand foreign sales of factory products has been most gratifying".[1] If American business men succeed in doing what the United States Consul-General in India has recently been urging them to do, to raise the present low proportion of the import trade that is theirs in that country,[2] their gain will be made at the loss of English business men. Whether they deserve to gain and the English to lose, or whether the change would be to the advantage of the Indian, are not relevant to the present discussion. The relevant consideration is that they would gain to their competitors' loss—unless, indeed, the purchasing power of the Indian rises. Only in the case of purchasing power being relatively flexible is the so-called "Mercantilist fallacy" really a fallacy.

In the ultimate and theoretical view purchasing power may not be rigid, or not wholly rigid. There is, in varying degrees, everywhere the spectacle of unfulfilled wants on the one side and on the other an unfulfilled productive power, demands unsatisfied and possible supplies untapped. At first appearance there seems every reason that India, half starved, should share in the vast potential but not fully realized productivity of the United States. The case, however, is not so simple as this. Here it is sufficient to remark that in practice the purchasing power of India is low and probably for as long as the present need concern itself with will remain low, and that any proportion of her supplies that she buys abroad will be relatively fixed: if one country gains the selection to provide these supplies the competitors who lose it will, if not precisely to that amount, yet in a considerable proportion of that amount, have a smaller volume of foreign trade.

In all truth might the citizen of New Orleans (when discussing the United States' policy in Central America) have cried out, "What nobler ideal was ever conceived by mortal man than to

[1] *U.S. Sec. of Com. Report*, 1928, Vol. XXII, et seq.

[2] U.S. *T.I.B.*, No. 87.

raise ten million people to the point where they have gotten purchasing power!"

II. Metals and Energy Resources: The Determinants of Competitive Status in Foreign Trade

With these general considerations in mind and with the tendencies disclosed by contemporary statistics we can now proceed to estimate Japan's prospects in the programme to solve the pressure of population by industrializing, that is by living, at least largely, on foreign trade. Japan will be able to sell her goods abroad only so long as the buying countries do not meet the demand themselves, or so long as they do not change their present suppliers for others who can meet the demand on more advantageous terms. Throughout the world, however, there is a tendency for the buying countries to meet the demand themselves, and reasons have been advanced for believing that the tendency will be accelerated in the future. If the Chinese further develop their taste for cotton garments or violins or sugar confections, Chinese themselves will arise in time to satisfy the taste.[1] On the other hand, though the Chinese demand for Japanese imports of these goods may not be permanent, it may last long enough to help Japan tide over her coming difficult period. The shortage of capital in China and the limited sources of adequate iron supplies will retard and restrict the industrializing process in that country. Even then, however, Japan has to maintain her position against the ceaseless competition of rivals.

The problem thus resolves itself into an examination of the advantages and disadvantages that Japan has in meeting the competition of her rivals. In most markets, notably in the markets of the Orient and Africa where purchasing power is so low, the price at which the goods can be offered will decide the place in the conflict.[2] Advantages and disadvantages revolve around costs.

[1] Chinese companies are already manufacturing wireless sets. Vide *Far Eastern Rev.*, April 1929, p. 185.

[2] Cf. Dept. of Overseas Trade *Review on British Malaya*, 1929.

Propinquity to the millions of China and the Indias and to the prospectively prosperous populations of Manchuria and Siberia will serve to reduce costs. The greater understanding that Japan may be assumed to have of these people will heighten this initial advantage. Far more decisive factors than these, however, are firstly the terms on which she can purchase the raw materials, and secondly the costs absorbed in manufacturing them into finished articles. For the time being it can be assumed that the purchase of raw materials will not disadvantage her, at least not more than Germany or England or other countries importing them; and if plans for growing cotton in Korea or in her South American plantations come to anything she may even have a slight advantage under this head. Production costs will therefore be the chief factor determining the price at which Japan can offer her manufactures, and production costs in turn are determined by the sources of iron and of energy-power at her disposal and the efficiency with which these are utilized. Japan's place in the competition for foreign markets will be primarily and ultimately decided by her possession of iron, coal, petroleum, and water power, or by her ability to secure these cheaply.

Here we approach a fact which is at the very root of modern life.[1] A moment's reflection is enough to show how much of it—almost all of its material environment—depends upon iron and the sources of energy. Not only is this so, but the world's fund at least of iron, and of most of the present known sources of energy, is strictly limited, and their nature is such that once used they are ended and cannot be replaced. A ton of wheat consumed can be replaced by another ton grown on the same plot of ground, but a ton of iron ore or a gallon of petroleum once used cannot be thus reproduced. It is this exhaustibility and non-reproducibility indeed rather than the operation of Diminishing Returns in agriculture that makes the possibility

[1] Cf. Lecture by the chemist, Professor Jaeger of Gröningen, in *Science*, 26.4.29, on "The Present and Future State of our Natural Resources". Also Carl L. Alsberg, "Progress in Chemistry and the Theory of Population", *Journal Indust. and Engineering Chemistry*, May 1924.

of "over-population" something more substantial than a hypothesis of the schools, and that in the future may be creating international issues of first-class importance.

The correlation between the "prosperity", or standard of living, of any given country and its supply of these fundamentals is a striking commentary on what they mean in modern life. In illustration of it an expert of the United States Bureau of Mines, Dr. F. G. Tryon, has prepared statistics from which a selection is made hereunder:

I. PER CAPITA CONSUMPTION OF IRON AND STEEL (1924–5)

	Pounds
United States of America	942
Great Britain	466
Germany	409
France (*plus*) Saar	475
Italy	110
Japan	75

II. PER CAPITA CONSUMPTION OF ENERGY (COAL, OIL, GAS, WATER POWER)

	B.T.U. (Millions)
United States of America	191
Great Britain	110
Germany	76
France	57
Italy	13
Japan	15

III. PRODUCTION OF COAL PER UNDERGROUND MAN PER DAY

	Year	Tons (Short)
United States of America—		
Bituminous	1923	5·15
Anthracite	1923	2·79
Great Britain	1913	1·28
Prussia	1913	1·32
France	1913	1·08
Japan	1913	0·83

IV. PRODUCTION OF IRON PER MINE WORKER PER YEAR[1]

	Ore (Tons) 1924–5	Metallic Iron (Tons) 1924–5
United States of America	2,039	975
Great Britain	962	289
Germany	373	119
France	1,174	411
Italy	372	184

The first and second tables show the average consumption of iron and steel and of energy in a year by each member of the population in six countries. The differences are very great: the United States rate is about twice as high as that of England, and higher still than the rates of Germany and France, and about ten times as high as that of Japan and Italy. The point is that there is a relation between these rates of consumption and the general standard of living prevailing in the countries concerned, not a mathematically precise relation, but one that is intimate enough. There are, of course, no statistically accurate measures of the standards of living available that would enable one to express them in terms of a common denominator; but there are some approximate indications, of which the level of real wages as estimated by the International Labour Office is perhaps the most useful. Calculations based on it and expressed in terms of London as the base 100 have been made and are in part given hereunder:[2]

United Kingdom (London)	100
U.S.A. (Philadelphia)	179
Germany (Berlin)	67
France (Paris)	53
Italy (Rome)	43

A far more convincing illustration, however, of the connec-

[1] These tables from data presented by F. G. Tryon of the Brookings Institution at the Round Table on Mineral and Energy Resources for Future Populations, at the Sixth Institute of the Harris Foundation, Chicago, June 1929. See Norman Wait Harris Memorial Foundation, *Population and Migration*, Repts. of Round Tables, 1929, Vol. III, pp. 625–678 (Confidential Memeographed Report). Also cf. Taussig, *International Trade*, chap. on Effectiveness of Labour.

[2] From the *Commw. of Australia Year Book*, 1928, pp. 550–1.

tion between these consumption rates and the standards of living is given in the third and fourth tables themselves. These show that the countries consuming the most iron and steel and energy per person are also the countries producing the most per worker; that is, they can consume the most iron and steel and energy because they can produce the most. The output of labour in the United States is about two and a half to three times that in England, higher still than that in France or Germany, and perhaps six or more times as high as that in Japan. The discrepancy in the output of the miners in the several countries is due not to their superior energy or intelligence but to the fact that the sources can be more easily exploited or are of richer content, or both. The per capita productivity of labour is high or low according to the nature of the resources. A year's labour of the American miner produces 975 tons of iron metal, while a year's labour of the German miner produces only 119 tons.[1] "In order to produce the coal and iron ore necessary to make one ton of pig iron you have to spend five hours of labour in the United States, and to do it in Germany you have to spend thirty hours of labour."[1] Further instances need not be multiplied. Absolute accuracy would not be claimed for the figures and nothing more than a correlation is inferred from them, but even then we are left with some very significant information.

The light they throw on the condition of England may be noticed in passing. Not only is our country contending with a changing world economy and with it vanishing markets, but also with a depletion of its basic resources. We have been importing vast quantities of iron ores (and even iron manufactures) since before the War,[2] in recent years not less than a third of the total quantity used; while in coal mining, to say nothing of the competition coal is meeting with in the old external markets from petrol and hydro-electricity, Diminish-

[1] F. G. Tryon, op. cit.

[2] Cf. U.S. *T.I.B.* 639, *Iron and Steel Trade and Industry of Great Britain; U.S. Com. Year Book*, 1929, Vol. II, p. 655.

ing Returns are manifesting themselves with more and more effect, though probably less than one-tenth of our coal reserves are yet touched.[1] Even before the War, according to the computations of Sir William Beveridge, the price of coal and iron were moving higher than the general level of our prices.[2] The early initial advantages of abundant available coal and iron—advantages that brought forth "the magnificent episode of the Nineteenth Century"—are no longer ours.

That priority has moved across the Atlantic. Officials of the Department of Commerce may believe that the "principal factors" behind the recent high rise of the standard of living in America are "human";[3] but it is in no derogation of Americans—whose economic aptitude and enterprise are indeed not less than believed—to ascribe it to other sources. The spectacle of contemporary America revolves around its unparalleled wealth in Energy and the Metals, "the sheer richness and abundance of its natural resources". Of the world's iron and steel it produces half, of its petroleum seven-tenths, of its coal two-fifths, of its water power one-third, and all of its natural gas.[4] It is interesting in passing to remark the accident that the first considerable experiment, if what is mostly unconscious can be called an experiment, in democracy as the order of social relationships, should find itself advantaged with such a richness. Never before has a new way of seeking the Good Life been so helped by its material equipment.

Here, then, is the fatalism of natural accident hanging like a

[1] *Report of the Royal Commission on the Coal Industry* (1925), Vol. I, pp. 17, 19, 115.

[2] Sir W. Beveridge, *Econ. Journal*, Dec. 1923.

[3] *Report of Sec. of Commerce*, 1927, Vol. XXX. An interesting illustration of this rise is given in the figures for silk consumption: this has more than doubled since the beginning of the War. U.S. now consumes the greater part of the world's commercial output. Europe, on the other hand, shows a marked decrease. Another illustration is the percentage of the population in technical schools and colleges—the highest by far in the world. Another is the statistics of travellers on Pullman trains in the summer season—a steep recent rise. Another is the appearance in even small towns of numerous "Beauty Parlours" and the quite common habit of using them.

[4] *Recent Economic Changes*, Vol. I, p. 79.

pall over human effort. A few countries enjoy a great aggregation of the basic resources, many have a moderate supply, some have none. Italy, though she were composed of men of the faultless efficiency of robots, could scarcely raise her standard of living much beyond that of a peasant economy. Were the United States, on the other hand, fortuned with the same ratio between numbers and basic resources as Italy, her citizens would be living in conditions of life little different from those of Benjamin Franklin's day. As it is, the indications point to the United States' prosperity rising higher and the depression of Europe sinking deeper still.

How does Japan stand regarding the basic resources? To become an industrialized nation selling in the markets of the world she will require a supply both in point of amount and in point of availability that will enable her to produce her goods not more expensively than her rivals.

In seeking to estimate Japan's resources the student is fortunate in having at his disposal the results of a study made at the request of the United States Council on Foreign Relations by Mr. H. Foster Bain, a mining engineer with practical experience in the Orient and recently Director of the United States Bureau of Mines. Mr. Bain's opinion may be regarded as authoritative as contemporary expert knowledge of the question can permit.[1]

Iron ore reserves in Japan are so scanty that a per capita rate of consumption equal to that in the United States would exhaust them in two years.[2] In North Hondo are very considerable deposits of the Kuji iron sands, from which in olden times the Samurai swords were made. Experiments have been conducted for utilizing these on modern economic lines, and

[1] H. Foster Bain: *Ores and Industry in the Far East.* Council on Foreign Relations, Inc. N.Y., 1927. Another study that has been very helpful is a series of bulletins appearing in the *Far Eastern Rev.* for Jan.–Feb. 1929, from J. H. Ehlers, U.S. Assist. Commercial Attaché at Tokyo (valuable statistical tables are included); also U.S. *T.I.B.* 573.

[2] Bain, p. 209. "There is only one deposit in Japan which warrants the establishment of smelting works located with reference to the ore supply." *T.I.B.* 573, p. 4.

though so far they have not been successful, hopes are high of ultimate reward.[1] For all that, unless success becomes higher than it is reasonable to believe, Japan will have to draw the bulk of her supplies from outside of Japan Proper, and much of them not even from her own dependencies but from foreign fields. At the present she herself provides about one-tenth of the ore consumed in Japan Proper and only about one-twentieth of the ore consumed in the Japanese Empire.[2] As far as is known Japan's reserves are representative of the general dearth or of the low-grade quality of iron ores in the Far East as a whole China's reserves are less than had been expected; at the American rate of per capita consumption the known reserves would be exhausted in less than two years, the possible reserves in less than three years.[3] The Philippines have large deposits of low-grade lateritic ores, but their commercial utilization is not yet within sight. In Malaya and the Netherlands East Indies, on the other hand, the deposits are heavy and of good grade. Siberia may be well endowed, but is not yet adequately surveyed.[4] (In discussing reserves in the Far East it is necessary to keep in mind the population of that area—from one-third to one-half of the world—and not reserves alone.) Fortunately for Japan—and significantly for international relationships—a considerable portion of the Chinese deposits are in Manchuria and, by virtue of treaty rights, are in Japanese control. As far as iron is concerned, then, Japan will be dependent on sources outside of Japan Proper. The ease or difficulty with which she will secure them will be not unconnected with their general paucity in the Far East, a paucity so notable that industrialization on the scale of North America or even of Western Europe is precluded from the region as a whole.

[1] Cf. Ehlers, op. cit., p. 20.

[2] Vide *T.I.B.* 573, p. 11 and infra, p. 152. Though the output of ores in Chosen (Korea) is now more than double that of Japan its reserves are even smaller than those of Japan. Cf. Bain. Cf. Ehlers, p. 19.

[3] Bain, op. cit., p. 304.

[4] Cf. U.S. *T.I.B.* 359, *Iron and Alloy Metals in Siberia*.

Reserves of coal are not so deficient, both in Japan and in the Far East generally. They are far from being extravagant, however, if the long point of view be taken. Dr. Foster Bain estimates that Japanese reserves would last twenty-five years if consumed at the United States rate of per capita consumption, and Chinese reserves according to the latest estimates would last sixteen years.[1] Since the rate of consumption either in Japan or in China is not, and probably never will be, in China at least, as high as the American rate, supplies will suffice for the present,[2] and for far beyond it. So far Japan has produced about as big a tonnage annually as she has consumed—some thirty million tons a year; but as there is a deficiency of coking coal several million tons of this has to be imported, being paid for by an equal amount of exported coal. Manchuria has a vital bearing on Japanese interests as regards coal, too; by treaty rights Japan has control over the two richest coal mines in the country, Fushun and Penhsihu.[3] The former indeed is the largest single deposit in the world, an unusually enviable possession. Including Japan Proper and the areas under her present dominion, then, it can be said that she is, and for as long a time as her present rulers need be concerned with, will be self-sufficing. But is she and can she be self-sufficing at an economical price?

There is a unanimity amongst observers of the matter, both Japanese and foreign, as to the price of coal in Japan being too high, especially of coking coal. The United States Assistant Commercial Attaché says that it is a "most unreasonable and inexplicably high price".[4] Dr. Harada says that it was more than twice the price of coal in the United States in 1925.[5] The cost of iron and steel, apart from extra costs involved in

[1] Estimates of Dr. Wong, Director of the Geological Survey of China. Bain, p. 208.

[2] Cf. *T.I.B.* 573; and J. H. Ehlers, in *Far Eastern Rev.*

[3] Vide *Report on Progress in Manchuria*, 1907–28, 85, p. 127. There is also iron as well as coking coal at Penhsihu.

[4] J. H. Ehlers, in *Far Eastern Rev.*, p. 86.

[5] Harada, op. cit., p. 36.

working poor grade or scattered ores, will be proportionately high. According to the calculations of Dr. Imaigumi, made a few years ago,[1] a given quantity of pig iron costs:

	U.S.A.	Germany	United Kingdom	Japan
Yen	10	14	16	32

That is, Japanese pig iron was then costing more than three times as much as United States pig iron and twice as much as English pig iron.

Whether this higher production cost is to be a permanent condition or not is yet to be seen; the expensiveness of Japanese coal is at the present due primarily to the low output of Japanese coal-miners—low, as has been seen, because of the fact that coal in Japan is less easily mined and of an inferior quality.[2] It is possible that greater imports of Manchurian coal would lower the costs. Arrangements between the Japanese coal owners and the company operating the Manchurian concessions severely restrict these imports at present.[3] But in any case to import coal for the iron and steel industry would involve importing into Japan both the iron ores and the coal (or some part of the coal). It is very doubtful whether it could exist on so uneconomical a basis. As it is, the industry did not pay its way until 1928; and it paid its way then because the high world prices, brought about as an effect of the European Steel Cartel, enabled it to make some profits.[4]

If Japan is to become self-sufficing in iron and steel, it seems that it can do so on an economic basis only by establishing and operating the industry outside of Japan Proper. If for some unforeseen reason the coal mines within Japan Proper should begin producing cheaper and better coal, the industry might then remain within it; but unless this happens, iron and steel

[1] Harada, op. cit., p. 36. Figures in Ehlers, pp. 85–6, show a much smaller discrepancy.

[2] Cf. *T.I.B.* 573, p. 16.

[3] *Trans-Pacific*, cf. *Far Eastern Review*, March 1929, p. 35.

[4] Cf. *U.S. Commerce Reports*, 15.4.29. It ought to be added, however, that there is a good deal of competent opinion as to the industry's quickly setting itself on an economic basis.

founding will either have to be run on imported ores and dear local coal, or on both imported ores and imported coal; in either case the production costs would be notably in excess of the world level.

This argues that if there is to be a self-sufficing iron and steel industry, or even one producing any considerable portion of what Japan will consume, it can only be in Manchuria, where coal is abundant and cheaper, and where there are also heavy deposits of iron ores.[1] And even then, according to some observers, the poor grade of Manchurian ores, the present higher price of coking coal there, and the distance between the ores and the coal, will make it difficult for the industry to produce on the same level of costs as the American and other foreign manufacturers. The following table shows the relative importance of Japan Proper, Chosen (i.e. Korea), and Manchuria in the production of ores:

PRODUCTION OF IRON ORES IN JAPANESE EMPIRE[2]

(INCLUDING MANCHURIAN LEASES)

(In Thousands of Tons)

Year	Japan	Chosen	Manchuria	Total
1914	121	181	—	303
1917	267	132	103	523
1918	379	430	189	998
1919	362	417	263	1,043
1920	314	447	175	933
1921	86	232	206	525
1923	55	306	213	575
1924	57	323	220	601
1925	75	376	220	672
1926	130	387	566	1,084
1927	159	422	630	1,212

[1] There are large deposits of iron ores in Manchuria, but their iron content is generally too low to justify the cost of transportation outside of the country. The ores require preliminary "crushing, roasting, and concentrating" before being put into the blast furnaces. Cf. U.S. *T.I.B.* 573, p. 5. Only at Penhsihu are ores and good coking coal found together.

[2] Ehlers, op. cit., p. 19.

And the following table shows the total consumption of iron ores in Japan Proper (only, and not in the Japanese Empire) and the sources from which they are drawn:

CONSUMPTION AND SOURCES OF IRON ORES IN JAPAN PROPER[1]

(In Thousands of Metric Tons)

Year	Total Supply	From China	From Straits Settlements	From Chosen	Total Imports (including those from other places than the foregoing)
1913	575	278	—	142	422
1914	—	297	—	163	461
1915	—	308	—	202	510
1920	—	650	—	332	995
1921	—	440	134	190	768
1922	948	645	170	90	908
1923	1,043	662	163	95	988
1924	1,259	800	265	137	1,201
1925	1,287	813	290	108	1,211
1926	1,022	503	290	99	891
1927	1,274	507	438	170	1,115[2]

It will be observed that in the last five years Japan Proper has supplied less than 9 per cent. of the ores she has consumed.

[1] Figures are taken from statistics given in *T.I.B.* 573, pp. 9–10. Though they do not precisely agree with other figures they are as accurate as can be obtained and accurate enough for our purpose. It ought to be added here that Chosen consumes about 75 per cent. of the ores she produces, turning them into pig iron. The pig iron is then shipped to Japan. Manchuria ships virtually no ores to Japan, but turns them into pig iron, most of which is then shipped to Japan. Though both Chosen and Manchuria have considerable pig iron industries they do not as yet make steel.

[2] In addition to ores, Japan Proper imports annually about two million tons of steel and iron, about half a million tons of iron bars, rods, plates, etc., and about half a million tons of pig iron. Cf. *U.S. Commerce Year Book*, 1929, Vol. II, p. 402. But these amounts seem destined to decline—cf. *Trans-Pacific*, 21.11.29, p. 11. Comprehensive figures both for imports and for production of ores, pig iron, steel, etc., can be found in League of Nations, *C.E.I.* 17, *Iron and Steel*, 38, p. 75.

Much of the above discussion as to the prospects of the Japanese Iron and Steel Industry is *a priori*, and can be judged by the reader for what it is worth; but there can scarcely be any room for difference of opinion as to even a moderate degree of self-supply involving foreign imports in increasing amount. Already about half the ores consumed in the Japanese Empire come from the foreigner.[1] Yet Japan is at the present losing nothing by this dependence. It is the opinion of the United States Assistant Commercial Attaché that the imported ores are costing no more than what is paid at Pittsburg;[2] and there seems no reason for these costs to mount higher in the near future. Nor will a steel industry based upon heavy imports of ore be singular. Great Britain imports about a third—five million odd tons annually—of its ores (and nearly as much iron and steel as it exports), while Germany imports nearly twenty million tons of ores and slags.[3]

What will be singular is the element that such a dependence introduces into Japan's Foreign Policy, an element not present in the British or German dependence because their supplies are not drawn as Japan's may be drawn from politically unstable regions. Until 1923 and 1924 two-thirds of her foreign ores were drawn from the Yangtze basin in China and serious dislocations and losses had to be endured in the steel industry off and on because of political conditions there, especially after the anti-Japanese Boycott of 1925. It was not for nothing that the Yangtze iron mines were among the famous Twenty-One Demands.[4] Since the Boycott Japan has been turning more and more to other sources, Malaya chiefly (where long-term leases have been acquired and several millions invested[5]), and latterly an arrangement has been made for drawing supplies

[1] Cf. Dept. of Overseas Trade, *Review on Japan*, 1928; also U.S. *T.I.B.* 573, and U.S. *T.P.S.* 76.

[2] Ehlers, op. cit., p. 85.

[3] Cf. U.S. *T.P.S.* p. 76, *Mineral Raw Materials*; U.S. *T.I.B.*, *Iron and Steel Trade of Great Britain*; and League of Nations, *C.E.I.* 17, pp. 21, 27.

[4] Vide P. J. Treat, *The Far East*, pp. 462–4. Also *T.I.B.* 573.

[5] Ehlers, op. cit., p. 21.

from the North-West coast of Australia.[1] But much more serious than the necessity of laying down plans for securing steady regular supplies from these and other external sources will be the constant preoccupation of Japanese policy with keeping hold on its Manchurian concessions; and these promise to be rather slippery to retain.[2]

Some degree of compensation, however, is the relative plenitude of hydro-electric power. Petroleum may be in uncertain and probably small quantities,[3] and coal may be dear, but the mountainous nature of the country assures a water power that is estimated to be from four and a half to six million horse-power.[4] As regards energy-sources and even as regards the metals, Japan is in a better position than Italy, which has no iron, virtually no coal except lignite, and but three-quarters of the water power of Japan.[5] The following estimates are interesting:

[1] Vide *Far Eastern Review*, June 1929, p. 260. It mentions one million tons as the contracted yearly amount.

[2] A valuable study of Mineral Production in Japan, 1877–1927, has been made by Prof. E. F. Penrose, published in Japanese. The present writer is indebted to Professor Penrose for copies of statistics and graphs from it.

[3] The annual production of petroleum in Japan has remained at about the same figure for the last decade, which is also the same as for 1913—about 80 million gallons (U.S.). Imports have risen nearly seven times the pre-war figure—from $6 million worth to $41 million (vide *U.S. Commerce Year Book*, 1929, Vol. II, pp. 394, 402, 728). Partly because of the manner and standard of living (e.g. relatively few motor-cars) and partly because of hydro-electric resources Japan is not a large consumer of petroleum.

Although a part of Japan is definitely petroliferous (cf. Bain, chap. on Petroleum) satisfactory estimates as to her petroleum resources do not seem to be available. There appear to be considerable prospects in Northern (i.e. Russian) Saghalien. Japan is now operating oil concessions there which are turning out rather better than expected, the output being nearly 70,000 tons in 1927, and was believed to have reached 133,000 tons in 1928 (cf. *U.S. Commerce Reports*, 1928, p. 418); but great difficulties have to be overcome (*Far Eastern Review*, Jan. 1929, p. 37). Most, if not all, of the Saghalien oil is taken by the Japanese Navy (Report of Dept. Overseas Trade on Japan for 1928).

[4] The Govt. Survey of 1923 estimated more than six million, *Jap. Yr. Bk.*, 1929, p. 354. Mr. H. Saito, then Japanese Consul-General in New York, puts the figure at ten million. *Annals Am. Academy*, 1925, Nov.

[5] For Italy, cf. *Revue d'Économique politique*, Mars-Avril 1929, p. 295 et seq.

WATER POWER

(*In Millions of Horse-power*)[1]

	Developed	Potential
The World	33·0	454·0
U.S.A.	11·72	35·0
Switzerland	1·85	2·5
Germany	1·1	2·0
England	0·25	0·85
Italy	2·3	3·8
Japan	1·75	4·5
Belgian Congo	0·000025	90·0
French Congo	0·0	35·0

This asset, though as yet but partially developed, is already making a mark upon the national economy. It has been said that more than half the motive power in Japanese factories is electric,[2] and it is reported that the Power Industry has a greater capitalization than any other.[3] It is noteworthy that the consumers of domestic light were more than double the consumers of domestic light in Germany, a country of nearly similar number.[4] And in 1925 (the latest year for which comparative statistics were available at the time of writing) the per capita ratio of domestic light consumers was even higher than in the United States.[5] It is conceivable indeed that the plenitude of electric power resources may bring about a new form of industrialization in Japan, one in which the massing of men in

[1] From *U.S. Commerce Year Book*, Vol. II, 1928, p. 715. Cf. *Far Eastern Review*, June 1929.

[2] But the author has not been able to verify the claim; it cannot be very far from the truth, however. This accounts for the relatively unsmoky atmosphere of Osaka and other industrial areas in Japan.

[3] *Japan Year Book*, 1929, p. 556. But the industry seems in need of "rationalization". There appears to be a good deal of over-production. Cf. reports in *Trans-Pacific*, e.g. 5.12.29.

[4] Vide figures in *U.S. Commerce Year Book*, Vol. II, 1928, p. 716.

[5] Ibid.

large cities and in large factories will give way to a kind of domestic industry dispersed throughout the countryside.[1]

As regards reserves of metals and energy, then, industrialization will be adventurous but by no means hopeless. It does not appear indeed that Japan would lose much by importing American steel. But if she resolves to go on with the programme of making herself independent of external supplies, much of the iron ore will have to be drawn from outside the Empire, and all but a little from outside of Japan Proper, while her coal will tend to be higher in price than that of the world market. In that case she will be dependent upon the foreigner and upon retaining her present status in Manchuria. Indeed, so essential is that country to any project of Japanese self-sufficiency in iron and steel, and probably in the future in coal as well, that the balance of reasons pro and contra is undeniably for setting up the industry there rather than in Japan Proper. In Energy resources, by reason of the national water power reserves, she will be at no disadvantage, rather at an advantage above the average.

To be satisfactory a survey of this kind should take in the reserves of Siberia, but on account of the uncertainty of information this is not possible. If a considerable mineral and fuel wealth is later revealed there, its effect on Japan's prospects would not be to invalidate the case for her industrialization as made out above; rather, in so far as it might have any positive effect, it would be to strengthen the case.[2]

III. Industrialization in Japan To-Day

It will be convenient at this stage to examine to what extent Japan is industrialized to-day—how far she has gone on the road to becoming a manufacturing nation.

[1] As a result of electrical development there is a cottage hand-loom industry in Belgium. Cf. *World Textiles, Manchester Guard. Commercl., Suppl.* 11, July 29, p. 19. Japanese authorities, in fact, were reported to the author as expecting an increasing use of electric power in village workshops.

[2] For Siberia, vide U.S. *T.P.S.* 36, *Siberia*, by Boris Baievsky. So far not much good iron ore. Also vide H. K. Norton, *The Far Eastern Republic of Siberia*, and *T.I.B.* 359, *Iron and Alloy Metals in Siberia.*

An indication of this is given in the statistics of the major occupations expressed as percentages of all the gainfully employed:

OCCUPATIONAL CLASSES OF BREADWINNERS

Country	Agriculture and Fishing	Industry	Commerce[1]
England and Wales (1921)	6·8	39·7	13·9
France (1921)	41·9	28·4	10·4
Germany (1925)	30·5	38·1	11·7
Italy (1921)	56·1	24·0	6·4
Denmark (1921)	34·8	27·6	10·8
Argentine (1914)	16·8	26·0	9·3
Australia (1921)	23·0	31·2	15·3
Japan (1920)	55·16	19·9	11·9

These statistics, particularly those for Japan, can only be offered as frankly approximate. They are not only approximate but somewhat out of date as well; and (for Japan) the proportion of workers given under Industry is probably too high.[2] As such they need modification. But when all allowances are made, and when they are checked by available figures as to the proportion of farm households to all the households—farm households are 53 per cent. of the whole—or by the distribution of population into urban and rural,[3] they do represent the broad truth that Japan is still primarily agricultural and that no

[1] Excepting for Japan, all the figures are taken from the *International Statistical Year Book*, 1927, p. 45 et seq., and where possible checked by reference to the official publications of the countries concerned. The figures for Japan are taken from *Résumé Statistique de l'Empire du Japan*, 1930, p. 10.

[2] Perhaps the figures in Harada, pp. 110 et seq., are more useful for to-day. He gives the percentage in Industry as 13·8. The official figures may include domestic industry craftsmen, though this is not indicated. So competent an observer as the U.S. Commercial attaché thinks that "industrial workers represent not over 5 per cent. of the adult population". U.S. *T.I.B.* 642, p. 7.

[3] Figures for Farm Households supplied by Jap. Dept. Agric. and Forestry. Figures for urban and rural in *Résumé Statistique de l'Empire du Japan*, 1926, p. 8; 1928, p. 7. Farm households also given in *Japan Year Book*, 1929, p. 491.

matter how important, even to the present national welfare, her industries may be, as far as the bulk of the people are concerned they stand at the circumference and not at the centre of her economic life. Probably Italy alone among the countries cited is as agricultural as Japan, while Australia or Denmark is considerably less so than she.

Further measurements of industrialization like the industrial production per capita or the amount of capital invested industrially corroborate this general truth.[1] It is for more than historical reasons that the Government is still without a Ministry of Labour.

And much of the present industrialization is on a small scale.[2] The number of wooden sheds and other small factory places in Osaka, the foremost industrial city, is surprising. Nor is Domestic Industry by any means a thing of the past. Throughout the villages one can see mats and footwear—both a big item in Japanese household economy—being made and numerous other crafts pursued, generally for part time only. Indeed, according to a communication from the Statistical Bureau of the Department of Commerce and Industry the bulk of the industrial output was still coming from the domestic industries, although (notwithstanding the absence of reliable figures) the Statistical Bureau could not "but recognize the general tendency" for Domestic Craftsmen "to decrease".[3] Though this opinion may perhaps somewhat overestimate the place of the Domestic Industries, it at least shows that Japan is no Lancashire or Rhineland—no "workshop" of the Orient as yet.

On the other hand, the change from a purely agricultural economy to a partly industrial one has been rapid, at least in the later stages. Dr. Harada has published figures showing

[1] Cf. Harada, pp. 61–3.

[2] Cf. photographs in *Geog. Rev.*, N.Y., April 1929, by J. E. Orchard.

[3] Letter dated May 20, 1929; cf. too T. Ueda as translated in Ogata, *Co-operation in Japan*, p. 103; Ayusawa, *Industrial Conditions*, p. 84; *U.S. Tariff Comm. on Broad Silk Manufacture*, 1926, pp. 8, 46, 92, etc. Brown, *Japan in the World of To-day*, p. 98; Ogata, op. cit., pp. 208, 213; Orchard, op. cit. Also G. C. Allen, *Modern Japan*, chap. on Industry.

that the population of cities of 10,000 or more has increased six times faster than the population as a whole since 1895.[1] The rapidity of the urbanization process is also exemplified in the wide discrepancy between the actual and the registered population of some of the larger cities—60 per cent. in the case of Tokio, and 96 per cent. in the case of Osaka, according to an investigation in 1919.[2] And inquiries into the previous occupations of urban workers show that "the majority . . . have been recruited from the peasant class".[3] In the decade ending in 1926 the factory workers virtually doubled;[4] and among them the men now outnumber the women.[5] That the volume of raw cotton imports has more than doubled since the pre-war years and that the per capita Foreign Trade[6] has more than trebled (which, even when allowing for the price movement, means a rate of increase at about twice the rate of increase of the population) are still further illustrations.

Proceeding to the industries themselves, we find that the most noteworthy are Textiles; Iron and Steel; Electric Power; Chemicals; Flour; Paper; and Sugar. The textile industry is incomparably more important than any of the others.[7] It employs more than half the total factory workers, and its exports comprise about 70 per cent. of the entire export trade.

Of the textile industries silk reeling comes first. Although its output is known as raw silk, it is as much an industrial product as spun cotton, and like it is ready for immediate weaving. Yet large-scale production is less developed in it than in the cotton industry—while in the latter, for example, the average number of workers to a factory is over 1,000, in the former it is only 92. It has been estimated that about 85 per cent. of

[1] Harada, p. 99. That the populations of Kobe or Osaka have nearly doubled in number between 1908 and 1925 is further evidence, vide *U.S. Commerce Year Book*, 1929, Vol. II, p. 392.
[2] Harada, ibid.
[3] Ibid., pp. 99–100.
[4] Ibid., pp. 109–11.
[5] Ayusawa, *Int. Labour Rev.*, op. cit., p. 197.
[6] Vide *Internat. Year Book of Agric.*, under Cotton. Also cf. U.S. *T.I.B.* 642, *Trends in Japan's Trade*.
[7] The Electrical Industry, however, has the most capital invested in it.

the silk is reeled in power-driven factories.[1] The remainder is reeled "in country districts where there still persists a household hand-reel industry employing many thousands of peasants"; over 700,000 in 1922,[2] and probably over a million now. Many of the power-driven factories are "mere sheds", and a large proportion of the basins are of the kind known as "sedentary reeling", a process wasteful of hand labour.

The part played by silk in the national economy is suggested by the fact that two-thirds or more of the world's export of raw silk comes from Japan,[3] and that (adding the small quantity of cloth) it amounts to nearly one-half of Japan's total exports.[4] The volume has nearly trebled between 1913 and 1928. Limited though Japan's condition of industrialization may be and with it her dependence on foreign food, yet so vital to her prosperity is her silk trade that any impairment of it assumes the magnitude of a national disaster. An estimation of Japanese resources therefore requires a close scrutiny of the industry's prospects.

Hopeful signs are the steady waning of European production,[5] thereby leaving Japan with fewer rivals to meet; and an unwillingness on the part of Americans to undertake silk raising because of the degree of hand labour involved in it.[6] Even more hopeful are the alertness and responsiveness with which both the Government and the producers are meeting the suggestions and requirements of their main market, the United States. Although a United States Tariff Commission Report says that the export industry is inferior in looms, in equipment, worker's skill, weaving technique, mill management, and dyeing, high praise has been given by a member of the United States National Research Council.[7] It may indeed be concluded

[1] U.S. Tariff Commission, *Broad Silk Manufacture and the Tariff*.

[2] Ibid.

[3] Vide *U.S. Commerce Year Book*, 1928, Vol. II, pp. 703.

[4] From 1925 to 1927 it averaged 40 per cent., or a little more, as calculated on the figures in *Fin. and Ec. Ann.*, 1928.

[5] Cf. U.S. Tariff Commission, *Broad Silk*; also League of Nations, *C.E.I.* 24, *Natural Silk Industry*.

[6] U.S. Tariff Commission, *Broad Silk*.

[7] Cf. Holland, *The Industrial Transition in Japan*, pp. 26, 41, 46, 51. U.S. Tariff Commission, *Broad Silk*, p. 92.

that as far as the Japanese themselves are concerned, no opportunity will be lost for conserving their market.

The future is disconcerting for other reasons. Leaving aside the possibility of competition from China (which will have to be reckoned with in the future), the disturbing features are firstly that more than nine-tenths of Japanese Raw Silk is taken by one country, and, secondly, that Rayon threatens the natural article with an unusually good substitute. Nine-tenths of the silk exports go to the United States. The vagaries of fashion in that country, as in any other country, are quite incalculable. In any case silk is not a necessity but a new luxury, made possible to its millions of American consumers by the steep rise in their country's per capita wealth, and therefore in their standard of living, during the last two decades. A temporary depression—not inconceivably arising from factors like unrestrained Stock Exchange movements—would immediately decimate the demand for such a dispensable luxury and at a stroke cut to the roots of Japan's economy. Even more incalculable than the stability of American demand are the movements of the American tariff. After a season's observation of the force and the manœuvring of the Interests' lobbies at Washington, the beholder can but infer that anything might happen there and that most things do happen.[1] The student is not without reason who writes that "it is possible that the rayon manufacturers in the United States, reinforced by the lumber interests and the belligerent cotton interests, may convince Congress not only to put a higher duty upon rayon imports . . . but even to put a duty upon raw silk". Even when taking the most hopeful view of the stability of the American market, it is still undesirable that Japan be so vitally dependent on any single country.

Rayon, or artificial silk, has developed from the early fibres made by Chardonnet, nearly fifty years ago, to the several

[1] An excellent article on the unreasonableness of manufacturers' tariff demands in 1929 is that of Prof. S. H. Slichter, an economist at Cornell Univ. in the *New Republ.*, Aug. 28, 1929. Also cf. Prof. Taussig, in *Foreign Affairs*, Oct. 1929.

highly successful methods of to-day. In price it is now considerably cheaper than the natural fibre,[1] and being an industrial product, while natural silk is an agricultural, the discrepancy may become greater still;[2] and in quality it is approaching nearer and nearer to the natural product.[3] It is this combination of similar quality at a much lower price that makes rayon so unequal a rival. The volume of world production of rayon was already two and a half times that of raw silk in 1927—surely a cause for thought.[4] The ratio seems bound to widen. Mr. Courtauld's prediction that the rayon business is virtually certain to increase appears anything but extravagant.[5] Some of the members of the Japanese silk business with whom the writer has discussed the matter think that rayon will do them no harm, probably some good, because raw silk will be mixed with it in the process of manufacture, and that wool and cotton have most to fear. This opinion seems less satisfying when it is found that cotton manufacturers are also claiming that rayon will do them no harm but rather will benefit their industry.[6] The fact is that the all-rayon fabric is now a *fait accompli*[7] and that both the silk and the cotton producers will probably feel the effects acutely. This seems the more likely because of the striking improvements that are following one another—yarns of fine filaments, a softer and more silk-like lustre, and a tensile strength even greater than that of natural silk.[8] That in England, Germany, and France the Rayon indus-

[1] Furuya, *Japan's Foreign Exchange*, p. 167, says that real silk is three times the price of rayon.

[2] For the effects of cheaper chemicals on rayon production, and for rayon developments, vide *Manchester Guardian Commercial Suppl.*, *World Textiles*, 11.7.29, p. 25.

[3] Ibid., pp. 23, 26, 29.

[4] Figures for commercial production of Raw Silk in *U.S. Com. Year Bk.*, 1928, Vol. II, p. 702; for Rayon in *Sum. of Tariff Information, Silk and Silk Goods*, U.S. Tariff Com., 1797.

[5] *Economist*, 16.3.29.

[6] Apparently they have received extra orders on this account. Cf. *U.S. Commerce Reports*, 7.1.29. That does not imply permanently enlarged sales, of course.

[7] Cf. *Manchester Guardian Commercial.*

[8] Ibid. Note especially articles "Fibres of the Future" and "Dull Lustre Yarns".

try should continue to prosper while the textile industries as a whole remain depressed is not without meaning. The prospects of the Japanese Silk industry are thus anything but reassuring: it is possible that the story of industrial substitutions—of synthetic camphor or manufactured indigo—is about to begin the most spectacular incident of all.

In face of this threat the Japanese are doing the next best thing. They are building up a rayon industry of their own. The following statistics of its output suggest the energy that is being put into it:

OUTPUT IN RAYON

(*In Metric Tons*)[1]

1922	113
1923	91[2]
1924	545
1925	1,350
1926	3,150
1927	6,800

Official figures are not available for later than 1927, but it is reported that the output in the first half of 1929 was four times the output of 1928.[3] The next decade will be years of crisis in the silk industry; but a good beginning has been made in meeting the threats. That Japan may become a great rayon manufacturer seems probable: the will to reap the chance is present, while in the Orient generally there is agreed to be a vast potential market for such an article.[4] If, however, Japan does find it necessary, by reason of the failure of natural silk,

[1] *International Statistical Year Book*, 1928, p. 89. Cf. *International Cotton Bulletin*, April 1929, p. 523; and Nov. 1929, p. 238.

[2] Year of the Earthquake.

[3] In the *Trans-Pacific*, 22.8.29. Also vide *Osaka Mainichi*, 16.8.30.

[4] *Manch. Guardian Commercl.*, op. cit. The importance of Italy as a rayon manufacturer is worth observing; after England she is the most important producer in Europe and her output is (up to 1928) three times as great as that of Japan. In British E. Africa—Kenya, Uganda, and Tanganyika—Japanese rayon dominates the rayon market, however.

to compete for the market, a great transformation in her economic and social system will have to be made. Hundreds of thousands of acres of mulberry plantations will be abandoned and millions of peasants now tending silkworms will be driven into factories.

The cotton industry is the second largest industry in Japan, not only in the number of its employees, but also in its position on the Export list—for there, too, it comes next to silk, following silk's proportion of 45 per cent. of the total exports with 24 per cent.[1] In point of industrialization it is more important still, being the most highly industrialized and highly "rationalized" industry in Japan, and having indeed little to learn in the lesson of modern efficiency from any textile industry in the world. It is well abreast of all the latest devices; the increasing output per operative,[2] a tendency that has been characteristic of both the cotton and the woollen industries, can be taken as one expression of its temper. And the degree of its "rationalization" is shown in the fact that the Japan Cotton Spinners' Association is credibly reported to control 97 per cent. of all the spindles and 40 per cent. of the looms in the country, besides numbering among its members most of the importers and exporters.[3]

The status of the Japanese cotton industry among the cotton industries of the world is shown in the following tables:

[1] In both, the averages are for 1924–7, latest available years, and all kinds —yarn, piece goods, etc.—are included, not only raw silk. Calculated from *Econ. and Financ. Ann.*, 1928.

[2] Vide *Jap. Year Book*, 1918, p. 581; 1920, p. 601; 1923, p. 553; 1929., p. 549. Also on the new Toyoda loom, *Far Eastern Rev.*, July 1920 p. 330.

[3] For this and for other information on Japanese cotton industry, vide Report of Arno S. Pearse, General Secretary of International Cotton Federation, *Japan and China Cotton Industry Report* and in *Intern. Cotton Bulletin*, July 1929, p. 557. Mr. Pearse spoke highly of the welfare work done in the cotton industry. and *Trans-Pacific*, 21.4.29; also in *Manchester Guardian*, quoted in *Trans-Pacific*, 18.7.29; and the *Economist*, 21.9.29; *Far Eastern Rev.*, Dec. 1929, p. 553. The biggest members of the Association, the Kanegafuchi Spinning Co., paid a 35 per cent dividend in 1929, vide *Trans-Pacific*, 13.6.29.

IMPORTS OF RAW COTTON[1]

(*In Millions of Quintals*)

Country	1909–13	1924	1925	1926	1927
Great Britain and North Ireland	9·027	6·54	8·021	7·226	6·419
Japan (including Korea and Formosa)	2·989	4·672	6·221	6·531	7·090
Germany	4·39	2·713	3·677	2·918	4·467
France	2·811	3·173	3·439	3·682	3·273

These statistics afford the most accurate available information as to the amount of cotton consumed in the four leading importing countries—they are the total imports less the total re-exports. It is seen that by 1927 Japan was the greatest importer in the world, exceeding in that year Great Britain herself. In 1928 (for which final official figures are not yet available) the excess was greater still.[2] Between them Great Britain and Japan import half the world imports of raw cotton.[3]

This evidence is definitive. Further evidence that might be adduced would either confuse the central picture or distort the true perspective. To compare the available statistics of the equipment in spindles, for example, with that of Great Britain is clearly to give a false impression—a very false impression—when these represent her as having only one-ninth of Britain's strength.[4] In view of this absence of adequate comparative

[1] *International Year Book of Agriculture*, 1927–8, Rome, p. 386.

[2] Cf. *Economist*, p. 512, 21.9.29. Also *World Textiles*, Supplement to *Manchester Guardian Commercial*, 11.7.29; and *Intern. Cotton Bulletin*, Nov. 1929, p. 222.

[3] *U.S. Commerce Year Book*, Vol. II, 1928. For Exports in 1928, vide *U.S. Com. Reports*, 8.5.29. For production, vide *Tokyo Chamber of Com. and Ind. Statistical Report.*

[4] Figures for spindles in *International Cotton Bulletin*, April 1929, p. 422; Nov. 1929, p. 226; or *International Statistical Year Book* (League of Nations). In any case Japanese spindles work a considerably longer time than the English. Cf. Mr. Arno S. Pearse on this point, *Japan and China Cotton Ind. Rep.*

statistical information on the Japanese cotton manufactory, it is wiser to estimate the industry by its imports of the raw material. In any case, Imports or Equipment or Total Output all place her in the very first rank of cotton powers: the United States and at least until recently England alone outplace her.

Japanese economists regard it as the most hopeful of their industries. Apart from its magnitude, what might be called the mentality of its leaders is its surest basis. Reference has already been made to the "rationalization". Perhaps the most significant indication of its "survival power" is its adaptation to the world shrinkage in demand for cotton yarn, that has followed on the rise of new spinning industries in so many countries. The following table gives the export of yarn and of piece goods:[1]

EXPORT OF YARN AND OF PIECE GOODS

(*In Millions of Yen*)

	1909–13	1923	1924	1925	1926	1927
Yarn	48·4	78·5	109·6	123·1	70·7	38·8
Cloth	26·0	186·0	239·0	301·0	270·0	258·0

It can be seen that the proportion of yarn to piece goods is changing markedly. Before the War cloth amounted to little over a half the exports of yarn; by 1927 it amounted to nearly seven times as much, and during the last two years the increase has been greater. Further, the amount of cloth is not only many times the amount of yarn exports, it is ten times the amount of its own pre-War figure. And such yarn as is now being exported is of higher quality and of finer counts.[2] The industry is thus accommodating itself to the new conditions; it is deliberately fashioning its product for export—cloth and high quality

[1] Calculated from the *Financ. and Ec. Ann.*, 1920, p. 95; 1928, p. 129. The amounts can be found in *Foreign Trade and Commerce*, Dept. of Overseas Trade, Dec. 1928, and earlier years.

[2] An indication of the change in spinning is given by the respective percentages of raw cotton imported from U.S.A. and Egypt and from India: the former is rising, the latter falling.

yarn, for both of which a market still exists. Nor is Japanese capital losing all hold over coarse yarn; instead of sending it to China it has set up its own mills there, and so enjoys the benefit of the Chinese tariff, of cheaper labour, and of local supplies of raw material. Of the three and a half million spindles in that country two-fifths are Japanese.[1] This same spirit of resourcefulness and vitality is shown in an invention like the now famous Toyoda Loom,[2] in the foreign trading of the industry, its shipping conventions, its missions and exhibitions, and above all in the improving quality of its cloth,[3] so good indeed that a report of the Department of Overseas Trade has to speak of it as breaking down "the exclusiveness of the reputation" of Lancashire.

It is not surprising to find it pushing its wares not only on its neighbours of the Orient—on China, Malaya, India, "the greatest cotton markets in the world", and the South Seas, but even as far afield as Eastern Europe. Lancashire has reason enough for regarding Japan as its "greatest potential competitor in the world's foreign trade".

How far the industry will succeed in finding export markets in sufficient quantities to enable Japan to pay for the increasing amount of foodstuffs that will have to be imported is difficult to say. Cotton yarn seems to have no prospects as a staple of foreign trade; and if cotton spinning can be developed industrially almost in any country of the world, and is being developed in very many unsuspected countries, what is to prevent the process from being carried a stage farther in the future by the development of weaving? And, as Dr. Orchard has pointed out, the very countries to which Japan is sending the bulk of her

[1] Vide *Jap. Year Book*, 1929, p. 546. Also *U.S. Commerce Reports*, 1928, p. 798. Also *International Labour Rev.*, Aug. 1929, p. 252. For Labour conditions in China, vide *U.S. Monthly Labour Rev.*, April 1928.

[2] Cf. *International Cotton Bulletin*, April 1929, p. 522; cf. discussion at Barcelona Cotton Congress, in ibid., Nov. 1929, p. 44.

[3] Cf. Dept. of Overseas Trade *Report on Trade and Commerce of East Africa*, 1929, pp. 17, 32, 33. Missions have been sent in latter years to S. America, Africa, and the Near East. It is worth mentioning that Japan is an eager buyer of British East African raw cotton. Vide *Intern. Cotton Bulletin*, July 1929, p. 580.

cotton frequently have more coal, the raw material itself, and cheaper labour.[1] They may even become foreign competitors. China is already exporting yarn to India, while India competes with Japan on the African littoral. Nor must the United States cotton industry be forgotten; already with an output that leads the world, its vast productive power is becoming more and more in need of external markets,[2] and no other country has such a power for acquiring these.

Before leaving the Silk and Cotton industries it should be remarked that Japan is building up a woollen industry as well, and that in the future it might easily become a competitor in foreign woollen markets. As an instance, muslin-de-laine, a light woollen textile originated in Europe as a suitable article for the Japanese and other Eastern markets, is now being exported to Europe by Japan.[3] The following illustrates the progress being made in local woollen manufacturing:

IMPORTS OF WOOL AND WOOLLEN YARN[4]

(In Millions of Yen)

	1920	1921	1922	1923	1924	1925	1926	1927
Wool	14·8	32·2	55·4	80·0	88·0	121·0	86·0	102·0
Woollen yarn	4·2	15·2	48·6	73·8	63·5	56·0	32·5	43·5

Japan in short, with her manufactures and exports of silk,

[1] J. E. Orchard, op. cit. In the summer of 1930 a powerful Textile Exporters' Assocn. was formed with the chief purpose of seeking out markets in Russia and West and South Africa. The Japan Cotton Spinners' Assocn. is one member of the group (*Japan Trade Review*, July 1930, p. 24).

[2] It should be made clear that the U.S. cotton industry rests on cheap labour, vide Blanchard, *Labour in Southern Cotton Mills*. Italy is also counting on Cotton exports—cf. *Giornale degli Economisti*, 1928, p. 237: Le Industria di Cotone in Italia.

[3] Vide *Japan Year Book*, 1929, p. 552.

[4] Vide *Financ. and Econ. Annual*, 1928, p. 130. The Japanese themselves are taking more and more to wollen clothes. It may be worth mentioning that an experienced German wool buyer in Australia gave it as his considered opinion that the Japanese woollen industry hindered itself greatly by unskilful and extravagant wool-buying.

cotton, wool, hosiery, and jute, is an all-round Textile power, though still with a very heavy lean on silk and cotton.

Other industries that should be mentioned are Flour Milling, Sugar Refining, Chemicals, Rubber Manufacturing, Iron and Steel, Paper-Making, and perhaps Pottery. The exports of flour milling and of sugar refining have been quadrupled since 1914, but as in both cases the export does not amount to more than 2 per cent. of the export of Textiles[1] its importance is not very great to-day.[2] Rubber is mentioned more for its potential than actual importance. Chemicals have made unusual progress and their exports promise a future.[3] Pottery and Paper are old specialities and still holding their ground, Paper, indeed, increasing greatly. Iron and Steel has been already discussed: It is receiving great efforts and is interesting here for its rising amounts of sheeting exports.

IV. Japanese Foreign Trade To-day

Proceeding with our examination of the general practicability of the programme of Industrialization for Japan, and in particular with our examination of the present character of the industrialization in that country, we now pass from a consideration of Industry to a consideration of Foreign Trade.

If the degree of industrialization is not large, relative to the population, neither is the Foreign Trade. Subjoined is a table giving the per capita foreign trade figures—that is, the total of exports and imports divided by the total population—for a number of countries:

[1] Calculated from *Financ. and Ec. Ann.*, 1928.

[2] This perhaps understates both industries somewhat.

[3] Cement especially. It is sold in E. Africa amongst other places. Cf. Overseas Trade Report, op. cit. For the volume of these—as of all of Japanese goods that are exported in noticeable amounts—vide *Board of Trade, Foreign Trade and Commerce Accounts*, 1926–8; and in addition to textiles, note especially figures for rubber goods, iron-sheeting, bars and rods, sugar and flour. On Chemical Industries generally, vide *T.I.B.* 217. On paper, vide *T.I.B.* 672, *Paper Trade and Industry of Japan*: The production of pulp and paper more than doubled between 1920 and 1928 and the exports more than trebled.

FOREIGN TRADE PER CAPITA[1]

(In Dollars)

Country	Year	Imports	Exports	Total
United States	1927	34·8	40·4	71·2
Chile	1927	32·0	51·0	83·0
United Kingdom	1927	130·5	88·0	218·5
Germany	1927	53·7	38·8	92·5
France	1927	50·8	53·1	103·9
Denmark	1927	129·0	120·6	249·6
Australia	1927	129·4	111·5	240·9
Japan (Proper)	1927	16·7	14·6	31·3
Columbia	1926	16·0	15·1	31·1
Paraguay	1927	16·4	17·2	31·6
British Malaya	1927	172·0	179·0	351·0
British India	1927	2·9	3·6	6·5
China	1927	1·9	1·5	3·4

It will be seen that Japan is low on the list, being in fact equal to Columbia and Paraguay, and exceeded more than ten times by British Malaya. The meaning of this must not be mistaken: a high per capita foreign trade does not connote a high national dividend. If it did, the Chilean would be better off than the American, and the inhabitant of British Malaya many times better off than either. Nor does it necessarily imply industrialization, as is evident from the above figures, especially from those of the United States. The meaning is to indicate, and that only roughly, how far a country is self-contained and how far it is dependent on the outside world. The more dependent on external supplies and sales a country is the higher will its per capita foreign trade stand. Thus the United Kingdom and British Malaya are highly dependent, while the economy of India and China is nearly self-contained. Japan is among those that are not so far away from being self-contained. Because of Japan's large population figure a

[1] *U.S. Commerce Year Book*, 1929, Vol. II, p. 743.

per capita average of this nature would somewhat exaggerate the degree of self-containedness. Nevertheless it would appear that the net imports of food amount to less than 5 per cent. of the food consumed.[1] But as the amount of food imports

[1] That was the conclusion of Dr. Grey after investigating the matter for the Health Section of the League of Nations. *The Food of Japan*, p. 12 et seq.

I. FOODSTUFFS IN JAPANESE FOREIGN TRADE

(In Thousands of Yen)

Year	Imports	Exports	Balance of Imports	Total Imports
1913	120,420	59,417	61,000	729,432
1924	333,282	106,800	226,481	2,453,402
1925	383,892	136,008	247,883	2,572,658
1926	338,510	143,912	194,598	2,377,484
1927	301,379	134,747	166,633	2,179,154

Rice, wheat, beans, sugar, meat, and eggs have from 1920–7 amounted to 12·23 per cent. of the Imports. These figures are taken from U.S. *T.I.B.* 642, p. 15, and *U.S. Commerce Year Book*, 1929, Vol. II, p. 401.

II. PERCENTAGE OF FOOD AND DRINK IN FOREIGN TRADE OF SEVERAL COUNTRIES

(In Thousands of Yen)

Country	Imports			Exports		
	1924	1925	1926	1924	1925	1926
United Kingdom	42·1	41·2	—	6·0	5·9	—
Germany	—	28·2	31·2	—	5·8	4·9
Netherlands	—	26·6	25·7	—	43·0	41·6
France	22·1	20·3	—	10·2	8·6	—
Denmark	23·6	23·8	—	77·7	80·4	—
Japan	—	12·11	14·92	—	6·04	5·9

The second table shows that Japan is less dependent than France on outside sources of food and drink, much less dependent than Germany, and very much less dependent than the United Kingdom. Excepting for Japan, the above figures are taken from *Memo. International Trade and Balance Pay-*

has been rising and the per capita foreign trade has also been rising, the direction of the country's economic movement is unmistakably manifested. Small as the foreign trade figures still are in comparison with her numbers, Japan's sustenance, above all her present standard of living, depend upon the disposing of her industrial products abroad in payment for the imports she needs. And in the future, as we now know from our analysis of Japanese demography, this dependence will grow greater and greater.

Her growing industrialism is also revealed in the relative

ments, 1913–27, Vol. I, p. 45 et seq.; those for Japan are taken from *T.I.B.* 642, p. 16.

III. JAPANESE IMPORTS OF RICE, SOYA BEAN, AND WHEAT

(*In Millions of Dollars*)

	1913	1926	1927	1928
Rice	24·003	23·887	37·410	15·627
Soya bean	3·535	23·102	19·532	23·057
Wheat	6·116	43·985	25·568	31·460

These (the figures are taken from *Com. Year Book*, op. cit., p. 401) are the main items in Japan's food imports. It will be observed that wheat is the biggest and that soya bean is nearly as important as rice. Soya bean, in fact, is so important and its importance has such a political significance that some reference should be made to it here. At the moment, soya bean forms the major protein factor in the food of the average family in Japan. Nearly a million acres in Japan are put under it annually, about 20 million bushels being grown, while about 4 million quintals (from 15 to 20 million bushels) are imported from the foreigner and somewhat less than half that amount from Korea (vide *Internat. Year Book of Agric.*, 1927–8, p. 352). The "foreigner" means Manchuria. So once again are we brought back to Japan's close relations (not to characterize them more strongly) with Manchuria; not only has she heavy capital investments there, one of the outstanding markets for her Textile manufactures, and a scarcely dispensable source of iron and coal, but she is drawing a large proportion of her chief protein food supply, and a considerable part of her agricultural fertilizers (because a by-product of the bean is bean-cake fertilizer) from there. Manchuria's prosperity is linked up with its production of soya. Between six and seven million acres are annually devoted to it, and more than half the world's supply is grown there (vide *Progress in Manchuria*, 1907–28, p. 47). On Beans, vide art. in *Far Eastern Review*, Feb. 1929, "Beans"; and for the part played by them in Japanese domestic economy, vide *Japan Year Book*, 1927, p. 480; above all, vide *Beans*, issued by S.M.R., Dairen, 1929.

proportions of the classes of goods in her import trade: thus raw materials are forming a larger proportion—by about 6 per cent. since the pre-War years alone—while manufactured goods are forming a smaller. Conversely the proportion of raw materials in the exports is diminishing while the proportion of manufactured goods is rising. That the volume of silk exports, the chief article of her foreign trade, should have nearly trebled since the pre-War years, and the volume of raw cotton imports should have more than doubled in the same period, is impressive testimony as to her increasing dependence on the outside world. Trends and tendencies rather than numbers and facts are what we are seeking, and here we have our finger on an outstanding, almost the outstanding, tendency, clearly pointing out the future.

A hopeful sign is the widening of the area to which Japanese exports are being sent. It is not possible to spend any length of time in studying the international trade in Textiles before becoming impressed with the extensiveness of Japanese markets and the energy with which they are being pushed. The reports of the Department of Overseas Trade on Africa and the Orient are eloquent of this.[1] It is not only in India, or China (Southern as well as North), or the Netherlands East Indies, or British Malaya, or Kenya, Uganda, Tanganyika, and Zanzibar in East Africa (where indeed Japan is the chief exporter, exceeding Great Britain herself), but also in Iraq, Egypt, and the Sudan, and even through Palestine, Syria, and Turkey into Roumania, and also in South Africa and Australia and across the Pacific into South America;[2] and a campaign is now being planned for Russia and West Africa and Canada!

[1] E.g. Overseas Trade Reports in 1929 on *British Malaya; Netherlands East Indies*; and on *Trade and Comm. East Africa.*

[2] Cf. Article by Sir E. Thompson, Chairman Cotton Trade Statistical Bureau, in *Manchester Guardian Comm. Suppl., World Textiles*, 11.7.29. Another sign that may become of considerable importance in future years is the importing of goods to re-export them; cotton, for example, is imported from India and re-exported to China more cheaply than China herself can import it directly. This "store-housing" re-export trade now amounts to four or five million pounds annually. Cf. Inoui, in *Trans-Pacific*, 12.9.29.

It is worth noting that Japan is creating a Bureau for Foreign Trade, vide *Economist*, 16.11.29, p. 911.

A characteristic of Japanese foreign trade that has received much attention and has been regarded with equal misgiving is its "Adverse Balance", the excess of imports over exports. For many years before the War and for every year since 1920 the excess has been considerable.[1] Does this imply a real deficit in the national account, or only an apparent deficit? And if a real deficit, what is its meaning?

In general, too much significance is attached to an adverse trade balance. Most countries, in point of fact, show an excess in their published returns; and among these Denmark, New Zealand, Holland, Belgium, Norway, Spain, Sweden, and Switzerland, and others, all show a greater excess than Japan. This general excess is in part cancelled out by the fact that import figures are usually calculated on a C.I.F. basis,[2] while exports are calculated on the local selling price, a variety in method that accounts for a considerable discrepancy; and in part it is cancelled out by a series of services known as "invisible exports"—shipping receipts, insurance premiums, etc.—and by a time gap, especially in capital and interest transactions. If every item could be ascertained a balance would be struck. The Economic and Financial Section of the League of Nations

[1] ADVERSE TRADE BALANCE: IMPORTS AND EXPORTS

(In Millions of Dollars)

Year	Imports	Exports	Balance
1911–13	307·4	265·2	42·2
1921–5	942·3	756·2	186·1
1925	1055·8	946·2	109·6
1926	1120·3	963·5	156·8
1927	1033·1	944·6	88·5
1928	1019·3	915·2	104·1

The above figures are taken from the *U.S. Commerce Year Book*, 1929, Vol. II, pp. 770–1, excepting those for the last column, which have been computed from the first two columns.

[2] I.e. price paid plus shipping freights, insurance, etc.

has compiled balance sheets for some sixty countries, most of which have an adverse trade balance, but which by including all the "invisible" transactions and by computing imports and exports on a common basis make a tally.[1] Japan is among the countries.

This would appear to dispose of any further concern with Japan's adverse balance, especially when we find a report of the American Bankers' Association, after the Earthquake, holding that the invisible transactions almost covered the deficit.[2] Unfortunately, the case is not so simple. Apart from the completeness or incompleteness of the analyses (they are admittedly incomplete), among the invisible exports loans from abroad may be included. To balance one's incomings and outgoings by recourse to loans is of course not to balance them at all, but merely to postpone the ultimate reckoning. For a short period, or as a solution to an abnormal difficulty like the post-Earthquake dislocation, this is sound enough; but over a long period it is disquieting.

Dr. Furuya, a Japanese economist, has calculated that there was a real deficit in the immediate pre-War years, made up partly by an export of bullion, but mostly by foreign borrowing.[3] During the War years Japan enjoyed "all the gains and none of the losses of belligerency" and accumulated a huge excess of credits over debits, nearly £300 million in all,[4] an accumulation that has probably in no small way staved off or disguised some of the consequences of the country's most serious economic defects. By 1920, however, the unfavourable balance reappeared and continued to appear each year; and to demonstrate that it was a real and not an apparent deficit, all the War-time gains were gradually eaten up. In 1924, 1925, and 1926,

[1] *Memorandum on International Trade and Balance of Payments*, 1913–27, Vol. I.

[2] *Japan—before and after the Earthquake*, Am. Bankers' Assocn., New York, pp. 40, 56, 57–8.

[3] Furuya, op. cit., p. 54 et seq.

[4] Cf. ibid., p. 90. Although this credit was accumulated, the industries that sprang up during the War lost nearly all their markets after it and failed to keep a stand.

for example, only by borrowing abroad could she strike a balance.[1]

This would seem to indicate that the excess of invisible exports over invisible imports is not great enough to cancel out the excess in the visible commodity trade. At all events it has not been great enough up to 1928. The adverse balance was actually and not merely apparently adverse.[2] Hence there has proceeded, in varying degrees, fresh borrowing abroad, the selling of her foreign investments, exporting of bullion (silver, until recent raising of the gold embargo) to creditors, and an unfavourable exchange.[3] The exchange indeed has manifested a consistent tendency to be unfavourable. This probably explains in part—though only in part—the trend since 1925 in the silk trade—a rise in the exports and a fall in the value received for them.[4]

Not to mention the losses that it has inflicted on the Japanese economy, it is a phenomenon that clearly cannot go on for ever. There is reason indeed for believing that its disappearance is within sight. An unwise credit policy on the part of past Governments and a defective financial system are not necessarily permanent elements in the national economy—improvements in fact have already been begun.[5] Speculation, made the easier

[1] Furuya, op. cit., pp. 116, 134. The exchange was at its lowest in 1924, when such a possible cause as inflation could not have been responsible, p. 141. For public debts to the foreigner, vide U.S. *T.P.S.* 83, *Public Finance of Far Eastern Countries.*

[2] Ibid., p. 154.

[3] For this phenomenon cf. values in *Fin. and Econ. Ann.* and volume in *International Year Book of Agriculture.* It is to be seen, too, in the coffee trade of Brazil and Columbia. Cf. *Memo. on Foreign Trade,* op. cit., Vol. I, p. 19.

[4] The exchanges of India and China being silver have no par, so that the Rupee or the Tael becomes dearer to Japan as the price of silver rises, even though Japan's commodity balance be in her favour. Cf. Furuya, p. 98.

[5] The gold embargo was removed at the beginning of 1930. Cf. U.S. *T.I.B.* 653, *The Big Five in Japanese Banking*; and U.S. *T.I.B.* 673, *The Currency System of Japan.* Just as a high degree of "rationalization" is being or already has been brought about in the Cotton, Flour, Shipbuilding, or Shipping Industries, so, too, is there a tendency to group the banks. Also vide report on Japan of Dept. of Overseas Trade; also G. C. Allen, op. cit.

and the more anti-social by such inadequacies, has exacerbated the malaise that descended on Japan in the post-War years. For since 1920 misfortune has followed misfortune in a sequence that the least trammelled of pessimists could not hope to continue: the world-wide economic disorganization after the Peace which treated Japan more harshly just as it fell on her earlier than other countries; the slump following the Washington Naval Limitation; the Earthquake of 1923, which cut off exports, yet at the same time necessitated heavy imports of reconstruction material; the slumps of 1924 and 1925; the new Indian Tariff; the damaging Chinese Boycott (which not only hit Japan in China but reached as far afield as Java and British Malaya); and the financial collapse of 1927, the severest in the country's history: these have shaken the entire economic structure. The seven or eight years following the Peace must be regarded as abnormal. In any case the deficit in the commodity trade has been growing less, and as imports of machinery can be expected to continue to shrink in the future, it will probably grow less still, while it is almost certain that the invisible exports are now increasing, and will continue to increase.[1] The adverse balance, then, appears to be a real deficit. On the other hand, it appears to be a temporary condition, the disappearance of which can be reasonably expected and is already under way; it is not an innate malady of the system. The adverse excess in Italy's trade is apparently much wider and much more disquieting.[2] Yet once again is one left with the impression that though Japan will probably scrape through the difficulty she will do so on a narrow margin.

[1] In connection with Japan's invisible exports mention should be made of her merchant marine, the tonnage of which is now exceeded only by that of the British and the United States merchant marines. Although the excess is great (U.K. = 20 million tons, circ.; U.S.A. = 14 million tons; Japan = over 4 million) it is much that she exceeds France or Germany or Italy.

[2] For Italy's position, *Giornale degli Economisti*, Gennaio, 1929, "il Crescente disavanzo della bilancia". Perhaps this study does not allow enough for the effects of putting the lira on the gold basis. Also vide *Popolo d'Italia*, 31 Maggio, 1930, address by U.S. Commercial Attaché.

A deficiency that cannot be explained in this manner and the future of which does not permit the same hopefulness is the narrow basis of Japan's Foreign Trade. This indeed is its foremost characteristic and as well its foremost weakness. Two staples, silk and cotton, amount to 70 per cent. of the total exports;[1] and two countries, the United States and China, are the markets for more than two-thirds of the exports.[2] Considering either the nature of the staples or the countries to which they are sent, it is a dangerous basis. The future of silk exports is quite uncertain, as has been seen, while cotton is bound to meet a hard-pressing competition and perhaps vanishing markets. To be dependent on China, who takes about 25 per cent.,[3] is hazardous for political reasons as the boycotts there have demonstrated, and is insecure because of the possibility of industrial developments in that country, though it is probable that Japan will continue to find a considerable outlet there in the immediate future for cotton cloth. To be dependent on the United States for the absorption of over 40 per cent.[4] of her trade—and that too nearly all in the form of silk—is more dangerous still. A country where every chance of exploiting every Business possibility is explored with not less energy than inventiveness must form a slippery prop to the economy of another nation. The securing from Congress by spinners of Schappe silk of a tariff of 40 per cent. *ad valorem* minimum ranging to 135 per cent.[5] cannot be overlooked by Japan. That she is selling her silk in the raw to American manufacturers at all—because a tariff of 60 per cent. to 90 per cent.

[1] Calculated from the *Financ. and Ec. Ann.* for the years 1924–7, the latest available.

[2] Calculated from *Financ. and Ec. Ann.*, 1928, for 1923–7, inclusive. It should be added that the U.S. Govt. considers the financial status of S. American countries not good when their trade is similarly specialized.

[3] That is, including Hongkong and Kwantung; excluding these, circ. 16 to 17 per cent. Vide *Fin. and Econ. Ann.*, 1928, p. 121.

[4] *U.S. Com. Year Book*, 1928, Vol. II, p. 744; *Financ. and Ec. Ann.*, 1928.

[5] Vide *Summary of Tariff Information on Silk and Silk Goods*, U.S. Tariff Com., 1929, pp. 1747–53, 1765. Also *U.S. For. Com. and Navigation*, 1927, Vol. I, p. 479.

ad valorem,[1] on silk piece goods leaves her no alternative—means that one of the most obvious and natural paths to wider industrialization is closed to her. Not only is the path closed, but it is not inconceivable that her raw silk might be debarred too. It can be accepted that the Rayon interests are not unaware of the potentialities of the market now taken by silk and that they are not unmindful of the efficacies of an agitation for tariff reform on such a matter. They already have a tempting official (though erroneous) statement that the wages of Japanese silk spinners are only 14 per cent. of the American.[2]

Not that there can be any contention, of course, that the United States is under an ethical or any other commitment to continue to buy (as she now buys) 94 per cent. of Japanese silk exports because these happen to be as the breath of life to the economy of Japan. It is, however, the business of the student, plainly and objectively, to indicate this as an element, among other elements, of weakness in Japan's present economic status. In view of the record of the United States tariff, and in view of the enormous productive power of American domestic industry still without consumers, it must be recognized that Foreign Trade with that country is incalculable.[3] When the foreign trade consists of a commodity with prospects so uncertain as those of raw silk, it almost ceases to be incalculable and to become predictably lost. Even at the present time the relation is one in which she *needs* to sell her silk to the United States incomparably more than the United States desires to buy it, and since 1925 the evidence shows a more and more unequal relationship. A unit of silk has been falling continually in value since that year. The author does not venture to interpret the phenomenon; but at least some part of its significance for Japan

[1] *Summary of Tariff Information on Silk and Silk Goods*, U.S. Tariff Commission, 1919, pp. 1747–53, 1765; also *C.E.I.* 24, p. 18.

[2] U.S. Tariff Commission, *Broad Silk*, p. 23.

[3] Cf. Dept. of Overseas Trade, *Review of the External Trade of U.S.A. in 1928*, London 1929; especially p. 25.

must be evident to all.[1] How much longer can her silk growers afford to accept a smaller and yet smaller sum for a larger output?

V. The Inferences

Between 1924 and 1928 less cotton yarn was exported throughout the world than in the five years preceding the War. This shrinkage was not due to any decline in the production of yarn, nor of course to any decline in the population of the world; for both in fact were bigger. Further, not only was there a smaller volume of trade, but the trade was "more equally divided among the exporting countries". The smallness of the volume and the lesser inequality in its division are due alike to one cause—the wider distribution of production. Many more countries are now manufacturing cotton yarn than formerly. Here in epitome is a movement passing over world economics: what has happened in cotton yarn may be expected to happen in other branches of production: countries are building up industries of their own and their economy is

[1] TERMS OF TRADE IN SILK

Year	Quantity		Value
	Quintals	Piculs	Millions of Yen
1924	223,950	—	685·3
1925	265,154	436,000	879·5
1926	266,761	444,000	734·05
1927	317,566	522,000	742·53

Official figures since 1927 are not yet available, but acceptable reports up till the middle of 1929 show that the movement was continuing. Cf. *Trans-Pacific* 13.6.29; 13.2.30. *Financ. and Econ. Ann.*, 1928, for Value, *Int. Year Book of Agric.* and British *For. Trade and Commerce* for Quantity. Besides Brazil and Columbia Coffee, this phenomenon is to be seen in the trade of Netherlands East Indies. Cf. Dept. of Overseas Trade *Review of Dutch East Indies*, 1929.

According to the document prepared by the League of Nations for the World Econ. Conference in 1927, not only had the price movement of silk remained lower than that of wool or cotton, but that it had remained lower than the U.S. wholesale price level. *C.E.I.* 24, *Natural Silk*, p. 17.

becoming more balanced. In embarking upon a programme of intensive industrialization, selling manufactured exports in return for imports of food and crude materials, Japan is therefore setting her face against the current of the times.

Her programme, however, is not necessarily invalidated on that account. The process of "breaking down local concentration" will take many years, and in them there will be room for the exports of such countries as herself. But she will be only one among several countries competing for the favours: the United States, the United Kingdom, Germany, Italy, to mention a few of the rivals, have a productive capacity that cannot be absorbed at home. They must, in all cases for their prosperity and in some cases for their very subsistence, win markets abroad. A competition thus fierce will be made the fiercer because the industrialized exporters will need to sell their wares far more than the importing countries will need to buy them: the choice of terms will rest with the importers and the terms may be so high that only a few of the exporting countries can meet them. How much longer, for example, can Japan afford to sell a unit of silk for the continually shrinking price that the United States is willing to give? The price may fall to the point where she will have to surrender such market as remains to her rival, China, which, having a lower standard of life, can produce at a lower cost than she.

The process of "breaking down local concentration" will take many years, and the complete balance will never be attained. The vision of the self-sufficing state is the most impracticable of fancies. The disparity in the distribution of natural resources, in Iron and the Energies chiefly—and whatever Applied Science may do in the utilizing of new sources of power and of conceivable substitutes for iron, it is a disparity that will persist for long into the future—predetermines an interchange of goods. One country will be more industrial and another more agricultural.

To mention this, however, is to recall a weakness, some believe a vital weakness, in Japan's programme: she herself lacks iron ores and coking coal. Even when the reserves of Manchuria and Chosen are drawn upon scarcely half the iron ore consumed in the Japanese Empire is produced within it, and its coking coal remains higher in price than normal. It is likely that the price of coal will go down, and Japan is losing nothing at present by importing iron ores which cost no more than is being paid at Pittsburg by American iron manufacturers. That weakness then is not yet vital. And for many years to come she can expect to draw on her present supplies; and even if they fail she would probably suffer nothing by buying American steel. The far away future when the limitation in the earth's reserves of iron begin to manifest themselves in competition, and in rising prices, for them probably need not enter into Japanese calculations of to-day. Before then she may have devised a method of utilizing the millions of tons of iron sands at Kuji. In any case she will be counteracting some of her natural disadvantages by the wealth of her hydro-electric power. She is already approaching self-sufficiency in iron and steel, and some expert observers even claim that the industry is on an internationally competitive basis; and though this profitableness may be in part due to the raising of prices by the European Steel Cartel, it at least indicates that Japan need not at the present and in the near future be fatally hampered on the score of iron and steel. While her way will not be lightened by the natural advantages of the United States in them, it will not be weighted by the natural disadvantages of Italy. For the time being and for the near future Japan stands a shade to the minus side of normal.

This leads us to expect that the great progress[1] made in recent years will not be reversed. Nor is she without positive advantages for continuing the rate: among others might be mentioned her propinquity to the densest mass of population in the world—population is always a potential market—and also a persistence in her political philosophy of a line of thought

[1] For this progress, cf. report on Japan of the Department of Overseas Trade in 1928; *U.S. Commerce Reports*, 8.4.29; U.S. *T.I.B.* 389.

that, like the Tudor conception of the State, abhors the wastefulness of *laissez-faire* and the disorderly preying of the stronger upon the weaker, and that would not quietly suffer the terrors of unrestricted capitalism as early nineteenth-century England suffered them. The Government is not there regarded as having no interest in economic matters: it is, and from the time of the Restoration always has been, closely and actively interested. Not only can the Government be expected to do work like that of the United States Department of Commerce, which indeed should be a lesson and an incitement to any nation needing foreign markets, but to be concerned with welfare as a national rather than as a sectional desideratum.

On the other hand, there are flaws in the structure of her industrial framework that cannot be tolerated if the strain of international competition is to be borne. The wide-spread bolstering up of deficiencies, rather than the attacking of them ruthlessly, must be abandoned, though no doubt the over-capitalization and the mania for large figures begotten of the War-time inflation are awaiting liquidation in other countries besides Japan.[1] The hot-house atmosphere of export bounties, prohibitive tariffs, tax exemptions, and price agreements, in which so many industries are living, should be dispensed with as soon as possible, for it breeds a stamina unequal to the rigours of foreign rivalry. Dividends and interest in general are still far too high, in the not infrequent cases of dividends around 30 per cent. to 50 per cent. absurdly high:[2] the difference between the interest borne by agricultural and the interest borne by mercantile and industrial capital, because it is artificial, should be an urgent concern of both Government and of Credit policy.

The darkest prospect for the approaching future, however,

[1] There is an article on the very serious financial crisis of 1927, in *L'Economiste Française*, 1928, p. 163. Cf., too, files of *Trans-Pacific* in June, July, and August, 1927; and above all the report on Japan of the Dept. of Overseas Trade for 1928. Also vide article by Dr. Washio in *Trans-Pacific*, 6.10.28.

[2] For Dividends and Interest, vide Harada, op. cit., pp. 48–56; *Trans-Pacific*, 12.11.27; Overseas Trade Report, 1922–3; and Furuya, p. 91. Also vide *Financ. and Econ. Annual*, 1928, p. 28.

rises from the narrow-based character of her present export trade and therefore of her industrialization as well: nearly half her exports consist of natural silk—raw, spun, or cloth—and a quarter of cotton, while two countries, the United States and China, take two-thirds of the total amount. Her markets are widening: there is a vigorous and hopeful extension all around the shores and into the hinterlands of the Pacific and Indian Oceans; and in commodities like rubber and chemicals, perhaps glass, paper, and potteries, too, there is promise of a growing diversification. But the vital weakness remains: a dependence on two commodities and on two countries. The prospects of natural silk leave no place for anything but candour, and candour for pessimism. Cotton-piece goods are in better plight: yet it is not unreasonable to expect that they will ultimately share the fate, in part if not wholly, of cotton yarn. Chinese markets remain, in many ways, a promising field for Japanese exports; but Japan will have to shift her course according as new industries arise there, for arise they certainly will; and what might be no less serious is the possible appearance of another boycott whenever political relations become strained, a not inconceivable happening in view of Manchuria's status. In the relationship between the United States and Japan the two weaknesses are combined—the uncertainty of such a commodity as raw silk and the dependence on a single country, in this case a country with elements as incalculable as the American tariff and American business expediency.

Serious as this narrow basis is and necessary as is the broadening of it, it does not necessarily form a final handicap. In striving to realize what it means one must guard against the danger of exaggeration. So too with Japan's programme as a whole. After all, Japan is still drawing but a small proportion of her food from the foreigner: only about 5 per cent. of what she consumes is drawn from external sources, while the proportion of foodstuffs in the imports (after deducting the exports of foodstuffs) is only about 7 per cent. of the whole. Java, British Malaya, and Ceylon all import a larger proportion of the rice they consume, and several European countries a much larger proportion of their foodstuffs. Were all contact with the outside world suddenly cut off, there would be no actual starvation in Japan to-day and probably none for several years to come.

The final advantage that can be cited on her side in every disquieting consideration is the advantage of time. Economic changes may move quickly, but they do not move with the overwhelming suddenness of natural cataclysms: economic revolutions are revolutionary not in point of time but in point of the magnitude with which they transform the structure of society. Natural silk may lose its market, but it will not happen overnight, and at sign of the coming change Japan can build up her rayon industry. The boundlessness of human wants is always present for exploitation. The moment may come when the soul of China will be vibrating to some American cry like: "Every Chinese his own wireless set," or a Siberian's conception of the Standard of Life will not be satisfied without woollen pyjamas. Time and the insatiableness of demand are her very strong allies.

The inference is that Japan's programme of industrialization will involve great difficulties and great efforts. The halcyon days of the industrializing country that nineteenth-century England knew are gone for ever. Not nineteenth-century England, but England of the post-War years must be her mentor. Japan will be like a man heavy-burdened who is climbing the narrow pathway hewn up the side of a cliff. If he loses his balance he is lost; yet the difficulty of the climb and the weight of his load tend continually to throw him off his balance. Japan will have to thread her way through the shrinking courses of twentieth-century Foreign Trade, with markets disappearing here because of the rise of industry in the formerly importing country, and disappearing there because the more richly endowed resources of a competitor enable it to sell at cheaper prices; she will have to bear the burden of higher production costs, or a persistent tendency to higher production costs, due to her poverty of industrial resources, the paucity of iron ores and the poor quality and dear mining charges of her coal, as well as a dependence on concessions in Manchuria that will be liable to challenge from Chinese Nationalism; she will have to scale obstacles that may rise in her way not once but again and yet again in the need to reshape her industrial activities, as in changing over from producing raw silk for America to producing rayon for the Orient, obstacles possibly so hazardous as to be beyond her powers of endurance; for all the time her mind will be a prey to the anarchy that comes from the wreckage of faiths no longer held and from traditions of millenniums' growth dissolving in new modes of life, strange ideas of alien import, and an atmosphere where the loyalties to Family and the Tenno, and where the old restraints and the calm of the rice-fields are broken in the clangour of factories, in the individualism of crowded hurrying cities, and in all that is connoted in passing from Status to Contract—impersonality, competition, recurring unemployment, and that despairing, bitter cry of an urban proletariat which men misjudge for Socialism and a theory of the State.

But the way is not unattainable. And from the record of achievements in the past twenty years, especially in the past five years, no less than from the will to succeed that manifests itself so clearly, Japan can be judged to have elected upon a course which is not hopeless and which is ultimately unavoidable for meeting the growing inadequacy of her agriculture.

CHAPTER VII

RELIEF THROUGH EMIGRATION

I. Can Emigration Relieve the Pressure?

It has been reported that the *Population and Food Supply Commission* has decided that Emigration (apart altogether from the practicability or impracticability of finding a place to send the emigrants to) offers no solution to Japan's problem. The decision is closely in keeping with many previous statements made by Japanese officials. Nor are the officials alone in professing the belief: Japanese students have published similar opinions.[1]

There is of course nothing revolutionary in such a point of view. Among many, perhaps among most, students of the subject it is agreed that emigration is futile as a means of solving over-population. Some American students have carried it much further.[2] Among them the extremer school of thought would go so far as to maintain that if Italy, to take a hypothetical case, had never sent a soul beyond her frontiers, her population would have been neither more nor less than it is to-day; and conversely, if America had never received a single immigrant the American population would still have been 120 millions. These are the extreme deductions from what generally passes for *Malthusianism*. That there is some truth in the idea is not to be denied. There is a close connection (though as yet a connection not demonstrable statistically) between economic resources and the population (related to the conception of the standard of life prevailing among that population) living on the resources. Nor is there any obscurity about

[1] E.g. S. K. Inoui, op. cit.; vide, too, *Trans-Pacific*, 28.5.27; and Dr. Nitobe at the Kyoto Conference of the Institute of Pacific Relations; report in *Trans-Pacific*, 21.11.29.

[2] H. P. Fairchild, *Immigration* may be taken as representative. The point of view that emigration does not relieve populousness in the long run seems to have been in the back of Burke's mind. Vide discussion between him and Johnson in Boswell's *Johnson* (Hill's edition), iii. pp. 762–3. Boswell probably missed Burke's point.

the proposition that a country cannot go on increasing its inhabitants and then count upon emigration to save it from the necessity of reducing its standard of life, if for no other reason than because the countries where immigrants might settle are strictly limited in number and area.

It can be agreed, therefore, notwithstanding the extravagance of the extreme deductions, that emigration offers no relief to excessive numbers in a country where the birth rate and death rate continue unchanged or only slightly modified. The history of Ireland whose immigrants have been flowing to many lands since the eighteenth century is relevant here.

The efficacy or inefficacy of migration, however, becomes a very different question when the birth rate in the emigrating country is falling and—or—its standard of life, or (what is more dynamic) its conception of the standard of life, is ascending. In either of those two eventualities the empty space left by the withdrawal of the emigrants is not immediately poured over by the newly arriving children. A heavily populated country experiencing one or both of these forces will in consequence gain temporary relief from emigration—and it is only temporary relief that such a country needs. Here then is a reason why Japan may be legitimately interested in emigration, for she is experiencing both a decline in her birth rate and a rise in her conception of the standard of life.

It is not enough to dismiss—as is frequently dismissed—the prospect that arises at this stage by saying that the Japanese are a non-migrating or non-colonizing people. Some, probably many, Japanese may not like leaving home just as some, probably many, Englishmen may not like leaving home; that of course disqualifies neither race from a capacity for migrating and colonizing. That there are a million Japanese abroad[1] is surely no uncertain implication. That the number is not larger, when there is a considerable amount of unemployment at home, is no more evidence as to their lack of aptitude for migrating than

[1] The official figures give only 700,000 for those abroad. There is reason for believing that they under-represent the true position.

the small stream of emigration from England in latter years when the unemployed and perhaps permanently unemployed are counted in their hundreds of thousands is evidence as to a lack of aptitude in Englishmen for migrating. A nation cannot have emigrants unless it can find a country to send them to, just as a nation cannot be a colonizing nation without having colonial territories. Japan is without colonial territories (that have any significance in this connection), and her emigration has always been countered with very difficult obstacles. In view of the historical facts the million abroad[1]—and in no country to which they have immigrated is their record anything than that of having made good to an unusual degree—are evidence of a *penchant* for emigrating rather than for not emigrating. Another fiction of the same order, and one that is generally used to explain the Japanese lack of aptitude for migrating, is that they cannot endure extremes of climate, either heat or cold. That the pearl industry in Torres Strait (North Australia) is and for more than a quarter-century has been dominated by Japanese divers,[2] or that they can exist in the Imperial Desert of California,[3] or that they prosper in the Philippines, or that they have migrated to their own not very favoured Mandated Territories, answers for their ability to survive tropical climates. And that they can live in Vladivostok or Karafuto (S. Saghalien) answers for their ability to endure cold climates. The unwillingness that was earlier manifested towards migrating to Hokkaido was due to the poorer people's not being able to change their loose and airy clothes for more appropriate wear, or to abandon the light, wooden, draughty houses of Hondo, heated with nothing stronger than a brazier, for warmer dwellings.[4] The ability of Japanese people to live

[1] The official figures give only 700,000 for those abroad. There is reason for believing that they under-represent the true position.

[2] Cf. *Queensland Parl. Papers*, Reports of Resident, Thursday Island, e.g. 1907, Vol I, No. 11; and other Reports, 1902–11.

[3] Cf. P. S. Taylor, *Mexican Immigration in the Imperial Valley*.

[4] On normal heating arrangements, cf. E. S. Morse, *Japan Day by Day*. This excellent work is not so well known as it deserves to be. Professor Morse was a zoologist at Harvard University, and went to Japan in the 'Seventies for a few years to teach at the Tokyo University. At the time

in non-temperate zones, in short, does not appear to be less than the ability of Englishmen or Dutchmen or any other temperate-zone people. On the contrary as Japan, a stretch of land in the ocean running from sub-arctic cold in north Hokkaido to sub-tropical heat in south Kyushiu, that is to say, running from the latitude of Scotland to that of Morocco, has an unusually wide range of temperature, it is probable that the range of climates that could be endured by her subjects is wider than can usually be endured by temperate-zone peoples.[1]

Not only then do the Japanese show a capacity for emigrating, but emigration can reduce the pressure of numbers in Japan because the birth-rate is falling and the conception of the standard of life is rising. Since she will be greatly needing some such temporary relief, emigration clearly must become a serious matter for her statesmen. The unemployment into which a very considerable number of men will be thrown by the displacing effects of the changes that are bound to be made in agriculture and industry during the coming generation, to say nothing of the prospects of the hundreds of thousands of youths who will continue each year to arrive at the employable age, make the problem of creating occupations one of the hardest and most persistent of her social problems. The possibility of drafting off a quota of the unemployed, say 50,000 to 100,000 a year, for migration abroad is one that is bound to be grasped by every means available. Emigration may stand between social revolution and social stability. And this is to say nothing of possibly more urgent forces inciting her statesmen to find an outlet or outlets across the seas.

The obvious question that rises at this point is whither can Japan send her emigrants? It is common knowledge to-day

Japan was hardly touched by Occidentalism, and as Professor Morse was a fresh and admirable observer, with considerable ability for drawing what he saw, his impressions are unusually interesting. The Morse Collection of pottery in the Boston Museum of Fine Arts was made by him.

[1] The same range of temperature in China should be recalled when discussing the variety of climates in which the Chinese can live: in the south it is sub-tropical, while the winters in the north are bitterly cold.

that few countries are wanting immigrants and none is wanting them excepting in a strictly regulated flow. Even in Canada, the foremost of the immigrating countries, rumblings of discontent and threats to raise the bars are being heard.[1] Nor does Japan claim the right, rather she studiously insists that she does not claim the right, to send emigrants to Australia or other unfilled Anglo-Saxon communities that are now exercising exclusion in the interests of maintaining a certain standard of living—Japan herself excludes Chinese and is arranging to exclude her own Korean subjects for the same reason.[2] All this notwithstanding, there are still spaces in the world not yet filled and countries where the bars are not too high for scaling. Four areas may be singled out as having a practical significance for our present inquiry: (1) North Eastern Asia, (2) the East Indian islands, particularly Borneo and New Guinea, (3) South Pacific Islands, and (4) Brazil.

In North Eastern Asia we have in mind Manchuria, Eastern Inner Mongolia, and Siberia. Manchuria and East Inner Mongolia offer no field for mass migration because of the growing numbers of Chinese there;[3] the Japanese peasant or labourer can no more compete with the Chinese than can any European peasant or labourer. But the professional classes (which at the moment are suffering from unemployment as much as any class) might find one outlet there somewhat as the overcrowded professional classes of Canada are finding an outlet in the United States. Siberia is in a different category. If the Japanese continue to develop their tendency to use wheat as a cereal, Siberia may come to occupy a very close relationship with Japan, providing much of her food and in addition absorbing Japanese peasants somewhat as the Middle West of America absorbed German peasants in the latter nineteenth century. For Siberia is "not the frozen land buried in snow and peopled with exiles only that it is imagined to be,

[1] Cf. *Manchester Guardian Weekly*, July 12, 1929.

[2] *U.S. Labour Review*, Nov. 1929, p. 177; and the Prime Minister, Mr. Hamaguchi, in *Trans-Pacific*, 8.8.29.

[3] Cf. Teichman, *Travels in Eastern Tibet*, p. 67.

even by many Russians. In its southern parts it is as rich in natural productions as are the southern parts of Canada, which it resembles so much in its physical aspects".[1] An expert in the United States Department of Commerce thinks that there may be as much as 200 million acres there—i.e. about a quarter to a third as much as the arable land of the United States—that can yet be brought beneath the plough, and that as easily as was Western Canada and the Western States of America in the last half-century.[2] These possibilities and their significance for Japan must not be over-emphasized. The population there is already considerable—probably 20 million, or more than three times the population of Australia. There is also a migration movement to it from Russia under way. And if Japan is ever to send emigrants to it, some favourable arrangement with the Russian Government is presupposed, which in practice may be impossible or extremely difficult to come by. And in any case a migration from Japan would have to be backed by a heavy capital outlay. For all that, it is not impossible and it may become probable that colonies of Japanese farmers will in the second half of this century be established in Siberia growing some of the wheat consumed in the home country.

Borneo is a large island, the area of five Englands, with a population of perhaps three million, a climate, tropical it is true, and not to be endured on the coastal flats, but in the mountains and on the plateaux temperate and even salubrious.[3]

[1] Prince Kropotkin, *Memoirs of a Revolutionist*, p. 169, quoted by H. M. Vinacke, op. cit., p. 403.

[2] U.S. Dept. of Commerce, *Trade Promotion Series*, 36, *Siberia*, by Boris Baievsky; also cf. F. Nansen, *Through Siberia*, p. 301 et seq.; H. K. Norton, *Far Eastern Republic of Siberia*, pp. 13–17; and M. Harrison, *Asia Reborn*, p. 272. Even along the Trans-Siberian railway there are hundreds of thousands of acres that strike a visitor as being easily tillable though at the present they are in waste.

[3] Facts on Borneo from Sir Hugh Clifford in *Encycl. Brit.*, 14th Edition. Also vide Owen Rutter, *British North Borneo*, Constable, 1922, and C. Lumsholtz, *Through Central Borneo*, Vol. I, p. 15, Scribners, 1920. The author believes he is correct in saying that the suggestion about Borneo originated with Professor Warren S. Thompson, at a discussion he heard at an American University.

Less than a third is British territory, the rest Dutch. Neither the British Empire nor the Netherlands Kingdom is needing or developing the island. A similar statement can be made regarding New Guinea:

It, too, is a large island (somewhat larger than Borneo) shared between the Dutch and the British, and so little developed that its actual resources have not yet been even superficially surveyed, but it is doubtless capable of supporting a large agricultural population, and, if the industrial resources turn out to be as good as they seem, an industrial population as well. Alongside these two large territories the smaller islands—and there are several—in Insulinde that could be added to them as also being incompletely utilized, are of secondary importance. Since Japan might find room in these East Indian islands for a stream of emigrants that would have no negligible effect upon the ranks of her unemployed and upon the menace now slowly but certainly rising before her, arrangements ought to be possible whereby she can turn the country to such good use.

As for the islands of the southern Pacific, there has long been throughout them a process of depopulation, now arrested for the most part but sufficiently far gone to have almost emptied some of the islands. Moreover, in nearly all there is scope for economic exploitation and for a larger population; and as the islanders themselves, according to the conclusion of the latest investigator, lack the will or the ability for such work, the potentialities of the islands will be realized only if Oriental labour be introduced. In the islands east of Fiji, Asiatics already outnumber the natives; and the same investigator looks forward to a continuance of this "Orientalizing" of the ocean. Here then is another outlet for the Japanese.[1]

Brazil is for the present moment the most promising field of

[1] S. H. Roberts, *Population Problems of the Pacific*. The mandated islands of Japan are of very slight economic consequence and may be ignored in such a survey as this. Also cf. MacMillan Brown, *Riddle of the Pacific*, p. 289 et seq., and G. H. Scholefield, *Pacific, Its Past and Future*, p. 240.

all.[1] The Government welcomes the Japanese.[2] In 1926 it offered a grant in the State of Para of twelve and a half million acres—not much less than the present area of cultivated land in Japan. The concession has been taken up (apparently in part only) by the Kanegafuchi Cotton Company, one of the most powerful and progressive corporations in Japan, and a prominent director of the company has taken up his residence on the grant in order to devote the closest attention to promoting it.[3] The largest stream of Japanese immigration, however, flows not to the State of Para, but to that of Sao Paolo. The rate at which the stream has been increasing is suggested by the fact that in 1923 the immigrants amounted to 800, in 1928 to 11,000, and in 1929 were expected to reach 15,000. In latter years they have been exceeded by the emigrants from the mother country, Portugal, alone.[4] The figures are expected to mount higher still in the future.

We see, then, that there are four areas whither it may be practicable for Japan to divert some of her numbers—North Eastern Asia (to which can be added her own possession of Karafuto); Borneo and other islands in Insulinde; the South Pacific Islands; and Brazil. To no one of these could the stream be large (unless certain international changes are effected, to be discussed later); but all four streams combined together, if engineered with foresight and statesmanship, could probably drain off a not inconsiderable proportion of the unemployed throughout the next twenty years or so—the period that will be the most difficult to tide over. Such a draining off, if only of several hundred thousand a year, would serve as a safety valve:

[1] Vide especially Dr. K. Takaoka, *Study on Immigration to Brazil*, 1926 (in Japanese: access to the facts in it were given to the author by Professor Hoshida). Dr. Takaoka even believes that the arranging of a systematic emigration to Brazil will be a major remedy for Japan's problem. Also vide Prof. Hori in Suppl., p. 23 et seq., to *Japan Year Book*, 1928.

[2] Cf. *Trans-Pacific*, 18.6.27; and Special Brazil Number of *Japan Times*, 15.8.30.

[3] Cf. *Trans-Pacific*, 21.7.28; 26.1.29; also *Survey International Affairs*, 1926, p. 390.

[4] *International Labour Review*, Nov. 1929, p. 727.

it would remove some of the most inflammable tinder from the sparks of the revolutionaries, and it would save the country from that paralysis of despair that has descended on the English unemployed and left them with a life that is but death.

There will of course be many practical difficulties in the way of carrying out an extensive emigration programme of the sort suggested here. It is not enough to have an over-populated country on the one side and on the other an under-populated, transporting men from the former to the latter. A shipload of Japanese unemployed cannot be merely landed on the shores of Borneo and the matter left, or even begun, there. Swamps on the coast must be drained, roads cut through the jungle up into the mountains and on to the plateaux, shelters built and food provided, and all this done before the newcomers land. But there seems no reason to doubt that both the capital outlay that this will demand and the construction work that will have to be undertaken could be provided.

That the difficulties will be surmounted we can confidently expect from what we know of the Japanese attitude of mind. A glimpse of this is given in the handling of the only emigration of account that is now taking place—that to Brazil. Museums are established exhibiting the life and customs of the country, and regular courses are given the emigrants a few weeks before embarkation on the food, clothes, religion, and general habits of its natives so as to facilitate a ready adaptation. Subsidies are granted and loans extended to emigrating families, and their interests are carefully safeguarded all the way.[1] The real difficulty will not come from the capacity of Japanese to manage the project, but from the prevailing attitude to territorial possession among the Powers.

The author cannot leave this discussion on outlets whither Japanese emigrants might go without making at least a reference to a delicate subject—the White Australia Policy. It is perhaps the more delicate for him because he is an Australian. He understands and sympathizes with the basic motives behind

[1] Cf. *Trans-Pacific*, 15.10.27; 21.7.28; 26.1.29.

this policy. It is both right and proper that anything so disorganizing to the labour market as immigration, and so depressing to a justly cherished scale of living (somewhat painfully achieved), should be very carefully controlled and regulated. Otherwise the community delivers itself over to a *laissez-faire* of the most disastrous kind. And it is no bad thing that the Australian should still retain so much affection for the "old country" (as he calls England) as to want to have only a British people out there. But facts are notoriously obstinate things, and it is to be feared that Australia will in no distant future be made aware of some of the more obstinate of certain facts. Firstly, there is a growing disparity in the pressure of populations on the economic resources at their disposal that is bound to make itself felt in international relations, especially in international relations in the Pacific, before very long. Secondly, the populations pressed by reason of their poor resources cannot remain blind to or uninterested in territories capable of exploitation and yet which are not being exploited by those peoples now holding them. Thirdly, Australia can hardly fail to recognize that she is one of these last peoples: she is not making use of the thousands of square miles in the tropical north, and she is not making use of them because she has no need of them.

Under such circumstances the time seems near at hand when a separating of essentials from non-essentials might be done. The one essential in the Australian case is to preserve the high standard of living. The old name of the policy is indeed a misnomer: what Australians really want is not a White Australia, but a minimum basic-wage Australia. That safeguarded, the rest can be treated as non-essential. By careful stipulations and wise handling, the Australian standard of living would not necessarily lose anything by having a non-British, even a non-European, people making use of the now unutilized and (judging from what one has seen of North Queensland and Darwin[1]) by Australians unutilizable tropical land. One does

[1] A sojourn in Darwin, one feels, would convince the fair-minded Australian that Darwin is more than a political nuisance; it is an object-lesson.

not ask, Is it just?—Australians cannot be expected to listen to ethical arguments based on an international communization when countries (for example, Japan) continue having an unequal distribution of the good things among their own people at home—one now asks, Is it really necessary? and Will it be expedient to try keeping this tropical land unused and unpopulated much longer?

What is to be said against drawing a line from east to west, following the Tropic of Capricorn, and arranging for Japan and Italy to take over the country lying north of the line? Both countries would find, to their astonishment, that an incomparably smaller proportion of this nothern land was utilizable than they had believed; but of this very small proportion they could make more good than the Australians because they need it. And the Australians would lose nothing by their doing so.

II. Does Japanese Policy Envisage an Emigration Programme?

In view of these facts it may be as well to examine once more the statements of Japanese statesmen on emigration in order to ascertain whether they are so unconcerned with the matter as they sometimes appear to be. If we do scan their statements narrowly, for example those of Baron Shidehara,[1] we find indeed that while disclaiming the intention of trying to send emigrants to countries where they are not welcomed—the United States or Australia, to take an instance—they do not disclaim intention of promoting any emigration at all.

Perhaps a clearer light will be thrown on the official attitude of Japan if we glance through the records of the two last international discussions on the subject, that at the Peace Conference in 1919 and that at Geneva in 1924. These are not recent dates, it is true, but it does not appear, so far as the author can discover, that the attitude has been changed since then.

At the Peace Conference President Wilson's surprising at-

[1] E.g. in *Survey of International Affairs*, 1926, pp. 389–91; also appendix.

tempt to insert a clause as to religious equality in the Covenant of the League was used by Japan for attempting to insert a clause as to racial equality. It may be remarked while passing that, in view of the serious problem of minorities in Central and Eastern Europe, such a clause would have appeared peculiarly fitting if not unavoidable, in the Covenant. Because the Japanese failed to gain a unanimous—they gained a majority—vote, President Wilson refused to accept the motion (though he had previously accepted a majority vote in another connection). The point, however, is that the Japanese seem to have been seeking something more substantial than a humanitarian gesture: it seems that they desired their racial equality clause to include the right to immigrate. At least that is the deduction to be drawn from a statement made by Mr. Hughes, at that time Prime Minister of Australia, in the Commonwealth Parliament. According to Mr. Hughes, he offered the Japanese delegation at Paris to accept their motion provided that the equality be understood as equal treatment of aliens already living in a country, and that the right to immigrate be excluded. The Japanese declined the offer. "It was not enough for their purpose", said Mr. Hughes.[1]

An attitude scarcely distinguishable from this was maintained at Geneva in 1924. In that year, as is well known, the Assembly of the League sought to "stop the gaps" in the Covenant by means of a series of alterations now spoken of as the Geneva Protocol. The question arose during the drafting of the alterations as to what would happen when a dispute arose between two States concerning an issue that was held by International Law to be a matter of domestic jurisdiction.[2] Immigration was clearly contemplated as a probable issue. As the Covenant then stood—and still stands—the point is ambiguous. According to Article XV, once a matter is declared by the

[1] Vide *Commonw. of Australia Debates*, Sept. 1919, p. 12607 et seq. Also Dillon, *Inside Story of the Peace Conference*, p. 489 et seq.

[2] The discussions in the Committee can be found in League of Nations *Official Journal*, 1924, *Special Supplement*, No. 24, especially pp. 45–57, 80–3, 88–91.

competent authorities to be a subject of domestic jurisdiction, it is at once withdrawn from the cognizance of the League. Immigration, according to International Law, is a subject of domestic jurisdiction: in the event, therefore, of a dispute arising between two States concerning the immigration laws of one of them, this article implies that the legislating State is free to enact what laws it may choose on the matter, and that is an end to it. According to Article XI, however, anything tending to produce war is a subject of concern to the whole League and can, indeed it must, be brought up for common discussion in the Council or the Assembly. Here, then, was one of the "gaps" to need and to receive attention. Japan sought to make Article XI explicit and to free it from its ambiguity by grafting on to the Protocol a clause to the effect that even if a question be held by the International Court or by the Council to be a subject solely within the domestic jurisdiction of a State, "such decision shall not prevent consideration of the situation by the Council or the Assembly".[1] It went further still and secured that "in the event of hostilities having broken out because one party had disregarded the judgment" as to the matter being within the domestic jurisdiction of the other, yet the recalcitrant "shall only be presumed to be an aggressor if it has not previously submitted the question to the Council or the Assembly in accordance with Article XI of the Covenant".[2]

Mr. Adatci explained to the First Committee that the object of his amendment "was to fix and define the duty of the Council in a question regarded as forming part of the jurisdiction of States". When the Committee appeared to be about to reject his claims the attitude of his delegation was left in no obscurity by a statement that he submitted: "It is", he said, "the profound conviction of the Japanese delegation that the League should . . . allow the application of the procedure . . . of the Covenant in the case of all disputes which may arise. . . . There would be otherwise this absurd consequence that the League will

[1] League of Nations *Official Journal*, 1924, *Special Supplement*, No. 24, p. 85.
[2] Ibid.; and vide *Survey International Affairs*, 1924, p. 58.

remain quite indifferent to the fact that the most flagrant acts of injustice are being committed under the purely technical and juridical cover of the alleged domestic jurisdiction of a State." "What is so illogical and so unjust is that any party should incur the risk of being declared the aggressor because it takes action when flagrant injustice has given rise to disputes . . . and the League has categorically refused, in virtue of purely technical and juridical considerations, to deal with the matter."[1]

We cannot concern ourselves here with the dangerous though quite intelligible conclusions to which Mr. Adatci's claims led, namely, that war should, in this very instrument outlawing all war, be yet allowed in the case of its arising out of a dispute on matters of domestic jurisdiction. Accepted though it was by the draftsmen of the Protocol—and an Australian presided over them—it is a claim that nullified the very purpose of the instrument. What is interesting for our present purpose is the frank claim that immigration should no longer be held to be exclusively within the sphere of domestic jurisdiction.[2]

The records of the discussions at Paris in 1919 and at Geneva in 1924 suggest, then, that not only was Japan still interested in immigration and emigration, but was even contemplating the possibility of using belligerent action at some time or other on their account. We may be assuming too much from the records and may be investing their attitude with an interest and a purpose that were in fact not present; but in the light of what a close examination of the recent statements of Japanese statesmen on emigration reveals, namely, that no renunciation whatever to promote emigration has been made, our assumptions seem not unfounded and scarcely unreasonable. While no doubt the Japanese attitude has in large part been dictated by an acute sensitiveness as to national honour and a very justifiable protest against clumsy classifications in immigration codes that lumped them *en masse* with Kanakas and East Indian Coolies, there is

[1] League of Nations, *Official Journal*, 1924, *Special Supplement*, No. 24, p. 85.

[2] Some part of the Japanese attitude was no doubt determined by a resentment felt for the stinging insult just suffered from the United States Congress in the matter of the Exclusion Clause.

a strong suggestion that it has also been instigated by practical considerations. How could a statesmanship of intelligence and alertness be unconcerned with a matter so vital to their well-being? Excepting perhaps Italy, no country to-day can hope for so much amelioration from emigration as can Japan. To secure an outlet for only 50,000 or so a year may save the country from social collapse; and what must encourage the pursuing of such a possibility is that there are still areas which might serve as this outlet.

It is difficult for the student to resist the conclusion that the Powers—if only in their own interest, for in any case they cannot ignore the international repercussions of Japan's domestic situation—should combine at the fitting time to place Borneo or/and New Guinea and some Pacific Islands (in whole or in part) at her disposal. The British Empire and the Netherlands, for example, might transfer Borneo (or some part of Borneo) to the League of Nations, which in turn might confer it on Japan as a Mandate. In a similar way the Marquesas, in the Southern Pacific, might be handed over to her. In the case of Brazil (and possibly other Latin American countries too), and perhaps also in the case of Siberia, satisfactory arrangements may be made with the sovereign States concerned without any concerted international action.

Once again, however, it may be emphasized that the significance of emigration for Japan should not be exaggerated. Emigration by itself can be only a palliative at the best, and sometimes not even a palliative; and even in the case of a country like Japan, experiencing as it is a falling birth-rate, a rising conception of the standard of life, and an increasingly productive economic system, an outlet large enough to absorb all the men and women who may be redundant at home could never be found. Japanese officials and Japanese students are aware of all this. But the point is that to drain off only a portion of the unemployed might serve as a much needed safety valve for the hot social vapourings of the coming twenty or thirty years, and in so doing preserve the tranquillity of the country.

By organizing streams to the four groups discussed, and by adding the flow of technical and professional men to Japan's own territories, it ought to be practicable to dispose of not less than 50,000 to 100,000 emigrants a year;[1] and 50,000 to 100,000 a year may be "the little more or the little less" that will save the peace. It was the last straw that broke the camel's back.

[1] For more than a decade before the outbreak of the War in 1914 Italy sent out nearly half a million permanent (i.e. settling) emigrants. Vide figures in *Piccolo Annuario Statist. Ital.*, 1928.

CHAPTER VIII

CONCLUSION

"If I come to an orchard and say, 'There's no fruit here', and then comes a poring man who finds two apples and three pears, and tells me, 'Sir, you are mistaken, I have found both apples and pears', I should laugh at him: what would that be to the purpose?"

Dr. Johnson

I. The Heart of the Problem

The Japanese population will not reach the higher of the figures expected both by many Japanese themselves and by many foreign observers. Factors are already at work, and in the future they will be at work more and more powerfully to exert a drag on its rate of increase. The marriage rate is shrinking, and it is likely that the 1930 census results will show (what is usually the same thing) a not insignificant retardation in the average age of marriage. Moreover, the fecundity of Japanese families, which has been declining throughout the last two decades, has now begun a fairly sharp fall. And the spread of contraception, perhaps encouraged and organized by the authorities, will guarantee the continuance of the fall. But the full effects of these skidding factors will be delayed for a generation or more by reason of the peculiar age-composition of the Japanese population. The death rate (the crude death rate) is about to decline, while the birth rate (the crude birth rate) will remain high, though not necessarily and not probably as high as hitherto. The death rate is about to decline because there will be born a lesser proportion of children to the total population, and because the old-age group will be unusually small; that is to say, the two groups where the death rate is highest will be unusually small in proportion to the total population, so that death will remove a smaller proportion each year than normally. And the birth rate will remain high because of the abnormally large proportion of the population in the child-bearing group. In consequence we are to expect that it will be twenty or thirty or more years hence before a pronounced turn towards a stationary level is made, and that at least 15 to 20 million persons will be added to the present numbers before then.

Within the next generation, then, some 15 to 20 million (or more) additional individuals will have to be fed and clothed. The Japanese economic system is already embarrassed by the size of the population it now supports. Can it be made to support an increase of this magnitude?

It is fairly certain that Japan cannot grow the extra rice needed for these 15 or 20 million, unless the rate of per capita consumption be considerably reduced. In order to feed her present population she is importing about 50 million bushels a year. And what little may be done to increase the harvest of the country, either by enhancing the yield per acre or by extending the acreage under cultivation, will not suffice to grow the hundreds of millions of bushels extra that will be needed later.

The truth is that Japanese Agriculture is already entering upon a crisis, irrespectively of the prospect of 20 million more Japanese requiring to be fed. The rice crop is costing too much to raise. Instead of the yield per acre promising a higher figure in the future it is already too high. It has been forced to its present height by the efforts of too many farmers to wring a living from the limited amount of land that can be cultivated, squeezing from it every ounce that it will yield. Their pressure on the soil is now beginning to result in Diminishing Returns, even though the full fatal consequences of Diminishing Returns are for the moment being countered by the profits from silk culture. But this cannot go on indefinitely: the end, indeed, seems even now to be moving within sight. Its movement, like all the other economic motions in Japanese agriculture, will be accelerated by the demands of the farmers for a better standard of living. Taking these two forces into consideration, the force of economic laws and the force of human desires, it is not easy to see how some very far-reaching changes in Japanese agricultural economy can be avoided over the next thirty years—changes, it must be repeated, altogether independent of the effects that will be worked by this addition of 20 millions to the population. All the probabilities point to a reduction in the number of farmers so as to permit an enlargement of the farm-holdings—or to a diminution in the membership of a farm household—in order that the amount of land supporting one individual will be less inadequate for supplying him with a reasonable income. With fewer farmers and with bigger holdings the severe degree of manual work that now prevails can be moderated in several directions by the use of machines, even though agricultural machinery on the American scale is not to be thought of in Japan. And in agricultural finance, and in buying and selling, as well as in actual production, there is wide scope for the ameliorating services of co-operation. Whether the changes are brought about by State action, as, for example, by Nationalization and redistribution of land, or not, is of secondary interest. The probable imminence of the changes is the point. Only through them can the wastefulness of Diminishing Returns be averted; and only thus, too, can any satisfaction be given to that rising demand for a higher standard of life.

A transformation along these lines will result in less men being required to grow the harvest, and in less economic effort expended on it, but it will not result in a bigger harvest; much more probably it will result in a smaller (though regarding the price per bushel always in a less expensive) harvest. Japan, in any case, can never raise all her own rice if the rate of per capita consumption remain unreduced. And even if she proceeds with substituting other foods, notably wheat, for the old staple, rice, she will still be obliged to import several hundred million bushels of cereal from abroad each year. In short, Japan of the future can only live as England now lives (though no doubt never to the same degree), by buying food from the foreigner.

To buy food from the foreigner requires having a means of paying for it; which is to say, requires having or building up manufacturing industries and exporting their products. That in turn requires a capacity for triumphing over rivals in foreign markets, where the competition in the coming years is likely to become more and more exacting. Japan is not well-fortuned for acquiring such a capacity: she has scarcely any iron, little and poor coal, few of the raw materials, and a basis to her present Industry and Foreign Trade that is quite insecure. To succeed against such odds will demand a vigilance and an effort that must never falter.

Can Japan win through by her own efforts and without being forced to seek other lands for her subsistence? We have seen that the kernel of the Japanese position to-day is that the Japanese raise raw silk so as to export it in payment for imports of raw cotton and by making up this raw cotton into yarn and cloth they can re-export enough of it to pay for the rice and other foods which they are now obliged to seek from the foreigner. It is a simple arrangement; depressingly simple. Can Japan multiply it to ten times or more of its present extent? Can she in the first place raise and sell so much more raw silk; and in the second place buy so much more raw cotton with the proceeds of it, make it up, and sell it abroad, as to purchase food for these additional 20 millions? To state the question is enough to show the extreme unlikelihood of an affirmative answer. If the present economic system cannot be extended to this degree, can other industries be built up to the height necessary for supporting the 20 million?

That is the heart of the Japanese problem: what goods can Japan put these people to manufacturing (and manufacturing at prices set by fierce international competition) which foreign markets will buy? To prophesy an answer one way or the other is not possible. Economic processes are so complex and their development in the future, because of technological and organization improvements, so unpredictable that the present writer hesitates even to suggest what the coming years may hold for

Japan. He can state only the contemporary facts and point out the more significant of their implications.

II. The Domestic Implications

The chief domestic implication is a problem that will never be completely soluble and will always be a case for palliative treatments only—unemployment. The coming economic changes will tend steadily to reduce the demand for labour, the reorganization of agriculture lessening the numbers of farmers required and the degree of mechanization of industry, that is inseparable from an efficient industrial system, displacing men from the factories; while in addition the steadily increasing population will be continuously swelling the supply of labour. Unemployment may assume such proportions that it will become a question—a question which in China is already being mostly answered in the negative—whether it be better not to introduce further machines and a more efficient technique of production when there is such a plethora of labourers without work, and to suffer the fall in the standard of life that would probably result from such a decision. And even then there would be farmers without farms to till and urban operatives with no hope of a job. If in the midsummer of this year (1930) the number of people needing relief in Tokyo district alone are reported to be half a million, what will the unemployed for the whole of Japan, urban and non-urban, registered and non-registered, amount to twenty years hence?[1]

The history of the post-War decade in England has shown that men without work or any hope of work, even when numbered in their hundreds of thousands, can be kept quiescent if only given enough to sustain mere physical existence. Unemployment, even on this grand scale, does not necessarily jeopardize the stability of society. An element, however, that might electrify the Japanese unemployed, and one that has been insignificant among the English, is—and still more will be

[1] Reported in *Japan Weekly Chronicle*, 31.7.30.

—the large number of college and technical graduates unable to find work suitable to their education. It appears that many of these will have to become clerks or even mechanics and manual labourers. That means an "intellectual proletariat". In Japan, where there is a two-fold style of living for non-peasant and non-labouring-class people, European clothes being worn at the daily work but the Japanese kimono at home, and generally, too, a part of the house designed for entertainment *à l'Occident*, the unsuccessful graduate will be obliged to doff his European clothes and to put on the habit of the workman. He will never be free from a most inflammable reminder of his economic and social failure. A more poignant accentuation of class differences could hardly be devised, and class differences, too, that are along a new and unvenerated alignment, the alignment of capitalist urbanized society. The Japanese are a sensitive people. And all the time will continue that steady dissemination of Western individualism and with it the potent yeast of Labour ideology. The persistent searching efforts of the Authorities to control *Dangerous Thoughts* among the student class, assuming though it does a form not easily understood by Englishmen, appears at least intelligible in the light of these facts.[1] For an intellectual proletariat, armed with the weapons of socialist dialectic and socialist emotion, and living in the midst of large crowds of disappointed workless labourers, will be a bigger threat to social tranquillity than ever was the discontented aristocrat of the *ancien régime* who set out to engineer the passions of a hungry mob.[2]

[1] On *Dangerous Thoughts* and the Government campaign against them, vide the files of the *Trans-Pacific* in the last three years. Continual references will be found. A bureau in the Home Office for directing thought was set up last year. Cf. *Trans-Pacific*, 11.4.29. Cf., too, *Japan Year Book*, 1927, p. 257; ibid., 1929, pp. 263, 273.

[2] The success of a radical revolution, it ought to be added, however, would be as difficult, we might almost say as impossible, in Japan, as it would be in England; and for similar reasons. The very sustenance of the nation will depend more and more upon foreign supplies, so that any prolonged interference with these would starve the country and therefore the *de facto* Government into submission. And as Japan has a powerful navy and as the probabilities of ever winning over the personnel of the navy to a radical *coup d'état* are negligible, the navy would at once blockade the country on the arise of a radical revolution and starve it into surrender.

It is because unemployment, and the character of that unemployment, will be the central problem arising from the pressure of numbers in Japan that emigration must have a very strong interest for her. The drawing off of merely 50,000 to 100,000 of her unemployed annually during the coming twenty or thirty years may save the stability of her society, not so much for the actual physical relief it can afford but because of its psychological effect—the infusion of a tranquillizing hope among unoccupied and despairing people.

It must be remembered at this point that Japan has little surplus wealth to help her tide over a critical period. She cannot afford the luxury of compromising with economic forces as some countries can. She lives almost entirely from hand to mouth. This is a condition that can scarcely be appreciated by Englishmen, whose surplus, for all their industrial depression, is still not inconsiderable, and (yet more to the point) whose ideas on such matters are still those inherited from the days of before the War and the latter half of the nineteenth century, when they possessed unfilled colonies beyond the seas whither any excessive population could be sent, held loans and capital investments reaping a generous return in every part of the world, their ships and manufactures used and welcomed in all countries, foreign lands ransacked for their food and apparel, so rich that agriculture at home could be largely abandoned and the countryside turned into a park taking on a loveliness beyond all compare—the spacious days that gave forth the life which lives again in Mr. Siegfried Sassoon's *Memoirs of a Fox-Hunting Man*, and whose distance even now we can measure in the poems of Rupert Brooke. Yet though those days have gone and gone for ever, England still has a margin that would be like opulence itself to penurious Japan.

But if Japan has no margin of wealth to fall back upon in a critical period she has an inheritance of culture that will serve her perhaps in equal stead—a fine æsthetic sensibility, a power for self-discipline, and a patriotism or sense of social obligation excelled nowhere. The patriotism of the Japanese, whether it take the more recognizable form of sacrificing everything for the service of the Emperor, or that of employers or other economic superiors realizing and carrying out responsibilities to their dependents in a way unknown to the West, is not less than the travellers describe, and contrasts strangely with the individualistic traits of the Chinese. Self-discipline is another distinctive characteristic ranging from its highest expression in the Zen sect to the stoical strong-nerved behaviour of a common crowd during an earthquake. And behind these high moral qualities is an æsthetic appreciation far more sensitive than usually goes with moral strength: a sense of artistic fitness and a horror of πλημμελέιν—of striking the wrong note or jarring the rhythm—is as instinctive among the Japanese as it was among the Ancient Greeks, though the solecisms committed by a few over-zealous Westernizers may sometimes disguise it from the foreigner. The feeling of the European student when for the first time brought face to face with this civilization is one of unexpectedness and sheer delight. The beauty of its Art, its old and tested wisdom, and the exquisite refinements of social intercourse come upon him as Discovery itself.

Such a civilization and the character it has bred will serve the country well in the coming years. It will probably save it on the one hand from merely hot-headed revolution, and on the other from anti-social behaviour on the part of the possessing class, infusing the one end of society with restraint and the other end with a consciousness of the common good.

It is conceivable indeed that the dual forces of a constant economic pressure to lower the standard of living and a rising demand for a higher standard may become so exacting on behalf of husbanding the resources and so intolerant of all extravagance that a new economic order unknown to any contemporary society may arise in Japan. For it is far from certain that the economic output motived by the play and counterplay of profit is as great or as regular as the productive capacity of any given community might permit: under the stress of her urgent problem Japan may find that the wastefulness of uncontrolled capitalistic enterprise will be a luxury greater than she can afford. Her position may become such that she will be required to live as it were in a state of siege, and in consequence economic direction may be taken over by the State as it was taken over by the State in European countries during the War, or may be supervised as it is now being partly supervised in Italy, a country, it has been seen, with a comparable problem. Since Japanese character is what it is and since the habit of subordinating private consideration to the well-being of the nation (here personified as the desires of the Emperor) is developed to a pitch reached by no other country, it is to be expected that what happens to be most conducive to the national well-being will be carried out either in part or in entirety as it would be in few other countries. And on account of the abundance of hydro-electric power it is conceivable that the economic system will not only be different in its system of ownership but different too in its system of production, small-scale mechanized village industries widely distributed throughout the countryside breaking down the usual Occidental concentration in vast factory areas. The coming generation in Japan may provide the world with a new and interesting form of social organization.

III. The International Implications

But even so the problem may be too great for Japan to carry through by her own resources. For though unemployment will probably not cease to harass her even at the best for the next thirty or fifty years, behind this looms the more sinister question: Will Japan be able through the economic resources of her own territory to find support for all her people, employed and unemployed alike? Must she, if not to avoid actual want of food yet to avoid at least a recession, and most likely a marked recession, in the standard of living, find additional resources outside of her own territory?

Let us be clear as to what this question involves. Obtaining access to outside lands can interest a country for two main reasons: firstly as a place to settle men as farmers of the fields which can no longer be found for them at home. Because Japan is experiencing the dual condition of a declining (true) birth-rate and a rising conception of the standard of life, emigration of this nature would be efficacious. To send ten million people abroad to support themselves as small rice farmers in Borneo or New Guinea or along the Queensland coast would relieve the pressure greatly. If, on the other hand, these ten million could in any way be kept at home and employed in manufacturing goods to pay for their imports of food, it would be preferable to Japan to do so; particularly as the other proceeding would have to overcome peculiar political (international) difficulties. In any case it would still leave ten million or more of the addition that is going to be made to the population to be dealt with. This does not rule out the efficaciousness of Japan's seeking relief through a mass migration of farmers, so much as bring us to the second reason for a country's seeking access to outside lands—to enlarge their supplies of necessary industrial materials. These are primarily (and in the case of Japan would be definitely) supplies of fuel and of metal. Will Japan need outside help in providing herself with these? At the present her Manchurian concessions assure her of them. But will these Manchurian resources stand the strain of a consumption scarcely less than ten times what it is at present and probably more? And if they will stand the strain, can Japan, notwithstanding her treaty rights, maintain a hold on them for the next fifty years? And even if the Manchurian resources prove insufficient or Japan fail to maintain her hold on them and it become necessary for her to draw upon the vast unused resources of the East Indian Islands, would that also compel her to acquire possession of the parts of the islands in which the resources are situated? Would it not be as easy for her to operate the areas as a concession, or indeed to buy the fuel and iron from there, providing these would be sold at a fair and reasonable price? Are outside territories going to be so indispensable to her either as places for settling large colonies of farmers or as supplies of industrial fuel and metals?

Once again is one unable to answer these questions because one cannot foretell the potentialities of future economic life. The present economic arrangements either in any one country or throughout the world as a whole are very imperfectly understood: they have somehow happened and they somehow work, but the connections, the subtle and indirect connections, between cause and result are guessed at rather than known. Certain though one may be about present trends and directions in Japan, one is uncertain about actual future necessities because the future holds changes, probably profound changes, in technology (we need only think a moment of industrial chemistry) and in that partially comprehended mechanism which brings ultimate seller and ultimate buyer together. We see the economic future, even of Japan, as through a glass, darkly.

But what is clear is the connection between Japan's predicament and her foreign relations. Japanese foreign policy will be determined by her population problem; and to say that is to mark out her population problem as the dominant issue in the Pacific Region.

One obvious and immediate line it will take is the securing of her interests in Manchuria. This in fact for some years now has been the corner-stone of Japanese policy. It can be taken for granted that in the event of any dispute arising over Manchuria, Japan, notwithstanding what Government happens to be in power at the time, will pursue a very definite and predictable course there.

Whether in the future her foreign policy will be extended to cover mass-emigration and the acquisition of land in Insulinde—perhaps, too, in North Australia—depends upon the answers given to the series of questions asked above. As yet these answers are unknown, and the present writer, though avoiding the pessimistic view of Japan's future with difficulty, does not dare to suggest what they may be. Yet even if mass-emigration and the acquisition of foreign territory do not become necessary, it is not easy to see how Japanese statesmanship can avoid being concerned with some programme of emigration, be it only to soothe an exasperated and despairing public opinion at home.

Arrangements ought to be possible for satisfying what after all would be fairly moderate demands or requirements on the part of Japan. A possible arrangement that occurs to one who has worked on the matter is that Japan, in the event of a Manchurian crisis arising, might be given a Mandate over Manchuria—or at least a part of Manchuria—from international society; or, if a Mandate be not possible, then a Protectorate under guarantees. By the end of the century probably neither the internal stability of Manchuria itself nor the security of Japanese economic interests would longer need such a contrivance, and the Manchurians could run their own government as they chose. Similarly a Protectorate or Mandate might later be arranged, when it became desirable, over parts of Borneo and over some of the Southern Pacific Islands. This for the moment is of secondary importance to a Manchurian arrangement. Taking into consideration the facts of history, the needs of all the countries concerned, and the benefits to be gained by the Manchurians themselves, it is not easy to think of adequate reasons why Japan should not continue her hold over the mines of Fushun or Penhsihu in Manchuria, and why China should not withdraw such claims as it can adduce. In civic life society no longer tolerates the full unfettered exploitation of private property by any one or more of its members: it regulates in no small way the use of possession; so, too, in international life, claims to unlimited control of certain countries, or parts of them, that have a more intimate connection with the well-being of a non-possessing than of the possessing country, should be over-ruled. Taking into consideration the position of Japan and its bearing on world-peace, International Society and not merely China is interested in Manchuria; and International

Society not merely the British Empire or the Netherlands Kingdom is interested in Borneo; just as International Society, remembering the condition of Italy—a condition not less serious than that of Japan's—and not merely France, or any other single Power, is interested in North Africa and Syria.

To have said that "arrangements ought to be possible" "from international society" is to indicate the one real threat to peace in the Pacific Region—namely, that to a large degree there is no international society at all. The influence of the League of Nations is, of course, in operation there as elsewhere, but, apart from the incompleteness of the League's present powers, two of the four strongest Pacific States—Russia and the United States—are not members of the League. Both States, it is true, have signed the Kellogg Pact; but if the recent conflicts between China and Russia are any evidence the Kellogg Pact appears to amount to scarcely more than a pious wish. Nor does the Four-Power Treaty of the Washington Conference seem much more substantial. Thus rather more so in the Pacific Region than elsewhere is there no adequate peace-providing machinery to-day. The maintenance of peace should be an obligation of international society as a whole; but so long as international society remains but partially organized and without coercive police weapons at its command there is no other arbiter over national claims and counterclaims than brute force. In consequence, if Japanese public opinion demands a certain course of action in foreign policy and another Power regards that action as an invasion of its own rights, there can be no other arbitrament between their claims than that of war.

In reflecting over the international implications of Japan's population problem, as in reflecting over any other great international issue to-day, we are brought to realize once more the paramount need of putting an end to the state of nature that still characterizes so wide a domain of foreign relationships, and of erecting peace-providing machinery that can determine—and enforce—a settlement of the disputes that arise and always will arise so long as human beings or their Governments have dealings one with the other. As things are at the present it is not foolish to speculate on a world two or three decades hence perplexed and menaced by an alliance between Japan and Italy and Germany and the ex-enemy group. Italian foreign policy in Central and Eastern Europe in recent years is of high significance. The Nationalist parties in Germany, as we know from the German Press, would welcome a *rapprochement* with Italy. What is to prevent an extension to Japan? Japan, Italy, Germany, all have claims on International Society. In the future their claims will become more pressing. If there be no legal means in existence for satisfying the claims, Necessity may force these Powers to attempt illegal means. It is a prospect to avoid which will be worth every effort: utility rather than justice demands it.

APPENDIX I

JAPANESE STATISTICS

As far as possible the statistical method has been the method of this survey, but unfortunately that has not been so far as had been hoped. More than once a programme of statistically illustrating a significant point on the discussion had to be abandoned because the necessary figures could not be found. Statistics in all countries are not complete or not always adequate; in Japan, notwithstanding the excellent statistical services in some fields, they are in general more fragmentary and merely approximate than is usual for a country of her importance. Where analyses of the economic life and demography would be relatively easy in, e.g., Italy or France, in Japan it is always difficult and sometimes scarcely possible.

No census of population (in the proper meaning of census) was taken until 1920. It was very limited in scope and apparently its results are not yet completely tabulated, or if so not yet fully available. The first adequate census of population was taken in 1925. And another and on the most satisfactory lines was taken in the autumn of this year. It will be several years before its findings are published. As regards population, then, it is possible to analyse its structure and movement at the present moment in a sufficient manner; but difficulty arises when an attempt is made to compare its present structure and movement with its past. Estimates of the population—they can hardly be called censi—go back to the early eighteenth century, earlier indeed than the figures of any European country. But in a study that seeks to be severely quantitative estimates are hardly enough; and when they are found (as they were found at the first modern national census) to differ by nearly three million from the counted figures of the population the research student is encountered with an extremely embarrassing discrepancy.

Not only have we in the years before 1920 an estimate and not a count of the population, but over large fields of the economic life there are no figures at all. There is no census of manufactures, none of production, none of occupations, no complete record of employment and unemployment, none or only fragmentary collections of many agricultural statistics, no cost of living index, and price indices unsatisfactory (vide S. Shiomi, in *Kyoto University Econ. Rev.* on Bank of Japan Wholesale Price Index, July 1926. Also Furuya, *Japan's Foreign Exchange*, p. 185).

The absence of figures for certain fields of Japanese life is perhaps best suggested by the omission of statistics on Japan in the statistical collections of international bodies like the League of Nations, the International Labour Office, and (sometimes) the Institut internationale de Statistique, and the International Institute of Agriculture, and in the collections of foreign statistics made by various States. Thus, significant omissions will be observed in the collection of data made by the League of Nations for the World Economic Conference; in the League of Nations' *Monthly Bulletin of Statistics*, the *International Labour Review*, the *Annuaire Statistique de la France*, the United States Dept. of Commerce Cost of Living Indices, the *U.S. Monthly Labour Review*, etc. A severe attack on a part of the Japanese statistical services can be found in the *Trans-Pacific*, 24.9.27.

A great need, as it strikes the foreign student, is to centralize and co-ordinate the various statistical offices. Instead of having statistical sections or sub-sections in the various Government departments, these might be consolidated into one large statistical office. The statistical services of the Government of the Commonwealth of Australia strike a student as being a model arrangement. The marked gaps and the marked overlapping in Japan would probably in this way be overcome. The admirable statistical work of the Japan Cotton Spinners' Association is an example of what can be done in Japan..

Most of the defects are, no doubt, due to a need for economy rather than to an inability to remedy them. The elaborate and costly statistical work of some Governments is apparently a luxury that the Japanese Government has felt it must deny itself (cf. Count Yanagisawa, who has been associated with the Japanese census, in *Bull. de l'Institut internat. de statistique*, Tome XXII, p. 67, Rome 1926). Moreover, judging by the methods and scope of the 1925 and 1930 censi, the defects will soon be remedied.

And notwithstanding these limitations, there is still sufficient statistical material available, and that available is still sufficiently accurate, at least to point the direction which Japanese economic life and the Japanese population are taking. It is not at all likely that a preciser and more accurate statistical information would reverse any of the deductions drawn in the preceding pages.

APPENDIX II

RICE CULTURE IN JAPAN

Rice culture, occupying as it does not only a predominant place in Japanese agriculture, but in the whole Japanese economic system, ought perhaps to be briefly described here. More than half the crop land in Japan is under rice.

The seed, after being carefully selected, is planted in small beds and the young plants are not removed to the fields until a few weeks later.

These fields are also small—there may be twenty or thirty or more to an acre—and are hedged in with a mound about a foot wide and about a foot (or less) high and are graded in such a way as to hold the irrigation water, but also to allow it to drain off when required. The irrigation, it can be seen, demands a special sort of field, one on fairly level land, or, if not level, on land that can be terraced into level fields. Terracing is done at a great cost of effort, and in some cases at a cost so high as to be scarcely worth the effort. Though terraced hillsides are not uncommon in Japan they are less common (probably because of the steeper nature of the Japanese hills) than in Java. In any typical rice-growing country the sides of a valley look like a giant's stairway, field rising above field.

Before the rice is transplanted the fields are broken up with mattocks or hoes, anything like deep ploughing being avoided because it would break the sub-soil and so ruin the water-holding capacity of the land. When the field has been broken up (by this hard digging) the water is allowed to flow in and soak it thoroughly. The water is put on to the fields by various devices—treadmills, small windmills, hand pumps, buckets attached to poles, are all to be seen—but human muscle provides most of the heavy labour exacted. For the first few weeks after the transplanting (the transplanting is heavy, back-bending work) the water is drained off the fields every morning, lest the sun should scorch the tender plants, and is run on again at night. After this period and throughout the growing season—until the end of the summer or early autumn—the fields are always under water, a slight flow being maintained so as to prevent stagnation. This involves continuous work at pumping or drawing. Beside this, is the work of weeding and hoeing and of manuring. After the water is drawn off the ground dries and the rice turns yellow and ripens.

At harvesting the stalks are cut, bound and stacked, and then threshed.

About one-third of the rice-fields are used for growing a winter crop —oats or barley or wheat, but green manure in particular. In the S.E. of the main island a second crop of rice is grown in winter, but excepting in this isolated region the winter is too cold for a second crop. It is probable, however, that a larger part of the land could be used for other crops than is used at present.

In addition to the rice culture described here—the rice culture of the Japanese "paddy" or irrigated fields—some rice is grown on dry land. It is of course a small proportion of the total acreage.

It will be observed that the central feature of rice culture is the arduous manual labour it demands. Rice culture indeed is by far the hardest of all the cereal cultures, and, as has been well said, it is gardening rather than farming. To see a farmer working a treadmill beneath the August sun, or to see him working in the fields with feet beneath the muddy water, suggests only too vividly the costly effort these men are expending to raise the nation's food.

BIBLIOGRAPHY

The following is not an exhaustive bibliography of the subject. Only for relevant official and statistical sources has the author made it as complete as possible; among the books and periodical literature there are many omissions, particularly in the section dealing with international relations in the Pacific. These, however, are all easily discoverable.

On account of a faulty method of note-taking there are a few cases of books being incompletely cited, either their date or their place of publication not being given. The assumption of new duties has unfortunately prevented the author from spending the time necessary to remedy these small defects.

There is no significance in the order of citation—no rule, alphabetical or other, has been followed. In several instances articles in journals are specified; that is not to imply that they are the only articles therein bearing on the subject. Thus only four articles in the *Journal of the Royal Statistical Society* are cited, whereas there are numerous studies in the volumes of the *Journal* bearing indirectly on the subject. With one or two exceptions publications have been cited only once, even though they may cover more than one part of the subject. Thus the *Résumé Statistique*, cited once only, is relevant to all five sections.

I. POPULATION

Official

Japan:

Diagrams and Numerical Tables showing Growth of Population and Vital Statistics of the Japanese Empire, Tokyo, 1913.

Résumé statistique de Mouvement de la Population de l'Empire du Japon, 1919–26.

Résultats statistiques du Recensement, 1925.

Résumé statistique de l'Empire du Japon, annual.

Financial and Economic Annual of Japan, annual from 1902.

Annual Statistics of the City of Tokyo, Tokyo Municipal Office.

Japan As It Is, compiled by H.I.M.'s Commission to Panama-Pacific International Exposition, 1915.

1920, Statistics of Population, Central Bureau of Statistics (in Japanese).

Day Census in Central Districts of City of Tokyo, S. Kanaya, Tokyo Bureau of Statistics, 1930 (arrived after completion of MS.).

Great Britain:

Annual Report Chief Medical Officer of Ministry of Health, 1928.

Summary Tables of 1901 Census, Cd. 1523.

Registrar-General's Statistical Review of England and Wales, 1928.

Australia:

Commonwealth of Australia Year Book, annual.

Commonwealth of Australia, Bulletin 39, *Population and Vital Statistics*.

New Zealand:

New Zealand Official Year Book.

United States of America:

Births, Stillbirths, and Infantile Mortality Statistics.

France:

Annuaire Statistique de la France (Statistique Générale de la France).

Statistique internationale du Mouvement de la Population jusqu'a 1905. Ministère du Travail, Paris, 1907.

Bulletin de la Statistique générale de la France, periodically.

Italy:

Annuario Statistico Italiano, Rome, annually.

Germany:

Statistiches Jahrbuch für das Deutches Reich, 1926.

COLLECTIONS

Institut international de Statistique, Le Haye:

Annuaire internationale de Statistique, 1920–1.

Aperçu annuel de la Démographie du Monde, 1922–5.

Aperçu annuel de la Démographie des divers Pays du Monde, 1927

Bulletin de l'Institut, periodically.

League of Nations:

International Statistical Year Book, annual, Geneva

International Health Year Book, 1927, Geneva.

C.E.I. 4 (1), *Natural Movement of Population during the First Quarter of the Twentieth Century*, Geneva, 1926.

C.E.C.P. 59 (1), *Estimates of the Working Population, 1931 and 1941*, by A. L. Bowley, Geneva, 1926.

C.E.I. 39, *Population and Natural Resources*, Geneva, 1926.

Others:

Japan Year Book, Japan Year Book Office, Tokyo.

Second Report National Birth Rate Commission, 1918–20, *Problems of Population and Parenthood* (ed. Marchant), Chapman and Hall, 1920.

JOURNALS AND REVIEWS

Journal Royal Statistical Society, London, S. de Jastrzebski, "Changes in Sex and Age Composition of European Population", *XCI*, Vol. II, p. 28; Presidential Address of G. Udny Yule, Vol. 88, p. 25; L. C. Connor, etc.

Journal American Statistical Association, Dublin and Lotka's study in volume for 1925; P. K. Whelpton, "Differentials in True Natural Increase", Sept. 1929; Sydenstricker and Notestein, "Differential Fertility according to Social Classes", Suppl. March 1930.

Eugenics Review, London, quarterly. Now largely devoted to discussions on or concerning contraception. Also see articles by Brownlee in *XVII*, 1926, and by Knibbs in Jan. 1928.

Sociological Review, Leplay House Press, London.

Metron: Rivista internazionale, Roma. An indispensable quarterly for the demographer and statistician. The number of essential studies that have appeared in it have been too numerous to be cited here; but special reference should be made to article on Irish Fertility, 1870–1911, by W. T. Russell, 31.3.28.

Rivista Italiana Statistica, Universitario di Bologna, Ottobre 1927, M. Boldrini "de alcuni fattori dell' aumento de popolazione"; also "Il Minimum di Mortalitá".

Giornale degli Economisti (Italian Economic Journal): e.g. Savorgnan, "Nuovi contributi allo Studio dell'Attrazione matrimoniale", and Ugge, "Gli Indice dell'Attrazione matrimoniale", Nov. 1929; article on "Infanticido Abbandono d'Infante e Procurato abborto nella Vita sociale", 1925, p. 401.

L'Illustration, Paris, weekly, L. Naudeau, "Enquête sur la Population de la France", articles appearing irregularly throughout 1929 and at least up to Aug. 1930.

Revue Mondiale, Oct. 1929, B. Nogaro, "Problème de la Population en France".

Annales de Géographie, Nov. 1926, article on "Mouvement de la Population de la France".

Revue Politique et Parlémentaire, 10 Sept. 1929, "Problème démographique en Italie", M. Mitzakio; and "Eugenisme et Natalité", M. Autun.

Economic Journal, C .T. Brunner, on Local Variations in Birth Rate, March 1925; Blackmore and Mellonie, on the Nineteenth Century Poor Law, May 1927; article by Dr. Bowley, in June 1924; discussion on Population and Unemployment, 1923 vol.; W. S. Thompson, etc.

Economica, London University, L. Robbins, "Notes on some probable consequences of a stationary population in Great Britain", April 1929; also article by Dr. H. Dalton, March 1928.

Journal of Political Economy, Chicago (very helpful survey, including bibliography, of the position of contraception, in articles by A. B. Wolfe, 1928–9).

American Journal of Sociology, S. R. Winston, "Relation of certain Social Factors to Fertility", March 1930.

Francis Galton Eugenics Laboratory Memoirs, *XVII*, p. 72.

Transactions Asiatic Society of Japan, G. Droppers, "Population of Japan in Tokugawa Period", *XXI-II*, p. 252.

Transactions Japan Society of London, Y. Okuma, "Japanese Marriage Law, Past and Present", *XXI*, *XXII*.

Kyoto University Economic Review, E. Honjo's studies; and Prof. Yamamoto, July 1927.

Trans-Pacific Magazine (Tokyo): J. Kayahara, "Abortion and Infanticide in Tokugawa Japan", 22.10.27; D. K. Overell, "Japan is not overpopulated", 7.7.28.

Journal Industrial and Engineering Chemistry, Carl L. Alsberg, "Progress in Chemistry and the Theory of Population", May 1924.

Science (Washington), Prof. F. M. Jaeger, of Groningen, "Present and Future State of our Natural Resources", 26.4.29.

Foreign Affairs, A. E. Taylor, "World's Food Resources", Oct. 1926.

Scottish Geographical Magazine, Prof. J. W. Gregory, "Inter-racial Problems and White Colonization in the Tropics", 1924.

Geographical Review (U.S.A.), W. Coulter, "Dot Map of Distribution of Population in Japan", 1926, p. 283; P. M. Roaxley, "Distribution of Population in China", 1925, p. 1.

Books

Harold Wright, *Population*, Harcourt Brace, New York, 1923.

A. M. Carr-Saunders, *Population*, Oxford, 1925.

A. M. Carr-Saunders, *The Population Problem*, Oxford, 1922.

R. R. Kuczynski, *Balance of Births and Deaths*, Macmillan, 1928.

Raymond Pearl, *The Biology of Population Growth*, Knopf, 1925.

Raymond Pearl, *Studies in Human Biology*, Williams and Wilkins, 1926.

Dr. Sweeney, *Natural Increase of Mankind*, New York, 1928.

Louis Dublin (ed.), *Population Problems*, Boston, 1926.

E. B. Reuter, *Population Problems*, Lippincott, 1923.

E. M. East, *Mankind at the Crossroads*, Scribners, 1924.

G. N. Newman, *Infantile Mortality*, London.

Dr. Newsholme, *Vital Statistics*, London.

Sir G. H. Knibbs, *Shadows of the World's Future*, 1928.

P. R. Wattal, *The Population Problem in India*, Bombay, 1916.

C. V. Drysdale, *The Small Family System*, London.

Edwin Cannan, *Wealth*, London, 1914 (discussion on "diminishing returns").

London Essays in Economics to Edwin Cannan, Routledge, 1927 (essay on "The Optimum Theory of Population", by L. Robbins).

Dr. Cooper, *Technique of Contraception*, New York, 1929.

Lella Secor Florence, *Birth Control on Trial*, Allen and Unwin, 1930.

II. AGRICULTURE

Official

Japan:

Department of Agriculture and Forestry, *Statistical Abstract of the Ministry of Agriculture and Forestry.*

Department of Agriculture and Forestry, *Rice Statistics*, 1929 (in Japanese).

Department of Agriculture and Commerce, *Statistical Reports*, 1917–21.

Department of Agriculture and Commerce, *Outlines of Agriculture*, 1910, 1914.

Home Office, *Rural Life in Japan*, 1914.

United States of America:

Department of Agriculture, *Agriculture Year Book*, annual.

Department of Commerce, Trade Promotion Series (henceforth cited as T.P.S.) 46, *Rice Trade in the Far East.*

Department of Commerce, T.P.S. 73, *Foreign Markets for Irrigation Machinery.*

Department of Commerce, Trade Information Bulletin (henceforth cited as T.I.B.), 41.

Great Britain:

Board of Trade, *Statistical Abstract for United Kingdom*, 1913–27.

Collections

International Institute of Agriculture, Rome, *International Year Book of Agriculture Statistics.*

International Institute of Agriculture, Rome, *International Review of Agriculture.*

International Institute of Agriculture, Rome, *Bulletin du Bureau des Institutions économiques*, 1910.

International Institute of Agriculture, Rome, *Agricultural Problems in their International Aspects*, Memo. to League of Nations and published by the League as C.E.I. 36, Geneva, 1926.

International Institute of Agriculture, Rome, *Statistics on Agricultural Populations and Tenure*, C.E.I. 36, Geneva, 1926.

League of Nations, *Monthly Bulletin of Statistics*, Geneva.

Journals and Reviews

Journal of Royal Statistical Society, especially studies by Harald Faber, in Vol. 87, and by R. J. Thompson in vol. for 1926.

Transactions Asiatic Society, Japan, 1913, "Studies in Japanese Agriculture".

Transactions Japan Society, London, Rev. Walter Weston, "Some Aspects of Rural Japan", and "Geography of Japan", Vols. XIX, XX.

Kyoto University Economic Review, articles by S. Kawada, in I, 1 (Tenant System), I, 2 (Agricultural Problems), III, 1 (Peasant farms); and by E. Honjo in I, 2 (Agricultural Troubles in Tokugawa period).

Journal Royal Institute International Affairs, article by Sir Daniel Hall, in Jan. 1929 on agricultural surplus.

Journal Political Economy, Chicago Univ., Dorothy J. Orchard, "Agricultural Problems of Modern Japan", April–June 1929.

Geographical Review (U.S.A.), Glenn F. Trewartha, Study on the Suwa Basin district, April 1930.

Quarterly Journal of Economics, Harvard, D. H. Buchanan, "Rural Economy of Japan", Aug. 1923.

Annals Association American Geographers, O. E. Baker, "Changes in Land Utilization in U.S.A.", 1927, 22.

Economic Journal, S. Sato, "Rice Industry of Japan", 1918, p. 444.

Giornale degli Economisti, U. R. Bucella, "Svoglimento ed il Sistema della Bonifica Integrale", Agosto 1929.

Foreign Affairs (U.S.A.), S. Nasu, "Agriculture and Japanese National Economy", July 1930.

New Republic (U.S.A.), R. Stewart, "Mass Production on Farms", 17.7.29.

Books

E. B. Copeland, *Rice*, Macmillan, 1924.

Shirosi Nasu, *Land Utilization in Japan*, Institute of Pacific Relations, 1929.

J. W. Robertson Scott, *The Foundations of Japan*, Murray, 1923.

S. Sato, *Some Historical Phases of Modern Japan*, Japan Society (New York), 1916.

Hokkaido Imperial University, Dept. of Agric., *American Influences upon Agriculture of Hokkaido*, 1915.

K. Ogata, *Co-operation in Japan*, King, 1923.

Egerton Charles Grey, *The Food of Japan*, League of Nations, Geneva, 1928.

F. H. King, *Farmers of Forty Centuries*, Madison, 1911.

D. Mitrany, *Marx v. the Peasant* in *London Essays to E. Cannan*, 1927.

E. G. Nourse, *American Agriculture and the European Market*, McGraw Hill, 1924.

III. INDUSTRIALIZATION AND FOREIGN TRADE

Official

Japan:

Financial and Economic Annual.
Tokyo Reconstruction Work, Tokyo Municipal Office, 1930.
Statistical Abstract for Tokyo, 1928, Tokyo Municipal Office.

Great Britain:

Dept. of Overseas Trade: Reports (published periodically) on—
Japan.
British Malaya.
China.
Netherlands East Indies.
U.S.A.
Board of Trade, *Foreign Trade and Commerce Accounts, 1926–8.*
Report of Royal Commission on Coal Industry, 1925, Vol. I.
Board of Trade *Gazette.*
Ministry of Labour *Gazette.*

United States of America:

Dept. of Commerce—
T.P.S. 13.
T.P.S. 76, *Mineral Raw Materials.*
T.P.S. 81, *International Cartels, Combines, and Trusts.*
T.P.S. 83, *Public Finances of Far Eastern Countries.*
T.P.S. 80, *International Trade in Petroleum.*
T.I.B. 217, *The Chemical Industry.*
T.I.B. 283, *International Trade in Raw Silk.*
T.I.B. 389, *Trends in Japan's Trade.*
T.I.B. 626, *Free and Dutiable Imports of the United States.*
T.I.B. 639, *Iron and Steel Trade of Great Britain.*
T.I.B. 642, *Trends in Japan's Trade.*
T.I.B. 653, *Big Five in Japanese Banking.*
T.I.B. 396, *Iron and Steel Trade of Pacific Area.*
T.I.B. 359, *Iron and Alloy Metals in Siberia.*
T.I.B. 637, *Foreign Trade of U.S.A., in 1928.*
T.I.B. 625, *Balance of International Payments,* U.S.A., *1928.*
T.I.B. 672, *Paper Trade and Industry of Japan.*
T.I.B. 673, *The Currency System of Japan.*
Special Agents' Series 218, *Netherlands East Indies and British Malaya.*
Commerce Year Book, 2 vols.
Report of the Secretary of Commerce, annual.
Commerce Reports, weekly journal.
United States Trade and Navigation, annual.

United States of America (*continued*):
United States Tariff Commission, *Broad Silk Manufactures and the Tariff*, 1926.
United States Tariff Commission, *Silk and Silk Goods*, Summary of Tariff Information, 1929.
United States Tariff Commission, *Cotton Manufactures*, Summary of Tariff Information, 1929.
Department of Labour, *Monthly Labour Review*.

Canada:
Canada Labour Gazette.
Dominion Bulletin of Statistics (1913–24).

COLLECTIONS

League of Nations:
Memorandum on Production and Trade, annual.
International Trade and Balance of Payments, annual.
Natural Silk Industry, C.E.I. 24.
Artificial Silk Industry, C.E.I. 30.
Cotton, C.E.I. 9.
Standard of Living of Workers, C.E.I. 26.
Iron and Steel, C.E.I. 17.
Electrical Industry, C.E.I. 16.
World Economic Conference: Reports and Proceedings, 2 vols., C.E.I. 46.
International Labour Review (I.L.O.), especially studies by Dr. Ayusawa.
Report of Albert Thomas to Governing Body of I.L.O., March 1929, on Japan, China, etc.

Bank of Japan:
Annual Report.

Osaka Chamber of Commerce:
Report (in Japanese).

Tokyo Chamber of Commerce and Industry:
Statistical Report.

France:
Bulletin de la Statistique Générale de la France, July–Sept. 1927 (Japan foreign trade before and after the Earthquake).

JOURNALS AND REVIEWS

Manchester Guardian Commercial, weekly.
The Economist, London, weekly.
Journal des Économistes, Paris, Librairie Félix Alcan.
L'Économiste Français, Paris.

Revue d'Économique Politique, Paris.
Revue Économique Internationale, Bruxelles.
Far Eastern Review, Shanghai.
Harvard Business Review.
Quarterly Journal of Economics (Harvard).
Geographical Review (U.S.A.), J. E. Orchard, "Can Japan develop industrially?" April 1929; same author in 1928, p. 374; also P. P. Goudkoff, "Economic Geography of the Coal Resources of Asiatic Russia", 1923, p. 283; H. F. Bain, "Our Mineral Heritage", p. 177, 1928.
Journal of Political Economy, Chicago, H. L. Lutz, "Debts Reparations and National Policy", Feb. 1930.
Journal of Geography (U.S.A.), W. O. Blanchard, "Iron and Steel Industry of Europe", Oct. 1928.
Annales de Géographie, 1928, p. 566; 1927, p. 481.
International Cotton Bulletin.
The Silkworm (U.S.A.), Feb. 1930.
The Protectionist (U.S.A.), "Progress of Japanese Woollen Industry", March 1930.
International Conciliation, p. 227, on Raw Materials.
Weltwirtschaftliches Archiv (April 1926, Y. Hirai, "Zur Korrektur der Japanischen Aussenhandelsstatistik").
Der Neue Orient (1926/7, Heft 5/6, "Die Japanische Baumwall Industrie"), etc.

Books

H. F. Bain, *Ores and Industry in the Far East*, Research Council on Foreign Relations (U.S.A.), 1927.
Schiuchi Harada, *Labour Conditions in Japan*, Columbia Univ. Press, 1928.
M. Takizawa, *Penetration of Money Economy in Japan*, same, 1927.
S. Y. Furuya, *Japan's Foreign Exchange and her balance of payments*, same, 1928.
M. Holland, *Industrial Transition in Japan*, National Research Council (U.S.A.), 1927.
E. F. Penrose, *Mineral Study* (in Japanese), 1928.
I. W. Ayusawa, *Industrial Conditions and Labour Legislation in Japan*, I.L.O., 1926.
Boris P. Torgasheff, *Coal, Iron and Oil in the Far East*, Inst. Pacific Relations, 1929.
Report of President's Committee, *Recent Economic Charges*, 2 vols., McGraw Hill, 1929.
F. W. Taussig, *International Trade*, Macmillan, 1928.
Arno S. Pearce, *The Cotton Industry of Japan and China*, Manchester, 1929.

IV. EMIGRATION

Collections

League of Nations:

Migration, C.E.I. 25, Geneva, 1926.

(I.L.O.) *Migration Movements, 1920–23*, Geneva, 1925.

(I.L.O.) *Reports on Legislation concerning Movement of Labour and Migration in general*, Geneva, 1926.

Journals and Reviews

Kyoto University Economic Review, II, 2, M. Yamamoto, "Principles of Emigration Policy".

Scottish Geographical Magazine, 1924, p. 257, Prof. J. W. Gregory, "Inter-racial Problems and White Colonization in the Tropics".

Preussische Jahrbücher.

Books

John W. Brown, *World Migration and Labour* (Report of World Migration Congress), Amsterdam, 1926.

H. P. Fairchild, *Immigration: A World Movement and its American Significance*, New York, 1914.

A. M. McLean, *Modern Immigration*, Philadelphia, 1925.

K. Takaoka, *Study of Immigration to Brazil* (in Japanese).

P. S. Taylor, *Mexican Immigration in the Imperial Valley*, Univ of California, 1929.

Owen Rutter, *British North Borneo*, Constable, 1922.

C. Lumsholtz, *Through Central Borneo*, 2 vols, Scribner's, 1920.

Robert F. Foerster, *The Italian Emigration of our Times*, Harvard, 1919.

R. L. Buell, *Japanese Immigration*, World Peace Foundation, 1924.

California and the Oriental, Sacramento (U.S.A.), 1920.

V. INTERNATIONAL RELATIONS IN THE PACIFIC

Official

Japan:

Annual Report on the Administration of Chosen, 1924–6. Seoul.

Report on Progress in Manchuria, 1907–28, S.M.R., Dairen.

Manchuria: Land of Opportunities, Dairen, 1922.

Beans, Dairen, 1929.

Great Britain:

Accounts and Papers for 1903, XLIV, Cd. 1639; for 1911, XVI, Cd. 5471; for 1917–18, XXIII, Cd. 8566; for 1918, XXIII, Cd. 9177.

Reports and Accounts, for 1921, XIV, Cmd. 1474.

Journals of the Parliaments of the Empire, 1920–9, London.

Australia:

Commonwealth of Australia Debates, 1902–5 (on White Australia Policy).

Mandate Report on New Guinea to League of Nations (1st, 2nd, 3rd), Melbourne.

Acts of the Parliament of the Commonwealth of Australia, Vol. I (for Immigration laws).

Queensland Parliamentary Papers, 1907, Vol. I, 1st Sess.; and 1908, Vol. II, 2nd Sess. (for Japanese in Thursday Island; and 1925, Vol. III, for report on Italians).

U.S.A.:

Foreign Relations.

League of Nations:

Official Journal, 1924, Special Supplement, No. 24.

Collections

Hertslet's *China Treaties*, 3rd edition, 2 vols., London, 1908.

J. V. A. MacMurray, *Treaties and Agreements with and concerning China, 1894–1919*, 2 vols., New York, 1921.

Journals and Reviews

Die Neue Rundschau (Sept. 1929, "Welt Politik in der Mandschurie").

Trans-Pacific Magazine, Tokyo, weekly.

Japan Weekly Chronicle, Kobe.

Osaka Mainichi, English edition of the Japanese daily.

Far Eastern Political Science Review.

Pacific Affairs, Journal of the Inst. Pacific Relations, Honolulu.

Asia, New York.

Japan, San Francisco.

Nuova Antologica, Milano.

Economic Record, Melbourne Univ. Press (e.g. article in Nov. 1927, on New Zealand and Asiatic immigration).

Round Table, London.

Journal of Royal Institute of International Affairs, London.

Foreign Affairs (U.S.A.).

North China Herald, Tientsin.

Far Eastern Review, Shanghai.

Revue Mondiale (Janv. 1930, "Désarmament naval dans le Pacifique").

South-Western Political and Social Science Quarterly, Austin, Texas, 1929 (J. Q. Dealey, "Policy of the United States in the Pacific").

Books

Proceedings Second Institute Pacific Relations (*ed. Condliffe*), Chicago, 1928.
Yamato Ichihashi, *The Washington Conference and After*, Stanford Univ. Press, 1928.
Paul Hibbert Clyde, *International Rivalries in Manchuria*, 2nd ed., Ohio State Univ., 1928.
Payson J. Treat, *The Far East*, Harper, 1928.
H. M. Vinacke, *History of the Far East in Modern Times*, Kopf.
N. D. Harris, *Europe and the East*, Houghton Mifflin, 1926.
Sir Frederick Whyte, *Asia in the Twentieth Century*, Scribner's, 1926.
Sir Harold Parlett, *Brief Account of Diplomatic Events in Manchuria*, Oxford, 1929.
Sir Frederick Whyte, *China and Foreign Powers*, Oxford, 1928.
A. J. Toynbee, C. A. Macartney, *Survey of International Affairs*, vols. for 1924, 1925 II, 1926, 1927, Oxford.
Stephen H. Roberts, *Population Problems in the Pacific*, Routledge, 1927.
Myra Willard, *History of the White Australia Policy*, Melbourne Univ. Press.
H. Temperley, *History of the Peace Conference*, Vol. VI.
E. J. Dillon, *Inside Story of the Peace Conference.*
H. B. Morse, *International Relations of the Chinese Empire*, 3rd vol.
T. W. Overlach, *Foreign Financial Control in China*, New York, 1919.
G. M. Crivelli et Pierre Louvet, *L'Australie et la Pacifique*, Paris, 1921.
Yosuka Matsuoka, *Economic Co-operation of Japan and China in Manchuria and Mongolia*, Dairen, 1929.
S. King-Hall, *Western Civilization and the Far East*, Methuen, 1924.
N. Roosevelt, *The Restless Pacific*, Scribner's, 1928.
Sir Frank Fox, *The Mastery of the Pacific*, John Lane, 1928.
P. T. Etherton and H. H. Tiltman, *The Pacific: a Forecast*, Benn, 1928.
P. T. Etherton, *China: the Facts.*
C. B. Fletcher, *The Pacific Problem*, New York, 1921.
J. Macmillan Brown, *Peoples and Problems of the Pacific*, 2 vols., Fisher Unwin, 1927.
J. Macmillan Brown, *Riddle of the Pacific*, Fisher Unwin, 1925 (anthropological).
H. C. Bywater, *Sea Power in the Pacific*, Constable, 1921.
W. H. Mallory, *China, Land of Famine*, American Geog. Association, 1926.
H. Kinney, *Modern Manchuria and the Southern Manchurian Railway*, Dairen, 1928.
Arthur H. Smith, *Village Life in China*, Revell, 1899.

Eric Teichman, *Travels in North-Western China*, 1921; *Travels in Eastern Tibet*, 1922, Cambridge.
Alleyne Ireland, *The New Korea*.
W. B. Pilkin, *Must We Fight Japan?* New York, 1921.
G. H. Scholefield, *The Pacific: its Past and Future*, London, 1921.
Margaret Harrison, *Asia Reborn*, Harper, 1928.
Upton Close, *The Revolt of Asia*, Putnam's, 1927.
Stanley Rice, *The Challenge of Asia*, Scribner's, 1928.
E. Hovelaque, *Le Japon*, Paris (Flammarion), 1921.
T. H. Longford, *Japan* (Nations of To-day series), 1923.
Y. Tsurumi, *Contemporary Japan*, New York, 1926.
E. G. Marks, *Watch the Pacific!* Sydney, 1920.
C. H. Sherrill, *Have We a Far Eastern Policy?*
Senator Pulsford, *British Empire and Relations of Australasia and Asia*, Sydney, 1905.
M. N. Golovin, *Problem of the Pacific in the Twentieth Century* (Transl. C. Nabokoff).
H. K. Norton, *Far Eastern Republic of Siberia*, London, 1923.
F. Nansen, *Through Siberia*, London, 1914.
Prof. Dr. Hans Molisch, *Im Lande der aufgehenden Sonne*, Wien, 1927.
Isaiah Bowman, *The New World, Problems in Political Geography*, New York, 1928.
L. Archimbaud, *La Conférence de Washington*, Paris, 1923.
Earl of Ronaldshay, *A Wandering Student in the Far East*, Blackie, 1908.
H. Croly, *Willard Straight*, New York, 1924.
T. Dennett, *Americans in Eastern Asia*, New York, 1922.
K. K. Kawakami, *Japan's Pacific Policy*, New York, 1922.
C. P. Howland, *American Foreign Relations, 1928*, Yale, 1928.
A. Gerard, *Ma Mission au Japon, 1907–1914*, Paris, 1919.
Prof. Dr. J. Witte, *Japan zwischen zwei Kulturen* Leipzig, 1928.

INDEX

For Product Safety Concerns and Information please contact our EU representative GPSR@taylorandfrancis.com
Taylor & Francis Verlag GmbH, Kaufingerstraße 24, 80331 München, Germany

www.ingramcontent.com/pod-product-compliance
Ingram Content Group UK Ltd.
Pitfield, Milton Keynes, MK11 3LW, UK
UKHW011001180926
475701UK00004B/505
9780415852364